CARLETON BEALS
A Radical Journalist
in Latin America

# Carleton Beals

## A Radical Journalist in Latin America

John A. Britton

**Library of Congress Cataloging-in-Publication Data**

Britton, John A.
  Carleton Beals : a radical journalist in Latin
America.

  Bibliography: p.
  Includes index.
  1. Beals, Carleton, 1893–    . 2. Foreign
correspondents—United States—Biography.
3. Foreign correspondents—Latin America—Biography.
4. Latin America—Politics and government—1830–1948.
5. Latin America—Politics and government—1948–    .
6. Radicalism—Latin America.  I. Title.
PN4874.B35B75  1987      070.4'33'0924  [B]      86–14661
ISBN 0-8263-0914-3

*Dedication*

This book is dedicated to Richard Greenleaf
and Lee Woodward,
mentors and friends.

# Contents

# Illustrations

# Preface

This project had its inception in January 1973 when Carleton Beals allowed me to look through the binders which contained nearly half a century of his personal correspondence. They occupied about twenty five feet of shelf space in his office and, on close inspection, left me with the impression that it would take many years to understand the story they contained. The first impression was correct. The broader outline of the importance of Beals's work as a journalist came into focus only after about a decade of research in his papers and other archives, and reading in Latin American and United States history.

One problem in this study centered on the controversial nature of much of Beals's writing. Historians, in particular specialists in twentieth-century Latin American history, have frequently faulted Beals's journalism. To some extent this type of revisionism is the inevitable result of what these two professions see as their main responsibilities. Journalists attempt to inform the public about current events by personal observation and quick analysis presented in an article, essay or book written, often hurriedly, to reach newsstands or bookstores before public interest in their subject fades. Historians, by contrast, procede more slowly. They attempt a lengthy survey of possible sources and consider different schools of historical interpretation before writing for their audience—historians, other humanists, and social scientists and interested lay readers. In this process, historians of the recent past often believe they have found flaws in the written record left by those who witnessed or were close to the events they described. Beals was certainly no exception in this regard. In recent decades, many historians have dismissed his work as overly impressionistic, excessively ideological, and sometimes inaccurate. It is my thesis, however, that while Beals was no paragon of objectivity, he did write on Latin American affairs from a much more consistent and considerably less superficial perspective than many students of recent history have understood.

I must acknowledge two historians whose work in seemingly unrelated fields helped me to place Beals's writing in its proper context. Eugenia Meyer's *Conciencia histórica norteamericana sobre la Revolución de 1910* contained a sweeping analysis of the publications of Beals and his contemporaries on one of the crucial events in Latin America in the twentieth century. She generously provided me with valuable advice for research which was essential to this study. The second historian, Lawrence Goodwyn, in his *Democratic Promise: The Populist Moment in America* developed penetrating insights regarding the radical nature of American populism, an ethos which Beals shared with his parents. Goodwyn's version of populism was vital to my understanding of Beals's leftist but non-Marxist approach to Latin America.

The author is indebted to many other colleagues who, through their suggestions for research and their comments on my early writing, contributed much to this volume. Many of them encouraged me to complete this study simply through an occassional kind word along with their critical evaluations. They are Barry Carr, Larry Clayton, Helen Delpar, José Luis Garcia Valero, Richard Greenleaf, Ed Holland, Philip Johnson, Charles Hale, Thomas Karnes, Lester Langley, the late Carey McWilliams, Don Olliff, Frederick Pike, Richard Salisbury, Charles Stansifer, the late Felipe Texidor, Darlene Unrue, Lee Woodward and Josefina Vázquez.

Financial support from the American Philosophical Society and the Francis Marion College Faculty Research Committee helped make possible my research in distant libraries and manuscript collections. The interlibrary loan staff of the James A. Rogers Library was prompt and efficient in handling my many requests.

The editors of *Journalism History* generously allowed me permission to use a substantial part of an article they originally published in 1979.

I owe a special note of thanks to Carolyn Beals, whose patience and cooperation was of great importance in this project, and Howard B. Gotlieb, Director of Special Collections of the Mugar Memorial Library of Boston University, whose organization of the Carleton Beals Collection has been exemplary. Finally, I acknowledge the editorial advice and typing skills of my wife Kathy and the understanding of Jeannie, Dan, and Maria. All four of them tolerated my frequent absences for research and writing in much better spirits than I was able to do.

## • 1 •

# Radical Roots

The journalist waited apprehensively as two United States Marine bombing planes, armed with machine guns, roared over the small Nicaraguan town of San Rafael del Norte. They made several passes, each one lower, in their search for the rebel forces of Augusto César Sandino. Recent events in that war torn country indicated that the Marine planes would fire on the 150 rebels who were hiding in the town. Some of Sandino's men peered from the doorways of San Rafael's adobe houses, one of which sheltered thirty-four-year-old journalist Carleton Beals. Unknown to Beals and his Sandinista companions, the Marines were under orders not to fire. The pilots soon turned their planes away. Their peaceful departure provided another narrow escape for Beals, an intrepid and at times foolhardy reporter, who a few hours earlier on that morning of February 3, 1928, had completed an interview with Sandino, in spite of the immense difficulty involved in this task.[1] Beals was the only journalist from the United States to accomplish this feat during the six-year undeclared war between Sandino's forces and the Marines. From Beals's account of Sandino and his movement, there arose a storm of controversy that added to the already heated debate concerning United States imperialism in Latin America. The Sandino story was neither Beals's first nor his last endeavor as a free-spirited advocate of leftist

1

causes in the Western Hemisphere; rather it was typical of his determination to expose the plight of the down-trodden and the exploited to the reading public of the United States. Beals's subsequent series of articles on Sandino for *The Nation* helped make the young journalist a leading spokesman of anti-imperialism and enhanced his reputation among United States government officials as a meddler in inter-American relations.

As one of the first twentieth-century journalists from the United States to specialize in Latin American affairs, Beals travelled extensively throughout the vast territory south of the Rio Grande. He found much evidence of social inequality, of the exploitation of the poor by the rich and of the overbearing presence of the United States. Beals publicized these conditions as often and as loudly as he could; he also stated his opinions on how to alleviate these problems. He endorsed the uplift of the impoverished masses by sweeping social change or, if necessary, by violent revolution. These views made him an enemy of many Latin American dictators, international business leaders and the U.S. State Department. With such powerful opponents Beals's unbending individualism received many severe tests during his long career.

Beals's career stretched from the 1920s to the 1960s, a period in which the United States exerted a predominant influence in the Western Hemisphere. Throughout these five decades, Beals insisted that the United States was an imperialistic power because of its use of military intervention, diplomatic intimidation, economic domination and clandestine manipulation. The heavy-handed assertiveness of Theodore Roosevelt and William Howard Taft gave the United States the Panama Canal and caused a number of military interventions by the U.S. in the Caribbean. Woodrow Wilson's moralistic justifications for similar actions did nothing to reduce U.S. involvement in the area. The failure of the Marines to capture Sandino in the late 1920s reinforced a tendency in the State Department to abandon "big stick" dipolmacy for less provocative methods of dealing with Latin America. By the late 1930s, the threat of world war led the U.S. to seek the good will and support of the other countries in the hemisphere; however, the facade of Franklin D. Roosevelt's Good Neighbor Policy often only masked the aggressiveness of the United States, in these times manifested through persuasion, co-optation or veiled threats. After World War II, Washington seemed to vacillate between overt intervention and less visible forms of influence and control. Through all of these policy changes, Beals criticized the United States for its violation of Latin American sovereignty.[2]

An advocate of revolutionary and anti-imperialist movements had a tenuous position in the major press institutions of the United States. The few relevant historical analyses of the work of U.S. journalists in what are now called Third World nations during the first half of the twentieth century indicate that Beals's outspoken brand of leftist reportage did not meld with the editorial perspectives of most of the wire services, newspapers, news magazines, and publishing houses.[3] His writings challenged the preconceptions of the reading public of the United States and those of the editors of major media organs. He attracted readers who had similar ideological perspectives or those who had a pragmatic interest in Latin America, such as diplomats and business owners.

Leftist interpretations of events in the critical region of the Third World challenged the American mass media's stereotypical images of the nations to the south of the Rio Grande. According to Anthony Smith in his *Geopolitics of Information*, most Western press coverage of developing areas tended to measure "progress" by the values of the modernized world, thereby imposing the alien standards of an urban, industrial society on people who live in a rural, agrarian society.[4] Beals avoided this form of cultural bias through his empathy for peasants and their traditions, a populistic inclination that strengthened his identification with the Left.

At first glance, Beals seemed to fit the model of the "political pilgrim" as described by sociologist Paul Hollander.[5] Beals often exhibited an affinity for radical organizations in Latin America and made no effort to conceal his preferences. A close reading of Beals's published writing and private correspondence, however, presents the picture of an advocate of revolution in the abstract, who became a critic of the leaders who claimed the mantle of revolutionary authority. A study of his commentary on radical movements and governments in Mexico, Peru, Guatemala and Cuba over a period of five decades reveals much more capacity for criticism of the Left than found in Hollander's selective, short-term examinations of American intellectuals' responses to revolutions.

Beals struggled, fought and survived as an outspoken leftist journalist, who in spite of his independent nature, worked with liberals and radicals of various ideological persuasions. His lack of commitment to institutions and organizations was both a strength and a weakness. On the positive side, his freelance status enabled him to collaborate with a number of different people including such leading liberals as Herbert Croly, Ernest Gruening and Carey McWilliams as well as with such influential radicals as Bertram and Ella Wolfe, Norman Thomas and Victor Calverton. The absence of institutional and organizational affiliation was a negative aspect when it left him isolated during crises and controversies. At times, his leftist friends and associates congratulated him for courage and intellectual acuity; on other occasions, they damned him for selfishness and narrow-mindedness. Apparently unaffected by praise or criticism, Beals held to his chosen course which seemed to vacillate between the periphery and the mainstream of the Left in the United States.

Beals was also part of the first generation of twentieth century American journalists and academicians to study contemporary Latin American affairs. The Mexican revolution that started in 1910 generated much debate in the United States during the next three decades. Beals joined the debate. Along with journalist Gruening, historian Frank Tannenbaum, economist Eyler Simpson, clergyman Samuel Guy Inman and ethnographer Frances Toor, he attempted to explain the Mexican revolution in order to defend it against the charges hurled against it by its conservative critics. Many of these Mexicanists soon enlarged their purview to other Latin American nations, where they usually defended land reform, labor organizations, and economic nationalism much to the chagrin of diplomats in Washington and business executives in New York. Beals was a leader in the first group of Latin American specialists to challenge the assumption, widely-held in the United States, that Latin America was a vast, resource-rich tropical paradise, waiting for the magical touch of Yankee ingenuity, investment, entrepreneurship and engineering to realize its immense potential.

## From Kansas to California

Carleton Beals's parents were determined leftists, who held to their beliefs through political and personal adversity. They met in the early 1890s, when Leon Eli Beals was a lawyer as well as the publisher-editor of the *Barber County Index*, a small weekly newspaper in Medicine Lodge, Kansas. His wife-to-be Elvina Blickensderfer came to Medicine Lodge as a schoolteacher. Their Victorian-style courtship moved more slowly than most because Leon was shy. In order to send flowers to the object of his affections in an unobtrusive way, he sent bouquets to all of the teachers in the local school, where in spite of this diversion, his real purpose was generally known. Soon after their marriage in early 1893, Leon secured an appointment as district attorney for Barber County, then a populist stronghold in south-central Kansas. Carleton was born on November 13, 1893 during a time of relative prosperity for the Bealses. Active in the Populist party, he and Elvina shared the disappointment of William Jennings Bryan's defeat in 1896. Leon's term as district attorney expired in 1897, and in the face of declining populist strength in Kansas, the family decided to move to California.[6]

When Leon and Elvina Beals left Kansas, they held definite leftist beliefs. Leon was no rustic hayseed Populist, but rather a well-read lawyer and politician. Born in Michigan in 1864, he held degrees from DePauw University and the law school of Washington University in St. Louis. Elvina was born in Iowa in 1868, attended Oberlin College and was active in the feminist and prohibitionist movements before her marriage to Leon. By 1897, both of them were close to espousing socialism, if they had not already done so. Carleton remembered that the family library contained the autobiography of Populist presidential candidate James B. Weaver and Karl Marx's *Das Capital*, a combination that reflected the Beals family's leftist brand of populism.[7]

Unfortunately, many disappointments awaited the Beals family in California. Leon chose not to make use of his training and experience as a lawyer for reasons that remain unclear and turned to other means of earning a living. His two major business undertakings, a chicken farm in Pasadena and a racket (or general) store in Oxnard, failed. He then supported the family through clerical work in Los Angeles and Pasadena. Although life was often a struggle, the Bealses managed to survive on his small salary. In 1900, Elvina bore their second son Ralph, after a difficult labor because of her poor health.[8]

The Bealses's economic plight seemed to strengthen their commitment to radicalism. Leon was active in a local labor organization that recruited Mexican-American workers in the sugarbeet industry. Carleton recalled attending labor meetings with his father in 1900 while his mother was in the hospital awaiting the birth of her second child.[9] In later years, Elvina ran for elective positions in Berkeley as a Socialist and eventually won a seat on the school board. The Bealses hosted the nationally known Socialist Eugene V. Debs for a night in their Pasadena home. Family discussions at the dinner table frequently included Marx, Engels and socialist interpretations of contemporary problems. Caught up in this atmosphere, four-year-old Ralph once startled an unsuspecting passer-by who paused momentarily in front of the Beals home. The stranger, attempting to be friendly, asked Ralph for his name; the youngster unhesitatingly responded that he was called "Socialist."[10]

Like many less radical parents in the early 1900s, Leon and Elvina were strict in their childrearing methods and had high academic expectations for their sons. Very early in life, Carleton revealed an outstanding intellectual ability but he also showed a troublesome lack of self-confidence in personal relationships.[11] His small stature made him the "little runt" among his peers. He was an intense, but ineffective, competitor in sports, and carefully avoided the rough-and-tumble combat so common among young males.[12]

At Pasadena High School, Carleton matured and gained self-confidence as a superior student with some social involvements. His one failure in a German class was, in his words, "the . . . the greatest disaster of my life up to that time." He repeated and passed the course, however, and continued with German in college. He also participated in extracurricular activities, including the preparation of floats for the Tournament of Roses Parade. This particular activity required special parental permission to stay out after 11 P.M. to work on the decorations, an indication of the careful familial guidance he received through his high-school years.[13]

## College Years

Beals's admission to the University of California at Berkeley in the fall of 1911 was a turning point for his family. He lived in an apartment in Berkeley for a few months before the entire family left Pasadena to take up residence near the university, primarily because of Elvina's interest in her older son's education. Leon Beals soon found a job in the Berkeley post office to support the family.[14] The parents were willing to make substantial sacrifices for their children, but Leon and Elvina probably found another benefit—the university community was more receptive to their radical ideas than their old neighborhoods in the Los Angeles area.

The second decade of the twentieth century was a period of expansion and rising prestige for the Berkeley institution. In the middle years of his two-decade tenure as president of the university, Benjamin Ide Wheeler not only improved the internal operations of the school, but also built a good relationship with the state legislature and with the general public. He gave students a larger role in university affairs. While maintaining stability in the growing institution, Wheeler recruited outstanding scholars for the faculty.[15] This dynamic academic environment stimulated Beals's developing intellectual abilities and gave him the opportunity to pursue higher education in a serious and enthusiastic fashion.

Apparently committed to a writing career before he entered college, Beals first chose mining engineering as a field that offered lucrative employment to support his real interest. His freshman science courses changed his mind.[16] He dropped out of Berkeley after his first year but returned in the fall of 1913, majoring in English with an economics minor.[17] Beals gained ample opportunity to develop his writing skills. One of his best remembered experiences was in a composition course entitled "An Essay a Day," taught by Professor Frederick Thomas Blanchard, an expert in English literature and a demanding teacher. In one paper, Carleton mistakenly used the word "alter" for "altar,"; Blanchard read a short selection from the paper aloud to the class to point out the error. Despite his sarcastic announcement that "Alter, spelled a-l-t-e-r, rhymes with halter," he afterwards took Beals aside and told him: "Son, you have the knack of writing. Don't let your pen be idle." Beals took this advice to heart; as a senior, he won the University's Bryce Historical Essay Prize with a study entitled "San Francisco as a Steamship Center."[18] He also was a preliminary winner in the upper division Bonnheim Essay Contest in the same year.[19]

While Beals made a good impression on the university's teachers and administrators, he also sharpened his taste for radical ideas.[20] Disappointed by the traditional approach used in the introductory economics course he and a few other students turned to Paul Blissen, a leftist economist then at Berkeley, and requested a special noncredit course in "heretical" economics, including the works of Ricardo, Engels and Marx. Blissen introduced Beals to Engels's *Socialism: Utopian and Scientific*, a book that made a deep impression on the eager student. One of Beals's heroes was another Socialist Eugene V. Debs; one of his biggest disappointments came with Debs's visit to Berkeley. Beals was scheduled to introduce Debs to a meeting held in a large tent. In spite of a heavy downpour outside, the tent was filled to capacity. Just as Beals began to utter his well-considered remarks, Debs entered the tent a bit early, probably to avoid the rain. The gathered faithful sensed Debs's presence and broke into spontaneous cheering cutting off Beals's speech. Debs's appearance was a memorable one; Carleton never gave his speech.[21]

In a series of short, but revealing, articles for a weekly campus paper *Student Opinion,* Beals flexed his intellectual muscles. He argued that the basic role of the university was the search for truth, which meant that students should engage in serious discussions of important issues. He noted in a disappointed tone that much of the informal conversation among students fell into "the ethereal realm of inanity."[22] Ralph Waldo Emerson's "The American Declaration of Independence" was one yardstick by which Beals measured his fellow students. The young radical scorned their complacent natures and their devotion to economic security at a time when larger social and political questions demanded their attention.[23]

Beals graduated with honors from Berkeley in the spring of 1916 and entered Columbia University Teachers College in the fall of that year to work for a Master's degree in education. In addition to a full course load, Beals took part-time jobs to help pay for his expenses. Living frugally, he took residence in an attic that had been converted into an inexpensive apartment. His stay in New York was brief—barely nine months—in which time, he earned the degree. His first teaching experience, supervised by the Teacher' College staff, was at a school just across the Hudson River in New Jersey. Beals soon discovered his main problem was discipline in the classroom. He would lose control of his students during the distribution and collection of papers and textbooks. His supervisors rated him as competent in the subject matter (English) but weak as a disciplinarian. Beals decided that he did not enjoy teaching, although he continued to lecture and give public speeches throughout his career.[24]

## Caught in the Draft

Beals's return to Berkeley with a Master's degree from Columbia in the summer of 1917 was overshadowed by his refusal to submit to the military draft. Given his ideological make-up, it was not surprising that Beals chose to declare himself a conscientious objector. His case arose when the United States had been a participant in World War I for only a few months, and the administration of Woodrow Wilson wanted to build support for the war effort. In particular, Wilson and Secretary of War Newton Baker hoped to avoid bad publicity about the recently instituted draft.[25] In spite of these larger trends, Beals became entangled in a bureaucratic snarl that lasted for seven months and resulted in three brief stays in prison for him.

Beals held a teaching appointment in the San Francisco Bay area for the fall of 1917, but he was unable to keep this commitment because on August 8, 1917, he received orders from Local Board No. 135 in New York City to report for a preinduction physical examination.[26] Instead of making the 3,000-mile trip back to New York, Beals exercised his right to select another draft board and chose the one in Berkeley. He presented his argument as a conscientious objector to Berkeley Exemption Board No. 2 and then refused to undergo the physical examination.[27] Upon the request of the Berkeley board, the local police arrested him on the charge of refusing the physical. While under arrest, Beals announced to the press that he opposed war in general, that he considered conscription to be "un-American and undemocratic," and that he intended to challenge the constitutionality of the draft law in the courts.[28] In spite of this inflamed rhetoric, the Berkeley police released him in a few days; but his troubles had only begun.

Beals's case remained in limbo for about three months because of confusion between the Berkeley and New York draft boards concerning jurisdiction. The New York board had original responsibility, but Beals was detained under the orders of the Berkeley board. Finally in early December, a judge and some military officials in the Bay Area placed him in a local jail, apparently on a charge of desertion. Released after six days through the efforts of some friends, Beals's next problem appeared in the form of a request dated December 13 by the New York board for him to report to the Berkeley board.[29] Four days after that communication, a United States marshall deposited

Beals in the Presidio, a military prison, at that time for refusing induction.[30] Five days after this incarceration began, the New York board, acting with consummate clumsiness, ordered the Berkeley board to send him to the nearest mobilization camp.[31] The Berkeley board refused to comply with this order. It left Beals in the Presidio and, thereby, won the administrative tug-of-war.

Soon after her son's placement in the Presidio, Elvina Beals contacted Roger Baldwin of the National Civil Liberties Bureau (N.C.L.B.) to help present Beals's argument as a conscientious objector. Baldwin immediately took Beals's case to Secretary of War Baker and wrote Elvina that all signs indicated "prompt relief. . . ."[32] The Civil Liberties bureau found the War Department cooperative in dealing with conscientious objectors in late 1917 and early 1918, and Baldwin's optimism was probably based on this general practice.[33] Beals explained his position as a conscientious objector in terms of his belief in the religion of Positivism, which considered humanity the supreme being and war a violation of the sanctity of life. He also stated his willingness to perform noncombatant service and concluded his appeal with the following sarcasm:

I have a rough knowledge of type-writing—this letter is a sample. Whether this constitutes sufficient ability to warrant my being placed at some other employment than my present one of shoveling coal is, of course, for you to decide.[34]

The War Department released Beals in February 1918 not as a conscientious objector, but as a physically unfit reject. The real reason for his release, as Beals recalled more than fifty years later, was that his presence had become such a nuisance that the company commander told the examining physician to find some major disability. The doctor promptly detected a serious heart problem and a hearing impairment and recommended a physical discharge. The company commander readily agreed.[35] On February 11, 1918, Beals left the Presidio with the selective service classification "5-G—a person totally and permanently physically or mentally unfit for military service.[36] Beals's escape from the military was a narrow one because during March 1918, the War Department began to take a hard line with draft resisters, in spite of the efforts of Roger Baldwin's N.C.L.B.[37]

Beals's experience with the draft intensified his feelings about the misuse of governmental authority. He deplored war, and detested the compulsory military service instituted by the government to fight the war. His attachment to Positivism was not permanent, but his skepticism about the workings of the modern state became a prominent part of his thinking in later years. Also his inclination and, at times, eagerness to challenge the established powers grew stronger with the passage of time. He inherited his parents' sympathy for the lower class and their willingness to adhere to radical ideas in the face of adversity. Although he had not formulated a consistent ideology, his dedication to an instinctive value system rooted in left-wing populism was a prominent feature of his thought throughout his career.

Four months after Beals left the Presidio, Eugene Debs made a dramatic speech to a large crowd in Canton, Ohio in which he denounced U.S. participation in World War I. Soon thereafter, federal officials indicted him for violating the Espionage Act; in March of 1919, they obtained a conviction. Debs was in federal prisons for nearly five years, during which time, he suffered from illness and depression.[38] Half a century later, Beals commented with much bitterness and remorse that Debs, "a great orator and a great human being . . . who could bring tears to your eyes," deserved a better fate.[39] Debs's sincere protest against the war and his authentically American brand of socialism made his incarceration seem a great injustice to Beals, who made no effort to mask his admiration for the Indiana radical.

Debs impressed many of his followers as a dynamic, even charismatic, personality with an important message. Their impressions, however, were insufficient to bring them into the Socialist party or to engender their ideological conversion. For Carleton Beals, however, his reverential attitude toward Debs was, in large part, the result of a broad commonality of ideas drawn from their similar experiences in the middle and western parts of the United States. Beals's intellectual heritage found symbolic expression through Debs's valiant, but futile, struggle to defend the interests of the common people—workers and farmers—against the onrush of industrialization and its highly structured class system, filled with social inequity and institutional imbalance. There is much of Beals's experience encapsulated in biographer Nick Salvatore's summary of Debs's role in United States history:

Debs came to understand the complex character of the American democratic tradition and publicly fought to define America's cultural symbols anew, in the changed context wrought by industrial capitalism. In so doing, he reminded all Americans that active engagement occupied the center of the national traditions. His life was a profound refutation of the belief that critical dissent is somehow un-American or unpatriotic.[40]

Beals held these assumptions too, but applied them to Latin America, an area in which the upsurge of the masses encountered resistance not only from the leaders of industrial capitalism but also from the lords of agrarian feudalism. Beals's travels in Mexico, Central America, Cuba and South America introduced him to new varities of rebellion and revolution, but his Debsian left-wing populism often guided his responses to political conflict and ideological disputation.

# • 2 •

# The Making of a Foreign Journalist

Beals's character confronted severe tests in the years from 1918 to 1923. His determination to be a professional writer carried him through editorial rejections, poverty and mental depression to find the subject matter suited to his talents. Journalism, not fiction, proved to be his forte; and the Mexican revolution gave him a topic of current interest to the reading public of the United States. When he crossed the Mexican border in 1918, Beals entered a nation that had been engulfed in violent revolution for seven years. The collapse of the dictatorship of Porfirio Díaz in 1911 seemed to herald the coming of democracy under the idealistic Francisco Madero, but the latter's idealism served him and his nation badly. By 1913, Madero lay dead—the victim of political assassination—and in the next few years, Mexico suffered through a brutal struggle that involved predatory generals, persistent radicals, voracious bandits and desperate conservatives. In 1918, the ultimate outcome of this struggle was in doubt; but the nation's new constitution (drafted in 1917) contained promises of a large-scale restructuring of Mexico's political, economic and social institutions for the benefit of peasants and workers.[1] The Mexican revolution appealed to Beals's populism and gave him first hand experiences that few journalists could match.

Carleton Beals and his brother Ralph set out for Mexico

14

from Berkeley in July 1918. While they had no definite plans, Ralph's eligibility for the draft and Carleton's unhappiness with his job for Standard Oil motivated the brothers to attempt what many considered a risky 1,500-mile trek to Mexico City. A few years later, Carleton wrote *Brimstone and Chili,* an entertaining, if exaggerated, version of their travels. Ralph remained in Culiacan, Sinaloa to work for a friendly German-American businessman before he returned to the United States. Carleton, however, endangered his health, and perhaps his life, to cross the rugged Sierra Madre Occidental on his way to Mexico City. He braved cold November nights at 10,000 feet, a severe case of influenza and unexpected meetings with anti-Yankee revolutionaries before he reached his destination.[2]

## Mexico City

Beals arrived in Mexico City destitute—without money or friends. By his own account, he was a disheveled, unshaven, dirty and barefooted vagabond, who must have resembled a peasant fresh from the backlands with his battered straw hat and a blanket thrown across his shoulders. During his first few days in Mexico City, he was disoriented and confused. He begged a few pesos for an occasional meal until he met Juan de Dios Avellaneda, a member of the Mexican Chamber of Deputies. Their meeting was by chance but Avellaneda, from kindness and perhaps curiosity, took Beals to his home. There Beals bathed and manicured himself, trimmed his beard and selected some clothes from Avellaneda's wardrobe. After a meal with the Avellanedas, Beals left, fortified with a full stomach and a more presentable appearance.[3]

Beals lived in a *casa de huespedes* (a cheap rooming house) in central Mexico City while he searched for employment. He decided to try for a job as an English teacher. His first interview at an upper-class British school proved to be a humiliation which he later blamed on his unsightly cap that he failed to conceal during the interview.[4] He earned a small income by tutoring a few people in English until he met George Politol, a young American with a good idea and four hundred pesos. Beals and Politol joined forces to set up the "English Institute" in a pair of rented offices at the corner of Independence and López streets in what was then a "fashionable" section of the city. Their joint enterprise became a quick success. Within six months after Beals's arrival in Mexico City, he had gone from penury to respectable prosperity.[5]

Beals's fortunes and self-confidence continued to rise during the next several months as his personable nature brought him new friends and acquaintances. In the summer of 1919, he obtained a high-school teaching position at the American School (the main educational institution for children of U.S. citizens residing in Mexico City). Beals gave his mornings to those duties and his afternoons and evenings to the English Institute. He also helped to organize a Shakespeare society for "some of the prominent club women of the American colony" living in Mexico City. Beals's college training in English literature served him well as a teacher and as an emcee of the Shakespearean group. Even though he quickly rose to the position of principal in the American School, he found the narrow interests of the American community to be stifling. With the issue of intervention clouding U.S.-Mexican relations in 1919, Beals refused to dismiss a Mexican student from the school, thus openly defying the wishes of the Americans. This idealistic stand, which revealed his unbending sense of moral certitude, cost him his job.[6]

His appointment as English instructor to President Venustiano Carranza's personal military staff was the high point of Beals's brief teaching career. In the requisite interview with the President, he was the victim of a potentially harmful *faux pas*. As he walked into Carranza's large office, his garter broke with a loud snap. Beals paused, raised his foot onto a nearby chest and repaired the offending garter and then completed a successful interview with Mexico's "First Chief," a decided contrast to his interview at the British school some months earlier.[7] While Beals's work with the presidential staff was short-lived because of Carranza's overthrow in May 1920, he did talk with the president several times and found him "a white-haired patriarch, without much warmth, chilly and inscrutable behind his flowing whiskers and blue spectacles."[8]

Although he was a teacher, Beals forsook the retiring lifestyle of a scholar for the boisterous adventures of a youthful playboy. His charming manner and wide interests brought him an unusually diverse group of companions. He enjoyed the "rough-neck" crowd at Fat-Sing's Chinese Restaurant on Dolores Street, whose favorite topic of conversation seemed to be real and fanciful tales of sexual excess.[9] Beals, himself, had many riotous adventures. One night, for example, after drinking and philosophizing in several bars, Beals and another American writer from the Fat-Sing group grabbed two flags (one Mexican, the other U.S.) from a storefront and launched a two-man offensive against an unsuspecting Mexico City policeman. Escaping arrest because the policeman was too bewildered to react, Beals and his friend continued their drunken revelry until sunrise. Beals then bathed, put on clean cloths, downed several cups of coffee and met his eight-o'clock class at the American School.[10]

Mexico City in this period was a fascinating mixture of stability and confusion, of beauty and ugliness, in which Beals immersed himself with great enthusiasm. Soon after his arrival, he walked through the Alameda, the park located near his *casa de huespedes*, where he lounged in the warm sunlight and listened to "the calls of the bootblacks, of the vendors of oranges, candy and ice, and the chirpings of the canaries." The dark green grass and the "balmy air" helped soothe the anxieties of his early Mexico City days and even inspired dreams of success.[11] From his room at the casa de huespedes, he looked out over Calle Dolores—the Street of Sorrows—which presented an entirely different scene. He saw an old, white-haired woman, whose "querulous voice, writhing from her toothless mouth, implored charity from each callous hearer," as she begged for food. A younger version of feminine street life on Dolores was "the Scarlet Señorita—trim ankle, slender, rounded body, curving face, snapping black eyes—who takes good men and bad, with her charms . . . ."[12] Mexico City possessed more than enough attractions to captivate the inquiring spirit of an impressionable gringo.

Beals was more than an observer of females; his boyish good looks and romantic nature attracted many of the females he met. He abandoned the life of the bachelor, however, on November 5, 1919 to marry Lillian Rhine, a twenty-five year old North American, who knew Beals from his earlier years in Berkeley and San Francisco. They lived in Mexico City for over a year after their marriage and met a number of writers, both Mexican and foreign.[13]

## Among Slackers and Radicals

In the late 1910s, Mexico City was home for an odd assortment of radicals, disillusioned liberals and communists from the United States, Europe and Asia. A special group of foreigners were the draft evaders from the United States, who found Mexico a convenient haven in 1917 and 1918. While their ideologies and purposes varied greatly and they often quarrelled among themselves, these exiles seemed to like the revolutionary atmosphere of Mexico.[14]

Beals knew a number of the cosmopolitan leftists in Mexico City. Among the most prominent was Roberto Haberman, a lawyer from California with a Rumanian-Jewish background. Haberman came to Mexico originally as a lawyer for a communal farm colony in socialist Yucatan. When the socialist administration of Governor Felipe Carillo Puerto began to weaken in the late 1910s, Haberman joined the labor movement in Mexico City, which at that time, was under the direction of Luis Morones. He became the liason between Morones and Samuel Gompers's American Federation of Labor.[15] Beals and Haberman became close friends. In 1920 Haberman helped Beals obtain a Mexican passport so that the latter could travel to Spain.[16] The two men renewed their friendship later in the decade.

Beals and Haberman co-authored a leftist article, which attracted the attention of U.S. military intelligence. Entitled "Mexico Abroad from the Radical Standpoint: The Mexican Government and the Workman," it appeared in the October 1920 issue of *The Liberator*, a socialist magazine published in New York, as well as in translation in a Mexican leftist sheet *La Vida*

*Nueva* during the same month. The article contained much Marxist terminology and was especially sanguine about the class consciousness of the Mexican workers. Beals and Haberman hailed the overthrow of Carranza and the rise of Obregón as victories for the Mexican labor movement. As early as December 17, 1918, U.S. military intelligence intercepted a letter from *The Liberator's* editor to Beals, in which he implied the young reporter was "a pacifist and a contributor" to that radical magazine. By 1920, military intelligence designated Beals as an active member of Mexico City's international leftist community.[17]

This 1920 article also contained some criticism of Morones, which forced Haberman to reconsider the advisability of publishing it. Many years later, Beals recalled that Haberman was "in very close with Morones and (Haberman) wanted it (the article) stopped, but I was already on my way to Spain. How could I stop it? He said it would ruin him if it came out, but apparently it didn't."[18] Haberman was able to hold important positions in the Mexican government for several years after the article appeared.

Beals also knew the Communist organizer Michael Borodin (né Gruzenberg), a Russian agent assigned to Mexico. Beals had several discussions with Borodin and came to dislike him because of his cold, calculating, revolutionary schemes. Borodin hoped to promote war between the United States and Mexico to help take interventionist pressure off Russia, a plan Beals later called "brutal and dastardly,"—a kind of Communist "realpolitik" reminiscent of the nationalist struggles of nineteenth-century Europe. Borodin also accepted the idea of eugenic experimentation and a totally mechanistic explanation of human nature, attitudes that Beals found repulsive.[19]

Beals observed the internal dissension that disrupted the Communist effort in Mexico through his relations with two of the most disputatious leaders Rabindraneth Roy and Len Gale. Roy was an Indian anti-imperialist who joined the Communist movement to help free his homeland from British rule. Beals saw Roy as a traditionalist, except for his desire to liberate India.[20] Gale, "a red-bearded American" who had left the United States for Mexico City to avoid the draft, founded *Gale's*

*International Monthly,* an official Communist publication. Beals and Gale developed a mutual dislike that emerged soon after Beals had roomed with Gale and his wife for a couple of weeks in late 1918 and early 1919. According to Gale, Beals left " . . . when, in January 1919 . . . the Gales' money ran out," thus forcing them to move into less expensive housing.[21] Beals had no respect for either of the organizations those two men tried to form. He revealed his contempt when he described the Communist faction headed by Roy as consisting of " . . . six members and a calico cat."[22]

Mike Gold was the radical who most impressed Beals with his non-conformist life style and his potential for intellectual growth. According to Beals, Gold was a " . . . rough-hewn, dark chap—earthy, elemental, brooding but devil-may-care, full of flamelike seriousness lightened by a whimsical sneer . . ." Beals saw in him a lyrical, literary strength that never completely emerged. Gold seemed to use Marxism as a "doctrinaire prop" so that he would have "proper confidence in himself, although his whole being, the poet and the artist in him, seemed basically opposed to rigid dogma." Beals was disappointed when Gold drifted into the role of propagandist for left wing causes in the 1920s.[23]

U.S. military intelligence was ever alert to the Communists in Mexico during these years. Beals's name, incorrectly spelled, appeared on a list of Bolshevik agents prepared by the agency. Intelligence sources reported that these agents were engaged in the spread of Bolshevik propaganda in South American and Mexico. All had " . . . received direct and personal instructions from Lenine [sic.] and Trotsky with whom they are in constant relation."[24] Beals knew the other two "agents" listed, but his work as a propagandist was limited to the article he and Haberman co-authored for *The Liberator.* His teaching jobs and his writing occupied most of his time. He did, however, know many Communists socially. More important were Beals's aversion to the dogmatic Marxist outlook and his amusement with left-wing factionalism. Unaware of his bemused disgust with the Communists, military intelligence described him as "an alleged slacker and Bolshevik leader," a description that continued to hold credence within U.S. government agencies for many years. Beals became vaguely aware of his reputation within the U.S. government when an American consular agent in Mexico refused to issue him a passport. The official told him, "I don't like the company you keep," probably referring to the nefarious "company" of Haberman, Borodin, Gale, Roy and Gold.[25]

## The Writer

From 1918 to 1920, Mexico City furnished Beals a stimulating atmosphere for writing. Revolutionary politics were tense with the widening schism between the moderate Carranza and the liberal Obregón. Beals's position as English instructor to Carranza's staff brought him close to the center of events; his contacts with Haberman, Borodin, Gale and Roy gave him insights into the machinations of left-wing organizations; and finally, Mexico City itself, through its colorful street people, venal politicians and ambitious soldiers, provided him with an ever-changing social-political milieu to ponder. The obvious contrasts between rich and poor helped to stimulate his egalitarian preferences and gave him a cause with which to identify—the Revolution.

Beals made a firm decision to write for a living during this period. His successful adaptation to Mexican culture, his growing mastery of Spanish, and his meteoric rise from vagrant to English instructor for the presidential staff gave him an improved sense of self-esteem and the courage to break away from "the American herd gospel: success, college friends, conventional engagement . . . a job in the shipping office." Also, the nonconformist attitudes that were to play a part in his writing began to take shape:

My experience had been like a sweeping fire that had burnt away the clutter of dead growth that is falsely planted by society in every young heart. Fear had disappeared—fear of poverty, fear of opinion, fear of love, fear of emotion, fear of future, fear of life.[26]

Beals was not an immediate success as a writer. He concentrated on nonfiction, writing descriptive and analytical material about contemporary Mexico. (His real interests may have been poetry and fiction.) In spite of considerable effort, he was unable to publish in any of these fields from March 1919 to April 1920. Finally on April 3, 1920, editor G. F. Weeks accepted one of Beals's poems for publication in *The Mexican Review*, a small, culturally oriented periodical based in Washington. There was no financial compensation, only an offer of free copies of the issue in which the poem appeared.[27] In addition to the piece he did with Haberman, three of Beals's articles appeared in magazines in the United States in the next few months. The first article in print was a 750-word essay "The Status of Prohibition in Mexico," which appeared in the May 1920 issue of *Current History*.[28] Neither the poem nor the articles had the probing journalistic bite of much of his later writing.

Beals's writing in 1919 and 1920, published and unpublished, indicated the presence of certain perspectives that he retained over most of his career. In an unpublished article entitled "Senador Caer," Beals attacked the U.S. Senate Foreign Relations Committee hearings on Mexico, chaired by archinterventionist Albert B. Fall, as prejudiced against the Mexican revolution.[29] His discussions of prohibition in Mexico pointed out the difficulties of enforcing such laws but concluded that most politicians favored these restrictions because of the debilitating effects of alcohol on the lower classes.[30] More interesting was his essay "The Mexican as He Is," in which he portrayed the Mexican national character as vain, sometimes cruel, often lazy, but artistically gifted and highly idealistic. He also noted that in spite of its anguished history, Mexico had produced a number of great political leaders.[31]

## The Revolution and the Discordant American Left

While Beals was sympathetic to the revolution, he maintained considerable skepticism about certain leaders and their programs. His independent brand of leftist analysis was similar to the highly individualistic approaches of the three most influential American radicals to write about the Mexican revolution in the 1910s: John Reed, Lincoln Steffens and John Kenneth Turner. Although Beals did not know any of them personally, he shared with them an obvious preference for the far left of the ideological spectrum and an equally obvious interest in the Mexican revolution. All four of these writers, however, held particular assumptions that carried them along separate tangents and usually resulted in different interpretations of the events in Mexico.

For example, both Reed and Beals had an intuitive populism that led them to identify with the cause of the downtrodden *campesino*. Fascinated with the audacious rebel and folk hero Pancho Villa, Reed never went much beyond a description of his adventures with the *Villistas* in northern Mexico. Mexican historian Eugenia Meyer observed that Reed's preoccupation with "the armed struggle" limited the value of his writing. Reed's achievement was more in his depiction of the vitality of Villa's rebellion than in the analysis of the causes or the direction of the larger revolutionary movement.[32] By contrast, Beals emphasized the social and economic results of the revolutionary process, not the military actions of the revolutionaries.

Lincoln Steffens had served as Reed's radical mentor in Greenwich Village in the early 1910s where the two reveled in the excitement of those Bohemian times. Their journalistic work in Mexico, however, followed divergent paths. Steffens's ideology was characterized by a belief in the capacity of strong men to lead mass movements in the proper, i.e. leftward, direction. On the other hand, Reed came to doubt the intentions of powerful leaders and the organizations they controlled. His admiration for Villa seemed to flow from the rebel's improvisational, almost anarchic style. For his ideal revolutionary leader, Steffens chose President Venustiano Carranza and denounced Villa as an ignorant bandit.[33]

The disagreement between Reed and Steffens underscored a fundamental source of discord in the American Left of the early twentieth century. Reed's preference for the impetuous Villa and his peasant followers implied a mistrust of powerful organizations that was to surface in Reed's later experience in Russia.[34] Steffens placed his faith in Carranza, a man he believed to be a true revolutionary and a dynamic leader. In fact, Carranza was neither, and the moderate and extreme elements of the Left in Mexico outmaneuvered him at the constitutional convention of 1917 and overthrew him in 1920. These two writers' attitudes, however, illustrate the basic conflict between those radicals who turned to the amorphous and ill-defined entity—the people (and their symbols such as Pancho Villa)— and leftists like Steffens who turned to powerful individuals who seemed to dominate mass movements.

Beals did not accept Reed's image of Villa as the vanguard of the people; he was even more opposed to Steffens's view of Carranza, in particular, and of revolutionary strongmen, in general. Beals observed the Mexican Left's growing disaffection with Carranza from 1918 to 1920 and regarded the coup d'etat led by General Alvaro Obregón as a triumph for the Mexican masses. Beals's writing on Mexico in the 1920s revealed a strong Debsian cast to his ideology. It was especially pronounced in his determination to evaluate the use of power in terms of benefits produced for workers and peasants. For Beals, the main characteristic of revolution was neither the political-military uprising, nor the ascension of a charismatic leader to authority; rather it was the ability of the revolutionary state to eliminate or, at least, to reduce social and economic inequities.

The American radical writer Beals most admired from the first decade of the revolution was the California socialist and muckraker John Kenneth Turner. In order to gather information on the reputed exploitation of workers under the Díaz dictatorship, Turner traveled through Mexico in 1908 disguised as a wealthy businessman looking for investment opportunities. First, in a series of articles in *The American Magazine* in 1910 and then, in a fuller book-length version *Barbarous Mexico,* Turner revealed the cruel plantation system that held its workers in virtual slavery. Turner was a proponent of the popular demands for land reform. Like Steffens and Beals, he was critical of the headstrong, unpredictable Villa. Given Mexico's endemic instability, Turner reluctantly accepted the conservative, bewhiskered "first chief" Carranza as an adequate leader for the massive social upheaval that would eventually remake the nation. Beals saw Carranza as a serious problem for the revolution. In general, however, he agreed with Turner's view that Mexico was caught up in a popular revolution that could not be denied in the long run, even by a revolutionary caudillo or an interventionist neighbor.[35]

Reed, Steffens and Turner provided no clear consensus for the American Left on Mexico in the 1910s. Beals, very much within their tradition of idiosyncratic radicalism, followed his own course in the next decade. All four of these writers grew up on the West Coast of the United States. Although they traveled widely and witnessed a variety of political movements, they seemed to stand in contrast to the East Coast radicals of urban America, many of whom were European immigrants or their descendants and who carried with them Europe's ideological preoccupations. Reed, Steffens, Turner and Beals were less concerned with the axioms and nuances of ideology than with the people who made up the revolutionary movements. Although Steffens placed his faith in the great leader, the other three were, in the last analysis, left-wing populists who looked to the masses in their efforts to understand the complexity of social revolution.

## Revolution in Mexico: 1920

Beals's doubts about the Carranza regime became irrelevant when in May of 1920, the army of Alvaro Obregón, heavily reinforced by Mexico's labor unions, ousted the incumbent president. Carranza had made a serious error when he opposed the leftist revision of the constitution at the Querétaro Convention of 1917. Thereafter, Obregón had the support of most of the worker and peasant elements as well as of the army. Carranza's power base eroded quickly, while Obregón consolidated his gains.

The overthrow of Carranza's government by the forces of Alvaro Obregón was the single most important event Beals witnessed and described in 1920. Obregón built up his military strength north of Mexico City, while Carranza attempted to impose an unpopular successor for the office of president. By May 5, 1920, however, Obregón clearly held the advantage in manpower and supplies. Beals discovered that Carranza's followers were hurriedly preparing to leave the capital for Veracruz, with all of the material possessions and money they could find. Beals was surprised to find the city in a light-hearted mood. Obregón's troops dashed into the outskirts of the city to find streetcars, buses and automobiles running as usual. Businessmen kept their stores open; their only precaution was to close the shutters over their shop windows. Most of Carranza's entourage escaped by rail before the rebels arrived, but the last train to depart was not so fortunate. Beals was on the scene soon after a spectacular train wreck. He pieced together the story of the pursuit of the heavy-laden *Carrancista* train by a locomotive run at full throttle under the command of a young Obregonistra officer. At the last second, the *Obregonista* jumped from the engine and "like the finale of an impossible movie film, the locomotive hurtled down the track, crashing in the rear of the Carranza train, utterly destroying three cars and disabling the remainder."[36]

When Beals left Mexico in the fall of 1920, he was much changed from the haggard, sickly person who had entered Mexico City two years earlier. His improved health reflected his new status as teacher and freelance writer. Cornelius Ferris of the U.S. military intelligence wrote the following description of Beals at the time of his departure:

Mr. Beals is about thirty years of age, short, florid complexion, light eyes, brown hair. While in Mexico, he wore a beard, light-colored and short, Van Dyke style. He will probably identify himself with educational influences and people of literary pretensions.[37]

Beals's identification with "educational influences and literary pretentions" placed him close to, if not within, the typology of leftist intellectuals devised by historian Christopher Lasch nearly a half-century later. A teacher and an aspiring writer, Beals was also a stubborn, rebellious individual who had resisted the draft and seen a revolution. The values and attitudes he inherited from his parents found reinforcement at Berkeley and in his first two years in Mexico. He was, in Lasch's words, "an outsider by necessity" who accepted and, at times, enjoyed his place beyond the environs of the comfortable middle class and its concomitant devotion to the status quo.[38]

## Italian Interlude

Beals and his wife Lillian visited Spain briefly and then settled in Italy for about two years. World War I was a traumatic event for most European nations, and Italy was no exception. They saw the economic reconstruction of Italy languish as political extremists exploited popular unrest to gain the upper hand. While Carleton struggled to write prose and poetry, Benito Mussolini seized power and built his fascist state,[39] a drama that the leftist writer could not ignore. Although neither Italy nor any other European country captured Beals's attention in a substantial way after 1923, his stay in Florence and Rome pointed him toward a career in journalism.

The Bealses found their time in Italy immensely trying. Dependent on his small savings and irregular income as a writer, they soon faced a bleak existence in a strange land where neither of them spoke the native language. In Beals's letters to his mother he described the depths to which they had fallen—a narrow survival on twelve lire (about $.70) a day. Beals calculated that he had seven months "to break in" as a writer; "otherwise, we are on the streets." He complained of their poverty, of living "so terribly close to the margin."[40]

Finances were only one of Beals's problems. He suffered from a recurrence of rheumatism he first contracted in Mexico and also from newly acquired respiratory congestion.[41] His most serious problem, however, was a deep and lingering depression that, some fifteen years later, he called "a nervous breakdown."[42] His anguish spilled over into a pathetic letter to his mother written in August 1921. He was despondent and had almost no hope of success as a writer or anything else; yet in this fit of depression, he showed a stubborn resolve to continue the struggle to write. In a poignant passage, both hopeful and bitter, he confessed that "the only thing I can do is write."[43]

Ironically, it was the Fascist Mussolini's rise to power that drew the leftist Beals away from creative literature to journalism and ultimately, to success as a writer. Beals's interpretation of Mussolini's regime, published in 1923, differed substantially from the image presented by most of the U.S. press. The majority of reporters accepted Mussolini's propaganda at face value and did not delve beneath the surface to expose the menacing aspects of fascism.[44] Beals's analysis of the Italian Fascist state was remarkable for its penetrating insights, even more so considering that he wrote in 1921 and 1922, before and soon after *Il Duce* assumed control.[45] Like other journalists, Beals found Mussolini a fascinating character. He was the first reporter, however, to expose Il Duce as a ruthless dictator. Beals understood him as a deft political manipulator, who was more concerned with power than with ideas. Mussolini possessed an excessively combative nature, an "uncontrollable hot-headedness," and a strangle hold on key political institutions. Lincoln Steffens's favorable impressions of Mussolini's ability to impose change contrasted sharply with Beals's warnings about the darker side of Il Duce's quest for total control. Beals described Mussolini's demogogic speaking style, enhanced by the jutted jaw, gleaming eyes, strutting posture—all combined with an actor's oratorical skills—which gave Italy's Fascist chief immense popular appeal to reinforce his authoritarian methods.[46]

Carleton and Lillian Beals left Rome for the hospitable environs of Mexico City in early 1923, thereby marking the end of Beals's first half-decade as a freelance writer. His years in Mexico and Italy were similar in that, in both cases, he was awed by foreign cultures, isolated from fellow North Americans, and impoverished for extended periods of time. In Mexico, he overcame these challenges by meeting a wide circle of people and earning a degree of financial security through teaching and, to a lesser extent, writing. In Italy, his responses were less successful. Even with the firm support of his wife Lillian, he was unable to adapt to life in Florence and Rome, nor was he able to find ready outlets for his writing. The depression that consumed him in 1921 and 1922 was the low point of his early career, but his resilience in the face of disappointment and melancholia was indicative of his unflagging desire to succeed as a writer. In 1923, opportunities arose that enabled him to combine motivation and dedication with his considerable talents for observation and written expression; Beals produced two books and a half-dozen articles. After 1923, the hard times were over—at least for a while.

# • 3 •

# The Revolution

Carleton Beals's return to Mexico in 1923 was marked by a potent mixture of journalistic success, intellectual excitement and personal anguish in the midst of a critical period in one of the first social revolutions in modern history. Beals soon realized that Mexico held the attention of a large segment of the reading public of the United States, much as it had in the previous decade. President Woodrow Wilson and his advisors had constructed their own understanding of the process of revolution in response to events in Mexico in the 1910s and Russia from 1917 to 1921. Both experiences indicated to Wilson and his successors Harding and Coolidge that large scale revolutions unleashed forces in society that led to economic disruption and political chaos. These conditions posed a threat to Wilson's idealized world system of peaceful, democratic nations engaged in orderly economic growth and commercial exchange.

Beals was one of the first writers from the United States to take exception to the Wilsonian view of revolution on the basis of events in Mexico. He observed the revolution closely and found its goals and, in most cases, its methods to be essentially beneficial for the people of Mexico. Beals joined with a new group of leftist commentators (Turner and Steffens no longer wrote about Mexico, and Reed had died in Russia in 1920) to emphasize that the social and economic reform programs initiated by President Alvaro Obregón in the early 1920s were intended to build a more egalitarian society. In short, Beals argued that the revolution had outgrown the disorder of the previous decade and that the Wilsonian view, accepted in large part by the Harding and Coolidge administrations, was no longer valid in the case of Mexico.[1]

Leftists in the United States were also struggling with the issue of revolution. The death of Lenin in 1924 and the rise of Stalin to power in Russia greatly complicated the debates about the use and abuse of power in a revolutionary context. Beals gave little attention to Russia in the 1920s, however, and formulated most of his ideas on revolution from his observations of events in Mexico. Within the diverse ideological framework of the American Left, Beals shared his views on Mexico with liberals Herbert Croly of the *New Republic* and Ernest Gruening of *The Nation* and radicals Frank Tannenbaum, later of Columbia University, and Norman Thomas of the Socialist party. By the last years of the decade, Beals, Gruening and Tannenbaum had become Mexican specialists who took their positions far to the left of the Wilsonians. They, nevertheless, displayed a willingness to find fault with the revolutionary state's excessive power, that for many ardent defenders of Bolshevik Russia was a painful, even forbidden subject.[2]

### Personal Anguish and Recovery

The personal anguish came as a result of the abrupt end of his marriage to Lillian in early 1924. The exact causes of their marital dissolution remain uncertain, but Beals's May 1924 letter to his mother gave the impression that he may have initiated the split. He wrote that "Lillian and I went into the arrangement on a 50/50 basis. If she suffered more than I it was her own fault. . . . I didn't intend to love anybody out of pity, kindness or respect for conventions." If Beals started the trouble that caused the breakup, he also suffered. In a fashion reminiscent of his depressed days in Italy, he complained to his mother of his poverty, his hopelessness, and his inability to write—all of which hit him soon after Lillian returned to her parents in California.

This letter, however, gave only one version of divorce. One of Beals's friends in Mexico City in those years, Katherine Anne Porter wrote a short story "That Tree," which probably contained a more objective portrait of the end of the marriage, especially its effects on Beals. Although not published until 1934, Porter incorporated an emotional quality in the mind of her unnamed central character, "the journalist," that must have drawn on conversations with Beals soon after Lillian left. Porter's Lillian (Miriam in the story) walked out of the marriage because she felt trapped in a Bohemian life style she despised. Beals clung to his dream of becoming "a cheerful bum lying under a tree in a good climate, writing poetry." He rejected the idea of a conventional job. Lillian, a schoolteacher with "a professional habit of primness," could not tolerate their disheveled, inexpensive apartment, his nonconformist, sloppily-dressed friends, his fondness for things Mexican, or the bleak future that his worse-than-mediocre poetry promised.

In this story, however, Porter saw Lillian's departure as a turning point in Beals career. Stunned by her sudden exit, Beals spent a night of sleepless misery. The unhappy marriage he had hoped to save was gone, and as a result, he finally discarded his futile ambitions in poetry. At this point, according to Porter, "he started out . . . to make a career for himself in journalism" to win Lillian back. It was his second choice. He thought, however, it "would impress his wife [and] the work was just intellectual enough to save his self-respect." Although the marriage never recovered, Carleton Beals became "quite an important journalist, an authority on Latin American revolutions."

It is impossible to determine how many of the psychological aspects of the story were the products of Porter's imagination and how many were observations of what she actually saw in Beals. So many of his documented characteristics in the early 1920s fit the story, however, that it is difficult to dismiss her account as purely imaginary. His desire to write poetry, his

Bohemian life-style, his radical friends, his career crisis (in Porter's story this occurs in Mexico, not in Italy) and his depression after Lillian left all find reinforcement in his published and unpublished writings. Also his propensity to dwell in mental anguish as described in "That Tree" was similar to his responses to later crises in his life in 1937, 1944 and the early 1950s.[3]

Beals's depression was relieved somewhat when he resumed an active social life that included relationships with many attractive young females. An early example of this revival was the short and, from his point of view, apparently intense and ultimately unsuccessful affair with Irene McKinnon, an American he met in Mexico. In an abrupt, almost angry letter she congratulated him on the publication of *Mexico: An Interpretation*. In the next sentence, however, she stated that "the autographed inscription [in the copy he sent her] was somewhat tardy and stupid, inasmuch as I selected my future "novio" [fiancee] some six months previous[ly]." This failure was soon forgotten in the excitement of a series of romances, with among others, the devoted Lupe, the beautiful Mercedes and the poetic Angie. Mercedes, the sister of model and photographer Tina Modotti, wrote him love letters in Italian, one of which included the phrase: "E por uno notte de amore e baci, baci, baci." [Translation: And for one night of love—kiss me, kiss me, kiss me.] Beals's busy love life probably reached its peak in 1926 and 1927. He kept photographs of many young women from this period, some signed with ardent expressions of affection.[4] Under such conditions, his divorce-damaged ego began to heal.

Beals's social activities after his divorce included more than female companions. As an important member of the U.S. expatriate community in Mexico City he frequented bars and restaurants in the central part of the city near the Alameda. His apartment, a room in a converted convent, was across the street from the offices of *Excelsior*, Mexico City's large daily newspaper. Within walking distance were a number of eating and drinking establishments that offered many levels of quality in food and drink. The U.S. expatriates enjoyed this environment. Beals, in particular, seemed at home in the somewhat boisterous environs of the "beer halls," populated largely by working-class types, where he and his companions inbibed *cerveza* and relished the ambience, at a slight risk to stomach and limb.[5]

## The Revolution and American Leftists

While Beals regained his personal equilibrium, he watched closely the efforts of Presidents Obregón (1920-1924) and Plutarco Elías Calles (1924-1928) to deal with the nation's problems. Both presidents had to cope with international pressures, largely from the United States and the demands of workers and peasants. Calles chose to continue Obregón's plans to strengthen the national government, in order to give it the capacity to deal with both challenges. Historians have come to debate whether the Obregón-Calles presidencies intended a revolutionary remaking of Mexican society or if they merely attempted to create a facade of reform in order to secure their grasp on the reins of power. There is no doubt, however, that many Mexicans and North Americans sensed that a genuine revolution was underway in these years.[6] The early stages of land redistribution and labor organization, the growing hostility toward U.S. business interests, the flourishing of left-wing art and literature, and the arousal of the lower classes convinced Beals and many of his colleagues that Mexico had embarked on a genuine restructuring of its social and economic systems.

American writers on the left side of the ideological spectrum saw in Mexico a land of great revolutionary promise. It was a nation that contrasted sharply with the conservative, middle-brow, commercial-mindedness of the United States. They wanted to build support for their own nascent organization among Mexican workers and intellectuals. Beals worked with these writers from the United States, who represented a broad cross section of leftist opinion from liberals like Herbert Croly, who was interested in the reform policies of the government, to Communists like Bertram Wolfe, who criticized the same government from a Marxist perspective.

Bertram and Ella Wolfe arrived in Mexico City in 1922 from Boston with two goals in mind. One was to teach English in José Vasconcelos's newly created ministry of education, and the second was to unify Mexico's factionalized Communist party. Beals, who had become highly dubious of the Communist movement in Mexico from his observations of the Roy-Borodin-Gold altercations from 1919 to 1921, found the Wolfes much more effective in their efforts among workers and especially intellectuals. Leftist infighting, however, would not die. Beals watched the growing rivalry between the Wolfes and the Communist party on one side, with Luis Morones, head of Mexico's largest labor union Regional Confederation of Mexican Labor (CROM) on the other side. Morones soon gained the upper hand, and apparently, engineered the expulsion of Bertram Wolfe from Mexico in 1925. Although Beals was friendly with both Wolfes, this type of internecine strife was potentially harmful for a journalist like Beals, who wanted access to people and organizations with a variety of ideological dispositions. In spite of these considerations, Beals gave serious thought to an offer from Ella Wolfe to travel in South America in the summer of 1925. She made the offer on behalf of the Mexican Communist party and its chief financial source the Soviet Union. Ostensibly, Beals was to study political and economic conditions, but actually he was to open contacts with the continent's leading intellectuals. Probably troubled by the financial and intellectual harness such an arrangement would entail, Beals turned down the offer and continued to stay some distance from the Mexican Communist party and the political storms that usually surrounded it. Instead, he chose to concentrate his attention on the highly fluid state of the revolution.[7]

Beals' ideology was sufficiently flexible for him to have a fairly close personal relationship with the Wolfes and, at the same time, to develop a good working relationship with Herbert Croly, editor of the liberal *New Republic*. While the initial thrust of innovative liberalism in the United States had dissipated during World War I, Croly showed considerable interest in the Mexican revolution. In early 1927, he visited Mexico City, where he met frequently with Beals for lunch. Beals was surprised by the conversational reticence of such an outspoken champion of liberal reform. "Our lunches," Beals recalled a decade later, "mostly consisted of sitting and following our own trains of thoughts, with occassional remarks to keep our rumination in the same channels." Beals also noticed Croly's "serious determination" to understand Mexico, a feeling that was reflected in several articles and editorials in the *New Republic.*[8] Croly praised the revolution's social and economic programs and condemned the United States's threats to interfere in the internal affairs of Mexico.[9]

Beals also worked closely with Ernest Gruening, who as managing editor of *The Nation,* came to have a deep interest in Mexican affairs. A 1912 graduate of Harvard Medical School, Gruening chose the more uncertain field of journalism. He rose rapidly from reporter on the *Boston Traveler* in 1912 to his position at the prestigious *Nation* in 1921. He began to take an interest in the United States's role in Latin America and made an extended trip to Mexico from the winter of 1922 through the summer of 1923. On Gruening's next trip, he invited Beals to his rented home in the Colonia Roma section of Mexico City. *The Nation* had published some of Beals's articles on Mexico and Gruening had formed a preconception of Beals as "an old man with a beard." The youthful Beals was amused to hear of this mistaken assumption. (Mrs. Gruening was less than amused at the antics of Beals's companion, the poet Witter Bynner, who was busily teaching the two Gruening boys how to smoke cigarettes. Mrs. Gruening politely rescued them from the clutches of Witter Bynner by ordering them to "try something else" for a while.[10])

Beals carefully nurtured his connections with the journalistic leaders of the liberal establishment. At the same time, however, he benefited from his friendship with Robert Hammond Murray, a quick-witted curmudgeon in his sixties who was quite capable of mounting conservative attacks against the revolution. Murray had been in Mexico for more than a decade, having arrived during the last years of the dictatorship of Porfirio Díaz. Beals met Murray, probably through Gruening, and soon found that he possessed a wealth of information about Mexico. Beals relished Murray's bluntness and listened closely to his acute observations. He remembered Murray as a "precisely dressed man, hard of hearing . . . [with] an earphone in his ear; [he] wore glasses, [had] a very keen mind, very sharp tongue, [and] a great deal of wit."[11] The Beals-Murray friendship lasted for three decades.

Murray was far to the right of Beals's leftist colleagues who founded the *New Masses*, a journal of radical opinion, in New York City in 1926. Beals was present at the selection of its first editor Mike Gold, whom Beals had known in Mexico City in the 1918 to 1921 period. The first few issues of the *New Masses* carried Beals's name on the masthead and contained articles by a number of leftists on a variety of subjects, including some by John Dos Passos on Mexico. Beals had no apparent objection to these issues, but he was distressed by editor Gold's devotion to "the Communist catechism," which made the magazine too much of "an official organ of the Communist party." Because of his lack of sympathy with Gold's strident ideological proclamations, Beals withdrew his name from the list of the magazine's supporting editors.[12]

Beals was more in accord with the conclusions reached by the supple intellect of Frank Tannenbaum. Working as a journalist, Tannenbaum first came to Mexico in the summer of 1922. He met Beals a year later, and the two soon developed an amiable relationship.[13] Tannenbaum, a member of the International Workers of the World, was a radical activist in the United States in the 1910s. He later became an out-spoken advocate of prison reform, in part because he spent a year in the Blackwell's Island Prison as a result of his agitation on behalf of the unemployed. After his release, he turned to academics and earned his bachelor's degree from Columbia University in 1921.[14] Like Beals and Gruening, he was captivated by the Mexican revolution and for many years gave much of his time to the study of its inner workings.

Beals was a consistent but nondoctrinaire left-wing populist who developed personal and working relationships with writers who held a variety of ideological positions. With the conservative Murray, liberals Croly and Gruening, Communists Bert and Ella Wolfe and the radical Tannenbaum, Beals exchanged observations and ideas—sometimes in a friendly manner, and at other times, in obvious discord. While ideology was important to him, Beals did not allow such disagreements to jeopardize most of these relationships. In fact, he usually benefited from his dealings with this varied assortment of friends and acquaintances.

### An Indictment of the Old Regime

Like many of his colleagues in Mexico, Beals was drawn to the revolution not only from journalistic curiosity but also from personal sympathy with the common people of Mexico. As early as October 1921, Beals wrote his mother that he wanted "to write the finest sociological study ever written in English on Mexico."[15] He was preparing a manuscript at that time and eventually submitted it to B. W. Huebsch, a New York publisher. Huebsch gave the manuscript a favorable reading, although he advised Beals to "reduce some of the heat which, though an evidence of earnestness, detracts from the dignity of the work."[16] Beals followed his advice to some extent, but *Mexico: An Interpretation* retained much of the vitriol of the original version. It was a book written in anger. Beals directed this anger on the Mexican aristocracy, the British and American diplomats and businessmen residing in Mexico City, and the Catholic church. He favored the peasants, the workers, and the reform-minded political leaders and insisted that the Mexicans could resolve their problems without foreign interference.

Beals directed his most caustic comments against the "selfish, willful, intolerant, arrogant" sons of the aristocracy who grew up to be "snobs and tyrants" in adulthood. Raised within the narrow confines of their class and educated abroad in the elite schools of France and the United States, these idle, frivolous gentlemen had no sense of identity with their nation and no sense of responsibility in public affairs. Most of them wasted their lives in endless rounds of late-night parties, and some engaged in flagrant sexual debauchery including incest. Beals observed "that the average young aristocrat is a wreck before thirty—a drunkard, a sexual pervert, and a cynic." That this dissipated and degenerate group be restored to the political power it held in the Díaz years was to Beals an absurd proposition that only U.S. diplomats and businessmen would entertain.[17]

Beals's contempt for the American colony in Mexico City rivaled, but did not quite equal, his disgust for the aristocracy. While serving as teacher and the principal of the American School, Beals gained some valuable insights about the attitudes of U.S. citizens in Mexico. He expressed admiration for those who learned something of Mexican culture and history. He denounced the blatant racism of many Americans who placed most Mexicans, Indians and *mestizos* alike, into the category of biological inferiority while they elevated only the aristocratic descendents from pure or nearly pure European stock to a plane of equality with Anglo-Saxons from north of the Rio Grande. The irony of the sober, hard-working, moralistic Americans advocating political power for the riotous, lazy, amoral upper class was not lost on Beals. He also scorned the passion for U.S. intervention of the *gringos*, who saw it as the only means to civilize Mexico and to restore the calm and prosperity of the Díaz years. In short, Beals found that many Americans were racist reactionaries who chose to reinforce their ignorance by isolating themselves from the vast majority of the Mexican people.

Beals's sympathies clearly lay with the common people of Mexico, the Indians and the mestizos (mixture of Indian and European). He did not romanticize the Indian past as some revolutionaries tended to do, but rather saw the Aztec Empire as a dictatorial system with an appalling record of violence and war. The future, Beals hoped, would bring out other aspects of the Indians' character—honesty, industry, self-abnegation and communalism, which together could overcome the fatalistic mysticism that often produced a debilitating passivity. The revolutionary emphasis on the positive, creative potential of the common people found an enthusiastic supporter in Beals. He was convinced that the clever, tenacious, adaptable mestizo was destined to lead Mexico out of its history of conquest and civil strife to a more peaceful existence based on an equitable distribution of property. Obregón's breakup of the large haciendas, his rural schools and his support for organized labor were early steps in the process of casting Mexico in a new image.[18]

The critical response in the United States to *Mexico: An Interpretation* was generally favorable. James G. McDonald of the *New Republic* saw Beals's social and political analyses as "sometimes profound and always interesting," although he warned readers of the book's pro-Obregón position.[19] Ernest Gruening wrote a similar review in which he praised the overall impact of the book but questioned a few of Beals's specific conclusions.[20] The most provocative review of *Mexico* came from the pencil of Robert Hammond Murray, who scratched marginal comments throughout his copy of the book. He agreed with Beals's diatribes against the Mexican aristocracy and the British and American residents of Mexico City, however, he disagreed sharply with Beals's advocacy of land distribution as a means of solving the agrarian problem. Murray believed that the large haciendas should be left intact in order to raise the level of food production.[22]

## Among the Revolutionaries

Encouraged by the modest success of *Mexico*, Beals again immersed himself in the revolution. The most obvious sources of information were government leaders like Obregón and Calles, both of whom Beals soon knew along with other key politicians. The politics of the revolution were only part of the story, however, and Beals sought out intellectuals and artists to study the cultural side of Mexico in the 1920s. He was also interested in the effects of the revolution on the peasants, who inhabited the isolated rural villages of Mexico's vast hinterland. Like many liberal journalists, Beals wanted the peasants and workers—the meek of Mexico—to inherit the benefits of the revolution, an expectation that sometimes failed to materialize.

His serious concern with the revolution did not prevent Beals from seeing the lighter side of Mexican politics. Alvaro Obregón was one of his nation's brightest wits, and Beals saw enough of him to appreciate his humor. While Beals was assisting a photographer friend in Chapultepec Park not far from the castle where the Mexican president lived, Obregón walked up to them alone, without any security guards. Beals remembered years later that Obregón "asked with a grin how much an assistant was paid.

'Not much. Three pesos a day,' Beals replied.

'Well, keep the job open for me. I don't know just how long I'll be sitting up there.' (He waved his left hand at the castle above us and grinned.)"[22]

More important than Beals's appreciation of presidential humor was his respect for Obregón as a national leader in a time of crisis. He found Obregón's military record in the violent 1910s to be especially praiseworthy.[23] He was most impressed, however, with Obregón's utilization of the relative peace his military prowess had helped establish to initiate reform.[24]

Beals knew Plutarco Elías Calles, Obregón's supporter and successor to the presidency. While Beals admired some of Calles's policies, he found very little to admire in his personality. He concluded that Calles was "a course, ruthless man of extraordinary intelligence and force and a glimmer of idealism," who was capable of using violent methods to achieve his purposes.[25] Beals had access to Calles's administration through an interesting source, Calles's personal secretary, María González. For a short time in 1923 or 1924, she had studied English under the tutelage of Beals. He cultivated this relationship because she was an important influence in the Calles government, opening or closing contact with the often reclusive president as she saw fit. Beals and many others knew that she was Calles's mistress as well as his secretary, positions that she filled until his death.[26]

The corpulent Luis Morones, a member of the Calles cabinet, was Mexico's most powerful labor leader in the 1920s.[27] Beals admired his tenacity in pursuit of the goals of the working class but became disillusioned by Morones's use of violence. By accident, Beals overheard a conversation in which the labor boss apparently ordered the assassination of a political opponent Senator Francisco Field Jurado. Beals tried several times to reach the senator without success. On the following morning, newspapers carried stories of Field Jurado's murder.[28] Beals had no solid evidence of Morones's involvement but thereafter saw him as ruthless and vicious character who was, ultimately, a danger to the revolution.

Beals was unaware of another of Morones's activities. Because of the tense relations between Mexico and the United States, President Calles authorized Morones to run the Mexican press agency which, among its other duties, monitored publications in the United States about Mexico. This agency often reported directly to the chief executive and included in its coverage the work of Beals, Gruening and their colleagues. The reports of the agency, and presumably Morones himself took special interest in criticisms of the Calles government.[29]

## An Appreciation of Rural Mexico

The political machinations in Mexico City contrasted with the return to calm in much of rural Mexico in the mid-1920s. Frequently disrupted by the civil strife of the 1910s, peasant society moved back to the quiet, but essential, quest for food and shelter. Beals spent much time in isolated villages. While there was little to report of immediate importance, he sympathized with the campesinos' struggle to survive in an unyielding environment.

The humble life-style of the Indian and mestizo peasants convinced Beals that they were morally superior to the middle-class, materialistic moneygrubbers of the United States. Certainly these peasants, he reasoned, were not far from starvation. Ordinary diseases claimed many of their lives and they were easily victimized by earthquakes and floods. But their inner strength enabled them to accept these losses and to continue to build and to rebuild, to battle the ferocity of nature and to appreciate its beauty, to worship life in its many forms and to accept death.

Beals enjoyed the simple aesthetics of life in Indian villages. His prose was poetic in its descriptions of these isolated havens of Indian traditionalism and natural grandure. In Tepotzlán, a centuries-old valley town in the mountainous state of Morelos, he watched in relaxed wonderment as the forces of nature put on an entrancing display. He rose early to catch the bright, clear sunrise. In the afternoon the clouds thickened and a thunderstorm threatened. Beals took refuge in the nearby church from where he saw

Sheets of flame ripple around the horizon; the thunder of smashing clouds descends in avalanches of terrorizing uproar upon the plaza. The bold stone escarpments of the mountain seem outposts of destructive malice as if Tepozteco (patron god of the village) . . . on El Cerro had seized, in his mailed fists sheaves of lighting, and boulders of thunder, and buckets of boiling oil-like water to hurl upon the huddling valley-dwellers—bent on destroying his people.

While the people of Tepotzlán could survive these storms and other natural traumas, they were threatened by the greater dangers of rapid expansion of alien institutions. They were "unwilling to admit their lives are shaped by force and historic tides not of their own will. But their checkered history is shattering their illusions." Beals likened outside intrusions to scars left by the violence of battle. The Catholic churches were large, monumental scars; the use of galvanized metal roofing, while not so imposing, was symptomatic of equally disruptive incursions of the industrial economy; and even the public library, with its homages to Plato, Cervantes and Molière, seemed to threaten the ancient Nahuatl culture. The most recent scar was the Bolshevik-inspired banners of the disciples of Lenin and Trotsky, who were far out of step with the Indians who had supported their own revolutionary Emiliano Zapata a decade earlier.[30]

With some hesitation, Beals accepted the idea that social

and economic change was necessary in rural Mexico. As with organized labor in the early 1920s, Beals was at first enthusiastic about land reform—the dismantling of the large estates and the distribution of their lands to the peasants. Simplifying the problem, he stated that any government which refused to enact land reform "must be adjudged criminal unpatriotic and bandit-minded."[31] By the mid-1920s, Beals saw a more complex picture. He especially realized the importance of high levels of agricultural production to supply food for consumers and raw products for industry. He even went so far as to deplore peasants' premature seizure of hacienda land through politicized local agrarian commissions, which he saw as injurious to the economy and a "legalized form of crop-raiding." His fundamental concern, however, lay with the peasants, who needed the land no matter how complicated the process of distribution.[32]

The narrow approach to land reform espoused by the Calles government eventually discouraged Beals. He argued that Calles never gave the *ejido* (or collective farm) system a fair chance. He felt that Calles had instead committed the revolution to the free enterprise theory of individual land ownership run on the basis of efficient modern technology. In addition, this policy did not receive a fair test because of corruption. Land reform officials became petty politicians, who used their authority as weapons with which to extract votes and money. In 1931, Beals described a dismal situation in which former debt peons, finally freed from their ties to the hacienda, could only drift aimlessly because of the unavailability of land. By contrast, he forecast that "the large *hacienda* will soon become once more the dominant factor in rural production."[33]

## The Campaign Against the Church

Beals worked closely with Herbert Croly, editor of *the New Republic*, on covering events in Mexico during the critical year of 1927.[34] In January of that year, Croly visited Mexico City, where Beals served as his guide to the intricacies of Mexican politics.[35] Both men recognized that the conflict between the Mexican government and the Catholic church that erupted into civil war in 1926 was a puzzlement to many non-Catholics in the United States and a justification for armed invasion to some prominent Catholic leaders. Since most American Protestants were aware that the Mexicans had been a Catholic people for over four centuries, moreover, the Calles government's policies directed against this venerable institution seemed inconsistent and vaguely ominous. Several prominent Catholics expressed anger more than confusion. The Knights of Columbus, a lay Catholic organization, demanded U.S. intervention to protect the church. Beals and Croly sought to unravel the jumbled church-state issue, in order to help discourage the movement for direct involvement by the U.S. military.

The causes of strife between church and state in Mexico went back at least to the 1700s when the Enlightenment-inspired Bourbon monarchs in Spain attempted to limit church influence in their American colonies in order to stimulate economic progress. The notion that the church was a barrier to material and social development persisted throughout the nineteenth century and was one of the primary reasons for the bloody three-year civil war of the late 1850s. The constitution of 1917, with a combination of radical and liberal twentieth- century ideologies, revived the campaign of the Left against the church. Calles was Mexico's first chief executive with the determination to enforce all of these restrictive and punitive provisions, and he did so with the intensity of an anticlerical zealot. The church, already on the defensive, responded to Calles by the declaration of a strike—the cessation of all baptisms, marriages and funerals—until the government relaxed its policies. This dramatic gesture caused great concern, even panic, among the faithful of Mexico.[36]

Beals's first attempt to explain the church-state crisis came in an article for *The Survey* soon after the strike started. He argued that the Catholic church was in decline because of internal factors, primarily its failure to adjust to historical forces that were in the process of uprooting the social and political traditions of Mexico. According to Beals, the Indian population had arisen from its former passivity; the government had asserted its authority against foreign powers, both secular and clerical;

and the intelligensia was committed to the importation of a liberal-leftist value system. The church, which had possessed the hearts and minds of the Mexican people for so long, seemed unable to meet these challenges.[37]

Croly wrote Beals twice in March 1927 requesting information on the church-state crisis.[38] Beals, who had been consistently anti-clerical in *Mexico: An Interpretation* and his 1926 article for *The Survey,* found himself in the throes of a troublesome "personal dilemma" in 1927. After a risky trip to war-torn Jalisco, he realized the extent of military abuse in the fight against faithful supporters of the church. In spite of this evidence against the Calles government, Beals hesitated to publicize the information because it would tend to strengthen the interventionists' argument in the United States. In a letter to Croly, Beals explained that "in painting [the] evils and abuses [of the government's campaign against the church] one's material is seized upon by the very people in the United States one does not wish to encourage."[39]

Beals's article for the *New Republic* was a carefully considered condemnation of military rapacity along with smaller, but equally, sharp barbs aimed at local political and agrarian leaders. The fight was no longer between an outdated church and a modern, revolutionary state; rather it was a bloody and wasteful struggle between loyal Catholics and Mexican militarists. The real victims were the peasants—who usually lost their crops, often their land and sometimes, their lives. Beals deplored all aspects of the civil war and faulted both sides. He felt the foulest deeds, however, were those ordered by the plundering generals.[40]

The Calles administration was sensitive to Beals's published interpretation of the Cristero War. In his December 1927 article "Whither Mexico," Beals expanded upon his thesis that the military's campaign against the Catholic rebels was out of control. He broadened his perspective beyond the wanton deployment of firing squads to include the entire revolution. He argued that it was on the verge of failure because of the uncontrolled depredations of the roguish generals and the widening gap between Callistas and Obregonistas.[41] The Mexican press agency included a summary of "Whither Mexico" in its bulletin, which circulated among high-ranking officials of the administration, including President Calles.[42]

For most of the decade, Beals had written favorably about the revolution and had been friendly with many of its leaders. Known to Obregón in an informal way, Beals had sent Don Alvaro a copy of *Mexico: An Interpretation* in 1924.[43] His mid-1920s evaluation of Calles was positive, making the harsh criticisms and dire predictions from his pen in 1927 even more of a blow to the unsettled chief executive.[44]

In the fall of 1927, Dwight Morrow arrived in Mexico City as U.S. ambassador. His special task was to improve the clouded relations with Mexico. Beals wrote to Croly that Morrow's arrival would bring at least a "temporary improvement" on several issues. Croly agreed, to some extent, because Morrow's unofficial legal advisor was George Rublee, an "old friend" of the *New Republic*'s editor. Croly asked Beals to help Rublee find his way around Mexico City, as did Frank Tannenbaum, who also praised him highly. Beals complied with these two requests and found Reblee a pleasant fellow with a disarming "embarrassed, absent-minded manner." Rublee remained in the background as Morrow helped to arrange a reconciliation between the Calles government and the Catholic church that eventually contributed to the ending of the destructive Cristero War in 1929.[45]

Mexico in the late 1920s defied quick analysis, and at times, elicited contradictory conclusions from some serious observers. Beals was, for most of the decade, an admirer of the Obregón-Calles administrations; but in 1927, he began to express some doubts. To Beals, the peasants were again the downtrodden, while Calles's generals were petty tyrants. Beals sensed only dimly what historian Jean Meyer said with greater clarity nearly half a century later: that the peasants fought willingly for the church and against the government to defend their religion.[46] Beals underestimated the peasants' identification with Catholicism as did Calles, Mexico's military leaders and even most members of the church hierarchy. Had Beals understood the full extent of peasant commitment to the church, many of his and his fellow journalists' assumptions about the revolution and Mexican society would have been severely tested.

## The Elusive Truth

In his efforts to explain the church-state issue and other aspects of the revolution, Beals exchanged ideas with his fellow journalists in Mexico, who were, in a sense, both friends and rivals. For instance, although his review in *The Nation* raised some questions about the limits of Beals's book, Ernest Gruening congratulated Beals on the high standards set in *Mexico: An Interpretation* for future writing about the country. Perhaps Gruening was reserving some areas for the larger study he was preparing, which appeared in 1928 as *Mexico and Its Heritage*.[47] Beals and Tannenbaum also exchanged letters on their views of the revolution. Beals expressed admiration for Tannenbaum's intensive study of the agrarian reform movement, a study that was the author's doctoral dissertation at the Brookings Institution and was published as the *Mexican Agrarian Revolution* in 1929.[48] All three worked diligently in their respective approaches, but their generally congenial relationships did not mean that they agreed on the revolution.

While they shared ideas and information, their ultimate conclusions about the revolution differed. All three said that the revolution could benefit the people, but they disagreed on what made the revolution work. Beals insisted that the long-term success of the revolution depended upon the interaction involving the Obregón-Calles political elite in Mexico City and the Indian and mestizo peasantry in the countryside. The politicians wanted extensive social and economic changes, sometimes at the expense of the tradition-bound peasants, who resented the intrusions of the modern machine age. Beals felt there was a need for innovation in the countryside but within limits that peasant culture could tolerate.[49] Beals seemed to fall between Tannenbaum and Gruening in his prescriptions for the revolution. Tannenbaum argued that individual peasant communities had to make their own headway after the national government provided adequate redistribution of land. Gruening looked at the revolution from the opposite perspective—Mexico City—which he saw as the main motivating force for the nation.[50] All three marshalled considerable evidence to support their theses and presented convincing arguments. The issues that they raised involving conflicts between tradition and change, and between the center and the periphery, have remained important and largely unresolved questions in the study of the revolution.

Of this trio, Beals was probably the most disillusioned with the revolution by the end of the decade. In a sense, however, he never completely lost faith in the potential for benevolent social and economic change by the government. The greatest source of his disaffection was the corrupt, heavy-handed leadership of Morones, and to a lesser extent, the entire Calles administration, which had brought about a near-fatal perversion of the revolution's ideals. At times, however, Beals's attachment to the original ideals was sufficient to counteract his disillusionment.

Beals's confidence in the revolution surfaced in his correspondence with Norman Thomas in the summer of 1928. Thomas wrote Beals to ask for advice on the complex church-state conflict in Mexico. Thomas had replaced the deceased Eugene Debs as leader and presidential candidate of the U.S. Socialist party. (This was a symbolic as well as a political position that carried a heritage of Debsian populistic radicalism.) Beals responded with a letter that apparently Thomas took to heart. In July of 1928, only a few weeks after the assassination of Obregón had endangered Mexico's recently achieved stability, Beals sent to Calles a Spanish translation of Thomas's statement, in which the Socialist leader reiterated some of the journalist's views:

In the last analysis, I have always believed that the government of Calles was right. I believe that its decrees have been unnecessarily restrictive. However, there is a justification for these decrees that does not exist in the case of open cruelty.[51]

From 1923 to 1928, Beals recovered from the rancor and dismay of divorce to achieve recognition as a respected authority on contemporary Mexico. He met Obregón, Calles and other powerful leaders in Mexico; he exchanged ideas with Tannenbaum, Gruening and other Americans interested in the Revolution. He developed an increasingly sophisticated understanding of Mexico. He moved away from the largely two-dimensional analysis in *Mexico: An Interpretation,* that branded everyone as either pro-or anti-revolution, to a recognition that the peasantry did not automatically benefit from land reform or from anticlerical policies. Beals's populist roots induced him to question policies established in Mexico City from the perspective of the common people. He did not, however, fully abandon his weakened faith in the revolution.

# • 4 •

# Revolution and the Anti-Imperialist Impulse

By the mid-1920s, Beals achieved an understanding of the modern conception of revolution largely from his observation of events in Mexico. The chaos and violence of the 1910s was, in his view, an unfortunate prologue for the central purpose of revolution: the reshaping of political, economic and social structures to shift power, wealth and status from the wealthy to the lower classes. Although he frequently expressed skepticism about the excessive authority of the central government, Beals argued that the Obregón-Calles regimes were, on balance, initiators of policies directed toward a revolutionary transformation of Mexico. Put briefly, Beals saw Mexico in the midst of what scholars like Samuel P. Huntington and Theda Skocpol would categorize about a half century later as a state-directed social revolution.[1]

Mexico's intensification of revolutionary policies in the 1920s jeopardized its fragile relationship with the United States. In response to pressure from peasants and workers, President Calles increased land redistribution and supported the demands of workers against their employers. Land redistribution threatened the large estates in Mexico owned by wealthy U.S. citizens, including the press magnate William Randolph Hearst. Labor's demands impacted the operations of American oil companies such as those controlled by California millionaire Edward Doheny. More importantly, the Mexican government's insistence that no matter who owned the property, the nation controlled the minerals and petroleum beneath the surface was a cause of much concern on Wall Street and in Washington. President Calvin Coolidge and Secretary of State Frank Kellogg reflected the anxieties of businessmen and bankers by their application of "hard-line" diplomacy to protect U.S.-owned property in Mexico.[2]

Beals was an outspoken defender of the revolution, even though he recognized its flaws. He was also an unyielding opponent of U.S. interference in Mexican affairs, whether by military means or diplomatic intimidation. In his view the revolution was not a justification for intervention but rather a justification for opposition to foreign involvement. As a result of his published objections to the Coolidge-Kellogg policy in Mexico, Beals earned the enmity of the U.S. State Department. He was frequently embroiled in controversy which made him not only a widely recognized journalist but, in the eyes of some American diplomats, a renegade propagandist in the service of the Mexican revolution.

### The Ghost of Imperialism Past

Beals's anti-imperialist reputation helped bring him an invitation to address the Conference on the Cause and Cure of War, sponsored by a liberal coalition of women's organizations. In the course of his attack on U.S. policy vis-à-vis Mexico, Beals started a controversy with former U.S. Ambassador to Mexico Henry Lane Wilson, who was to Beals and to most Mexicans, a symbol of Yankee imperialism from the early years of the revolution.

The well-known women's rights leader Carrie Chapman Catt was the organizer of the conference and invited Beals to speak. She wrote Beals that the conference was supported by nine of the most important women's organizations in the United States, and that he should expect an intelligent and well-read audience which would include some delegates who had lived in Mexico. She asked Beals to speak on U.S.-Mexican relations with special reference to the Monroe Doctrine. Beals readily accepted the invitation to appear before the conference on December 9, 1926 in Washington D.C.[3]

In his discourse on the history of U.S.-Mexican relations, Beals included the role of Ambassador Henry Lane Wilson; he portrayed Wilson as one of the villainous architects of President Francisco Madero's overthrow and an indirect participant in Madero's brutal murder. Mrs. Rufus Dawes, sister-in-law of Vice-President Charles Dawes, rose to defend Ambassador Wilson. In a trembling voice, she called Beals's remarks "the lowest note of the week" because they were filled with "charges of bribery and corruption against men not here to defend themselves." Beals retorted that he assumed his listeners were "an adult audience which would understand that self-criticism is the highest form of patriotism." After this exchange, Mrs. Dawes walked out of the room.[4]

In the storm of protest that followed this meeting, Catt expressed her support for Beals. She wrote him that his remarks and other criticisms of U.S. policy in Latin America had "created quite a controversy" among conference delegates. A vocal minority of the women felt the U.S. had received unfair treatment. This minority succeeded in establishing a special committee to arrange for defenders of U.S. policy to speak at future conferences. Catt relished the heated debate, calling it "a splendidly good thing."[5]

The excitement of intellectual confrontation was soon followed by concern for more practical matters. Henry Lane Wilson swung into action after learning from Mrs. Dawes that Beals's remarks were scheduled for publication in the proceedings of the conference, a project supported by the Carnegie Endowment for International Peace. Wilson wrote to James Brown Scott, secretary of the endowment, objecting to the inclusion of Beals's statements. Scott wrote to Nicolas Murray Butler, president of Columbia University, warning of the possibility of a libel suit involving the endowment. Butler then wrote to Catt urging her "to eliminate from the record that is to be printed and circulated with the aid of funds of the Carnegie endowment anything that could be regarded as actionable by Mr. Wilson or as passing the limit of fair and proper criticism."[6]

Catt suggested that Beals revise his comments on Wilson in the proceedings, but she expressed admiration for his point of view. Her main concern was to secure the financial backing of the publication. In a letter to Beals, she lamented "the sad fact is that to call a scoundrel a scoundrel is libelous in this country." Beals agreed to omit his condemnation of Wilson, although the published version remained a stinging denunciation of U.S. policy in Mexico.[7] Catt informed Wilson of the revisions, but she also defended Beals against charges that he was a paid propagandist for the Mexican government. She insisted that Beals was "an intelligent student of Mexican and American affairs" who dealt fairly with these two countries in his lectures and writing.[8]

In Wilson's exchanges with Catt and Beals, he recited his version of the events of February 1913, and also described his successful efforts to block publication of the other side of the story in the United States. The charges of Wilson's complicity in the overthrow and death of Madero first appeared in English in the writing of Beals's old friend Robert Hammond Murray. Although he did not name him in his letters to Catt and Beals, Wilson referred to Murray as a "disreputable newspaper correspondent." Wilson obtained court judgments against Murray in two libel suits that stopped publication of Murray's articles in 1916. Ten years later, he secured a retraction from the *Living Age*, which had carried translations of incriminating Mexican government publications that appeared in the Mexico City press.[9] Murray revived the controversy in a scathing attack on Wilson in a Mexico City newspaper in that same year.[10] Beals carried Murray's version of the Madero affair north of the border; he quickly discovered that Henry Lane Wilson had sufficient influence to block the publication of the story that was by then thirteen years old.

The dispute with Wilson was only one of the controversies that Beals's outspoken manner and leftist ideas helped to create. Beals's criticism of Wilson was not expected, but Beals's discord with bulwarks of institutional liberalism, such as President

Nicholas Murray Butler of Columbia University and the Carnegie Endowment for Peace, represented a new type of dilemma for him. His fiercely independent nature, however, was not subdued so easily in later years, even when the opposition came from the left of the political spectrum.

## Offensive Against the Interventionists

The confrontation between Beals and Wilson was but one episode in a long-running battle between proponents and opponents of the Mexican revolution in the United States. Among the most ardent critics of the revolution were American diplomats who saw Mexican social and economic reform as a menace to U.S. diplomatic and business interests in Mexico. The State Department took note of articles and books about Mexico that appeared in the U.S., an interest that led them to Beals and his colleague Ernest Gruening.

Even before Beals and Gruening began to publish on the social aspects of the revolution, the State Department was aware of their activities, particularly in connection with Gruening's position on the recognition issue. Because of the threat of the expropriation of foreign-owned property posed by the Mexican Constitution of 1917, the Harding administration refused to recognize, i.e. initiate normal diplomatic relations with, the Obregón government. Gruening was highly critical of this application of pressure on Obregón, and he and Secretary Hughes had a public confrontation on the recognition issue in the pages of *The Nation.* Gruening called for the publication of internal State Department documents relating to the recognition of Mexico; Hughes, in a sharp rebuttal, refused to comply.[11]

The diplomats were quick to stereotype the inquiring journalists. In June 1922, the State Department noted the presence of Frank Tannenbaum in the city of Veracruz by designating him as one of "an organized group of American 'Red' agitators."[12] In early 1923, Gruening went to Mexico where he, too, fell under the vigilance of the State Department. Diplomatic correspondence portrayed him as a "Harvard Jew," who wrote for radical magazines, such as *The Nation*, and therefore, was an individual who required careful attention.[13]

The State Department was also disturbed by the Obregón government's English language propaganda campaign in the United States. The Mexican president hired the English writer Emile J. Dillon, who wrote two books and several articles highly favorable to Obregón. Obregón also sponsored other types of publications in the United States which were intended to improve Mexico's image north of the border.[14] The reaction of the State Department indicated a deep concern with the spread of public information unfavorable to U.S. foreign policy. From this experience, the State Department suspected that any writer critical of American policy in Mexico might be subsidized by the Mexican government.

The United States ambassador to Mexico from 1924 to 1927 was James Sheffield, an avid defender of his nation's political and economic system. According to a careful study of his three years in Mexico, "he preached law and order and property rights with evangelical fervor." Nor did he hide his revulsion for the Mexican Indian at a time when the revolution brought about a new popular appreciation of native culture. The Ambassador showed his disdain for the revolution even more clearly by his association with survivors of the Porfirian elite, an insult to the Calles government. In Sheffield's distorted vision of Mexico, President Calles and Minister of Labor Morones were Bolsheviks, attempting to spread their radicalism throughout the hemisphere.[15]

The publications of American journalists sympathetic to the revolution was a source of concern for Sheffield and his staff. Sheffield was convinced that they were tools of the revolutionary leaders. He reported to Kellogg that they "are said to be on the payroll" of the government. Sheffield observed a number of Americans, including Gruening. He complained that the American public was grossly misled by the writings of these journalists, and as a consequence, they "would not support a movement for armed intervention in Mexico."[16]

In an unpublished memoir of his years in Mexico, Sheffield gave a summary of his impressions of the leftist American press:

There was also a small group of Americans living in Mexico City, some of them carried on the pay rolls of the Mexican government, who were actively engaged in spreading false and misleading reports about the work of the State Department and the American ambassador. Some of this group were communistic in ideals and anti-American in practice, but they were able to get their views published in many magazines and newspapers in the United States and to some extent influence public opinion north of the Rio Grande.[17]

In 1926, the State Department alerted its representatives to monitor the movements of Beals and Gruening. In a memorandum from the division of Mexican affairs, Gruening was described as "a radical and professional propagandist."[18] The department attempted to determine if either received financial rewards from the Mexican government but had difficulty in obtaining evidence. In a report to Kellogg on December 11, 1926, Sheffield stated: "I have no definite proof as yet that either Gruening or Beals is regularly in the pay of the Mexican Government, but it is a moral certainty that the former has received money from it, and it is probable that Beals has also."[19]

Of the U.S. journalists, Beals was the most dangerous in the estimation of some State Department officials. Beals's association with a few members of the Russian Embassy staff excited suspicious diplomats. A letter from Joseph C. Grew in Washington supplied Alexander Weddell, the U.S. consul general in Mexico City, with a highly imaginative and largely unsubstantiated description of Beals. In addition to being a so-called radical socialist, "the subject was also in charge of Bolshevik propaganda in Mexico, having been left with funds by both Gruzenberg and Manabendra Nath Roy. He was formerly Treasurer of the Communist Party established there by the two above-mentioned parties."

Grew's summary of Beals's Bolshevik connections from the 1920 military intelligence reports omitted any mention of his quarrels with Communist leaders Borodin and Gale and his rejection of their ideological tenets.[20]

The embassy's excessive concern about the ideas and actions of Beals and Gruening was an outgrowth of Sheffield's conviction that bolshevism dominated the Calles government.[21]

This attitude, along with Sheffield's trepidations about the future of American-owned property and the religious question, led the ambassador to urge the State Department to follow a more agressive policy with Mexico. The leftist American journalists were not fully aware of the internal correspondence of the State Department, but they sensed some of the hostility directed towards them from Sheffield and his colleagues.[22].

While not always in accord with Sheffield's more extreme recommendations, the State Department openly proclaimed its unhappiness with Mexican affairs and created the impression that intervention was under consideration. Twice during the Calles administration, Secretary of State Kellogg publicly criticized the Mexican government. In June 1924, Kellogg issued a pointed denunciation of Mexico's failure to establish domestic order and to protect American residents. In January 1927, Kellogg gave a stern warning against the Calles government's extension of land reform and petroleum regulations. In spite of the adamant position he took in public, Kellogg was uncertain about future Mexican policy.[23] By contrast, Sheffield was an unwavering proponent of a belligerent approach and urged Washington to move in the direction of intervention.[24]

The January 26, 1927 editorial of *The Nation* assailed Kellogg and Coolidge as warmongers, who were willing to risk "the lives of thousands of Americans and the peace of a continent." The editorial further called for an aroused public to resist any move towards war or intervention in Latin America. In the same issue, Beals accused Kellogg of attempting to weaken and perhaps to overthrow the Calles government by diplomatic intimidation.[25]

In an article solicited by Herbert Croly for the *New Republic*, Beals presented an analysis of American-owned petroleum property and its status under the new regulations of 1926. According to Beals, of the 147 American petroleum companies only 21 failed to comply with the new law; of these, the five companies owned by Edward Doheny were the most significant producers (36.05% of the total Mexican output). Beals called for the United States government to investigate the "outlaw" companies in Mexico, so as to determine the extent of the disagreement between the two countries in this area. Beals felt that the protection of the Doheny oil holdings was not worth a rupture in Mexican-United States relations.[26]

Beals and Croly led a chorus of news media voices that vehemently opposed United States intervention in Mexico during the first seven or eight months of 1927.[27] While the impact of this protest on the State Department is difficult to assess, there is no doubt that Kellogg's policy began to change in these months perhaps as early as March 1927. In July, Ambassador Sheffield resigned and, thereby, removed himself as a barrier to the betterment of Mexican-American relations.[28] The arrival of Dwight Morrow in Mexico City in October 1927 marked the beginning of a period of reconciliation between the United States and Mexico. Morrow seemed to be willing to accept the Revolution as a *fait accompli*. Also, he was more receptive to Beals and Gruening than Sheffield had been.[29] Only in the case of Beals's article about the negotiations between the United States and Mexico on the petroleum question did Morrow indicate displeasure with leftist reporting in Mexico.[30]

The improvement of U.S.-Mexican relations suffered a temporary setback in November 1927 when the newspaper chain owned by William Randolph Hearst published several falsified documents. The documents purported to show that the Mexican government engaged in conspiratorial activities against the United States, including the encouragement of anti-American rebels in Nicaragua and the bribery of U.S. senators in exchange for favorable consideration in Washington. Another allegation in the documents was that Ernest Gruening had been paid ten thousand dollars by the Calles government, apparently to foment labor unrest in England. Hearst's motive in publishing these stories was unclear, but perhaps resulted from the threat to his vast Mexican properties posed by Calles's land reform program.[31] Beals had heard rumors "about the so-called forged documents" several months before Hearst published them.[32] On Croly's request, Beals compared the Hearst releases to similar documents from Mexican government files supplied to him by Enrique Jiménez D., private secretary to Minister of Education José Manuel Puig Casauranc.[33] Beals's

findings anticipated what Hearst admitted to a Senate committee—that the documents were forgeries.[34]

The forged document episode did little to discredit Gruening, Croly and other opponents of U.S. meddling in Mexican
affairs; rather, it seemed to lend credibility to their case against
the Coolidge-Kellogg policies and to enhance their image as
crusading anti-imperialists.

### Among the Left-Wingers

While Beals established himself as a leading critic of U.S.
policy in Mexico, he also became a central figure in the cosmopolitan community of leftists who congregated in Mexico
City in the 1920s. These writers, political activists and artists
felt that Mexico contained the ingredients for monumental social and economic change.[35] A member of this group Mexican-
born Anita Brenner gave her impression of the ambience that
surrounded the community:

> We were all eventually close friends, we were sort of looking
> for the same things, working in the same channels. And it was
> not like the social friendships of now, it was a revolutionary atmo-
> sphere, almost like a workshop atmosphere, so we could all get
> into each other's 'thing.'[36]

Most of the leftists lived in Mexico City, a growing urban
center which was undergoing important changes in the 1920s.
On his return from Europe in 1923, Beals found the city "tam-
er" with "order [and] stability more apparent" than in 1920.
Also apparent was the rapid rate of suburban expansion as
middle-class families built homes and displaced the "semi-In-
dian" rural communities on the outskirts of the city. Most of
the expatriates, however, saw little of the suburbs. They
seemed to prefer the older, central part of Mexico City that
extended from the presidential palace on the Zócalo (large public square) west along Francisco I, Madero Street and its continuation, Juárez Avenue, for about a mile to the Juárez Monu-
ment. Within the square mile area bisected by Madero and
Juárez were the national government's executive offices, the

national congress, the Palace of Fine Arts, the Alemeda, the National University, and a number of hotels, restaurants and apartment buildings. The expatriates saw this section as the political and cultural center of the revolution; they also made it the center for activities, which included a heady mixture of Bohemian social life and radical intellectual discourse.[37]

Beals included some Communists among his friends and acquaintances. He saw Bertram and Ella Wolfe quite often, although he avoided involvement in their rivalry with Mexican labor czar Luis Morones for control of the growing union movement. The Wolfes finished a poor second to Morones, who became head of the ministry of industry and labor in the Calles administration.[38] Probably through the Wolfes, Beals met several members of the Russian embassy staff, including the remarkable diplomat and feminist Alexandra Kollontai.[39] With the Russians as with the Wolfes, Beals carefully minimized his official contacts and maintained these relationships largely on a social basis.

Mexico's most famous Communist of the 1920s was Diego Rivera, the muralist. He was a close friend of Beals and the Wolfes. This quartet, along with Rivera's wife Lupe, enjoyed many informal times together. Rivera's striking murals depicting the struggle of the peasants and workers to overcome their exploitation at the hands of capitalists and dictators captured the attention of art critics in Latin America, the United States and Europe. Rivera's corpulent physique and outspoken manner seemed to enhance his position as the revolution's leading cultural figure. Beals and other expatriates sought Rivera's company, praised his work and granted him a prominent place in their community.[40]

Anita Brenner was one of Rivera's most active supporters. She was primarily an art historian and critic, who saw in the creations of Rivera and other painters strong indications of the appearance of a Mexican national culture.[41] She and Beals grasped the artistic and historical importance of Rivera's murals on the interior walls of the National Preparatory School in Mexico City. In 1924, they were moved to action by the threat to the murals posed by riotous students of the preparatory school.

The students, mostly the offspring of wealthy, conservative parents, attempted to deface Rivera's work. They justified their vandalism by claiming that the murals created a negative image of Mexico in the eyes of tourists from the United States. Brenner and Beals circulated a petition among foreigners resident in Mexico in support of Rivera and the murals. The petition helped to prevent the cessation of Rivera's work in the preparatory school.[42]

Katherine Anne Porter was another frequent traveler to Mexico who grasped the relationship between art and the revolution. After her return from Mexico to the United States in the early 1920s, she wrote to Beals, requesting help in the location of "a simple job of work that would keep me in Mexico for at least two years." Her unhappiness with the United States and her desire to be in Mexico broke through in her complaint that "life . . . is not worth a damn here when one wishes to be in Mexico." Before she achieved wide recognition for her fiction, Porter wrote several magazine articles and a book on Mexico, concentrating on the renaissance of Indian art as a manifestation of the popular basis of the revolution.[43]

Beals also admired Frances Toor, a dedicated student of Mexican folk art and culture. She devoted many years to the observation and description of the Indian customs of rural Mexico, a subject that also interested Rivera and other Mexican painters. Beals first met Toor in the mid-1920s and, on first impression, found her "a strange Jewish woman . . . [with] thick glasses and apparently very obtuse in manner." He soon understood her deep feelings for the common people of Mexico, however, and came to value her friendship. Beals agreed to help her start a magazine devoted to Mexico's Indian culture entitled *Mexican Folkways*.[44] The magazine was a success within the limits imposed by such a specific field. In 1947, Toor published *A Treasury of Mexican Folkways*, a massive compilation of information on Mexican folk culture.[45] In her modest way, she helped bring the attention of English-language readers to the rural masses of Mexico.

The quiet personality of Frances Toor differed considerably

from the tempestuous life styles of Tina Modotti and her lover-tutor Edward Weston. Weston was a photographer of excellent reputation, who found Mexico filled with fascinating subjects. Modotti was his student from 1924 to 1926 and later became an art photographer in her own right. Weston met Beals in 1924 at a party in Mexico City that was boring except, in Weston's words, "for the author of a new book on Mexico [who] was the most interesting person there."[46] Soon Weston, Modotti, Toor and Beals became frequent companions for parties and outings in Mexico City. In November 1925, Beals secured the use of a government car and drove with Weston out to Chapingo, the national agricultural school, to observe Rivera's progress on his murals on the walls of a small converted chapel. Tina and Rivera's wife Lupe served as nude models for Rivera's symbolic rendering of fertility, his choice of theme for the agricultural school's mural.[47] About two weeks later in Mexico City, Weston and Modotti hosted a "wild party" that included Diego and Lupe Rivera, Toor and Beals. The gatherings at the Weston-Modotti residence convened on a weekly basis and were the main attraction on the social circuit of much of the expatriate community.[48]

Beals and Modotti became good friends during these years. He took special interest in her maturation as a photographer. In an essay for the magazine *Creative Art*, he pointed out the expansion of her interests beyond pure photographic technique to socially relevant content. She turned to populistic themes, like manual labor and mass political rallies, to symbolize the emergence of Mexico's proletariat. Beals concluded that her mastery of technique seemed to presage "the formulation of a truly personal and artistic philosophy."[49]

Beals, Modotti, Brenner, Toor and their leftist colleagues expressed an appreciation for what seemed to them to be a genuine rising of the Mexican masses. For most members of the community, Diego Rivera's murals and leftist ideology symbolized Mexico's struggle to build a new society free of the injustices of the past. Beals saw in the revolution one of the most important foundations for his anti-imperialism. In his view, the revolution deserved the opportunity to follow its own course, without any interference from its excitable and aggressive neighbor north of the Rio Grande.

## A New Intellectual Context

By his praise of the revolution and his rejection of imperialism, Beals joined other leftists from the United States in the denunciation of business values, middle-class materialism and the myopic sense of well-being that reigned supreme in the America of Warren G. Harding and Calvin Coolidge. While they pricked the sensitive nerves of government officials and business leaders, most leftists were not quite sure where to turn for an alternative to the United States as a model for political, economic, and social organization. Lenin's Russia emerged from the gloom of World War I as a possible answer; but by the mid-1920s, many liberals and radicals began to doubt the intentions of the dictatorial Joseph Stalin. Russia's promise dimmed as orthodox Marxist-Leninism remained in flux. Leftists searched feverishly for a framework that would give them sustenance and inspiration.[50]

Neither Beals nor any of his colleagues had a ready answer, but they were groping toward new approaches in a new field. Scholars studying the responses of U.S. intellectuals to the Mexican revolution have attempted to impose this corpus of writing on the customary framework of U.S. intellectual history in the 1920s. In so doing, they have neglected its most important and most innovative aspects.[51] In their analyses of revolution and imperialism in Mexico, Beals, Brenner, Gruening, Tannenbaum and a few others were wrestling with the problems of what social scientists since World War II have called the developing nations. The Mexican revolution, with its programs for land reform, public education and labor organization, attempted to speed up the process of modernization to benefit the masses. Presidents Obregón and Calles undertook these programs not only to enhance their own political power, but also to strengthen their nation against the ever-threatening neighbor to the north.[52] Beals understood this point and began to argue that only through broadly based structural reform could Mexico avoid domination by the United States.

Beals saw many possible complications flowing from the changes initiated by the revolution's leaders. Although he frequently commented on the conservative nature of the peasants' demands to restore land and sovereignty to their villages, he did not see reform as a return to a simple rural utopia. Studies of the impact of the revolution on political and cultural thought in the United States have tended to squeeze these perceptions into the Jeffersonian-Jacksonian agrarian mold.[53] For Beals, the revolution was too complicated for such historical conveniences. The long-standing gaps between the rich and the poor in Mexico were too great; therefore, he had no patience with wealthy estate owners, corrupt politicians, and *gringo* businessmen who grumbled about the harmful effects of social reform and plotted to prevent it. The idealized world of Jefferson and Jackson had little relevance to the complex political machinations and elaborate economic arguments that often engulfed the work of the revolution in rural Mexico.[54]

Beals's ardor for reform cooled somewhat, however, when he understood a certain aspect of the peasant point of view: Illiteracy and poverty were cruel oppressors but to the peasants, the possibility that the sudden, wrenching change made solely to implement the government's revolutionary programs for modern education, political unity and technological innovation, might bring dislocations that were nearly as painful as life under the old system. To achieve its goals, the revolution had to produce structural alterations to benefit the poor. At the same time, it had to protect the common people from severe disruptions of familiar patterns of existence. In the 1920s, Beals began to sense that the Indian heritage offered several stable traditions in art, music and community values that lived on in many areas in the countryside.[55] The government's large-scale, bureaucratically controlled programs designed to bring the peasant class into the mainstream of national life had to move with great care to avoid the destruction of the essential, surviving elements of Indian culture.[56]

If Beals questioned the effects of rapid socioeconomic change, he expressed no reservations in his condemnation of imperialism. The threat of direct U.S. military intervention stimulated some of his most acidic prose, which he aimed in the general direction of the Coolidge administration. Beyond the obvious danger of intervention by force, Beals detected a more subtle form of Yankee domination, the use of diplomatic, political and economic pressure to manipulate Mexico's leaders into enacting policies more amenable to special interests in the United States. When the revolution initiated land reform, undercut the authority of the Catholic church and asserted the right of the nation to expropriate foreign-owned property, business and government spokesmen in the United States made strenuous objections, couched in ominous language. Beals saw these objections as a new attempt to dominate Mexico by depriving that nation's leaders of the right to govern as they saw fit.[57] He and other defenders of the revolution took a public stand against what contemporary scholars call "informal imperialism." Although not as precise or systematic as recent students of informal empires, Beals became increasingly aware of this dimension of imperialism, which for the most part, escaped other prominent authorities on the subject in the 1920s.[58]

While Beals's connections with the intellectual Left of the United States were somewhat distant, many of his ideas and attitudes (and those of some other expatriates) bore a close resemblance to what historian John Diggins has called the Lyrical Left. In Diggins' conception, the Lyrical Left was born in 1912 in the heady atmosphere of prewar optimism. Young Bohemians living in and around New York issued pronouncements that revealed a "passion for social justice," a "thirst for esthetic experience" and a desire to find a leftist synthesis of human experience. While Beals did not participate in this episode in the history of the intellectual Left, his small-town Kansas and California background, his identification with the common people, his Bohemian adventures, his sensitivity to the mystical in nature and his struggle to maintain a holistic view of life was in accord with the style and tone set by Floyd

Dell, Mabel Dodge, John Reed and other Lyrical Leftists of the second decade of the twentieth century.[59]

In spite of his acceptance of these values, Beals worked on a subject matter that was beyond the purview of most of his leftist colleagues. Much of what he wrote in the 1920s did not fit into the broader pattern of leftist thought in the United States because the central object of his analysis—socioeconomic change in a Third World nation—had not achieved the recognition or the importance accorded it since World War II.[60] Even Beals did not fully appreciate the significance of his writing on this subject until later in his career. Nevertheless, his qualified advocacy of modernization by revolution and his unqualified condemnation of imperialism made him a prominent member of a small, but growing, group of journalists, academicians and activists whose pioneering efforts established the basis for a new framework for understanding and explaining the complex process of change that was underway not only in Mexico, but elsewhere in Latin America, Africa and Asia.

# • 5 •

# In Search of Sandino

The elusive Nicaraguan rebel Augusto César Sandino was a highly controversial figure in the United States when Beals, working for *The Nation*, interviewed him in the village of San Rafael del Norte on February 3, 1928. From that interview and observations made on the harrowing trip that preceded it, Beals wrote four articles that gave a sympathetic view of the Sandinistas much to the dismay of the U.S. State Department. In early 1928, a force of over 2,500 United States Marines pursued Sandino without success; yet Beals, with aid from the rebel underground, was able to find Sandino and file a story which captured public attention throughout the Western Hemisphere and Europe.

Sandino was the central figure in a polemic that grew out of two decades of United States intervention in the domestic affairs of Nicaragua. Many Latin Americans and most liberals in the United States denounced the intervention and supported Sandino. President Calvin Coolidge, Secretary of State Frank B. Kellogg, and special emissary to Nicaragua Henry Stimson called Sandino a bandit and insisted that the United States presence in Nicaragua was a necessity. They complained that heavily biased press coverage favored the rebels. Beals was already known to be sympathetic to liberal causes, and Kellogg's State Department observed his movements in Central America with great interest.

Beals's reportage on Sandino appeared in the United States when both leftist intellectuals and the general public were interested in the Nicaraguan and his movement. By the mid-1920s, many leftists were disillusioned with the Russian revolution and its harsh Stalinist government. In their quest for a more acceptable radical phenomena, many turned to anti-imperialism. In 1928, only three years after the publication of Scott Nearing and Joseph Freeman's *Dollar Diplomacy* and only two years after the release of Parker Moon's *Imperialism in World Politics*, U.S. intellectuals found Sandino.[1] At the same time, the general public had an unusually strong appetite for news about Sandino, perhaps because he seemed to fit the mold of the heroic individual in a manner not dissimilar to the style of Charles Lindberg.[2] Beals was in the right place and had the necessary experience to write dramatic, yet essentially objective, reports about Sandino.

In the summer of 1926, on his first trip to Central America, Beals noted the weight of foreign influence in the area. His criticisms of the United Fruit Company in Puerto Barrios, Guatemala, and of United States military and financial intervention in Nicaragua were typical of the criticisms made by many opponents of "dollar diplomacy."[3] He took a different approach, however, in his discussion of the expansion of Mexican influence in Central America. Citing an aggressive Mexican embassy staff in Guatemala City, including First Secretary Luis Quintanilla, Beals suggested that the Mexicans used the common Spanish heritage to strengthen ties between these two countries, and thereby, rival the influence of the United States. In Nicaragua, Mexico sent direct military aid to Sacasa's Liberal government, which was in rebellion against the Conservative government of Emiliano Chamorro.[5] These statements drew a response from Quintanilla, a friend of Beals from earlier days in Mexico City. He complained that Beals's *Current History* articles "exaggerated" the intentions of his staff in Guatemala and that the press in the United States twisted this article to accuse

President Calles of spreading Communist propaganda.[6] In addition to opening an argument with Quintanilla, this trip acquainted Beals with some of the complexities of Central American politics.

## Background of U.S. Intervention in Nicaragua

The history of United States-Nicaraguan relations in the early twentieth century was confusing. With the government and economy of this Central American nation in chaos in 1911, the United States assumed the administration of Nicaraguan customs income in order to stabilize public finances. In the following year, United States Marines moved into Nicaragua to help put down a revolt.[7] The United States maintained this two-pronged intervention until the State Department surrendered control of finances in 1924, as a result of pressure from the Nicaraguan government.[8] The Marines withdrew on August 3, 1925, in spite of pleas by President Carlos Solórzano, a Liberal party member, who insisted that they were needed for the preservation of political order. Solórzano's fears became reality when Conservative Emiliano Chamorro led a revolt in October 1925. Chamorro was unable, however, to gain recognition for his government from the United States and other Central American nations. After a year of pointless struggle, Chamorro capitulated to United States demands and allowed Adolfo Díaz, another Conservative, to become president on November 11, 1926. In the spring of that year, meanwhile, the Marines returned. Their number continued to increase as the political situation remained uncertain.[9]

The rise of Díaz to the presidency did not ensure Liberal quiescence. Juan B. Sacasa set up a rival Liberal administration in Puerto Cabezas on the Caribbean coast of Nicaragua on December 1, 1926. Mexico quickly recognized the Sacasa regime as the legitimate government. Alarmed by these events, President Coolidge insisted that Díaz, not Sacasa, was the rightful head of state and that Mexico was supplying military assistance to an "illegal" government in eastern Nicaragua. Secretary of State Kellogg added that Bolshevik influence was growing in

Mexico and Central America. He stated that the All-American Anti-Imperialist League was the agent of international communism active in that area and that it acted on direct orders from Moscow.[10]

The importance of Nicaragua in U.S. foreign policy was underlined by the mission of Henry Stimson to that troubled country. Given broad discretion by President Coolidge, Stimson managed to work out a compromise acceptable to Conservatives and Liberals with one exception—the Liberal military commander Augusto César Sandino. Sandino's recalcitrance troubled Stimson who believed that he was an opportunistic brigand. A few years later Stimson wrote:

I was told that Sandino had lived in Mexico for twenty-two years, where he had served under Pancho Villa, and only came back to Nicaragua on the outbreak of the revolution in order to enjoy the opportunities for violence and pillage which it offered.[11]

Another source of irritation for Stimson was the coverage of Nicaraguan affairs in the United States press. He complained that much of the information that reached the United States was distorted to favor Sandino. Stimson suggested that because the rebels controlled several ports along the east coast of Nicaragua, they had easier access to the North American press that did the Conservative and Liberal politicians who lived in the western part of the nation. Stimson concluded:

I found when I came to conduct my own investigation that this comparative superiority of facility enjoyed by revolutionist propaganda in reaching America had quite seriously warped the accuracy of American news, insomuch as most of the political statements which reached the American public came from revolutionary sympathizers—many of whom had not visited Nicaragua for years, and consequently, had no first-hand knowledge of existing conditions and opinion.[12]

## Sandino

On January 5, 1928, Oswald Garrison Villard, editor of *The Nation*, wired Beals in Mexico City. He suggested that Beals return to Central America to gather information on the popular response to the United States intervention in Nicaragua and, if possible, to interview Sandino.[13] Beals agreed to leave immediately but he urged Villard to withhold any early publicity on the trip to avoid censorship in Central America and also to ensure his own safety.[14] Beals decided to try to interview Sandino and planned his trip with the help of Pedro José Zepeda, the rebel leader's chief publicist in Mexico City. In Guatemala on January 10, he wired Freda Kirchwey, *The Nation*'s managing editor, that he hoped to contact Sandino supporters in El Salvador.[15] José de Jesús Zamora, a medical doctor in San Salvador, supplied an important connection with the Sandino underground organization.[16] A few days later, Beals reached Tegucigalpa, Honduras, where Froylán Turcios, publisher of *El Ariel* (a pro-Sandino paper) made arrangements for the final stage of the journey to the rebel camp in Nicaragua.[17]

Beals's trip through Central America was filled with difficulties involving both local officials and local terrain. While in Ed Salvador, the customs agents made a thorough search of his luggage and confiscated some of Beals's possessions. They arrested his guide, apparently on suspicion of being one of Sandino's operatives.[18] The demands of the various customs agencies, police forces, and other government officials proved to be a constant source of irritation for Beals.[19] He set out from Tegucigalpa on or near January 21, 1928, accompanied by a second rebel guide General Santos Siquieros, a veteran of earlier Central American civil strife.[20] The party moved by horseback into the rugged district around San Jacinto and encountered a succession of bad weather conditions: heavy mist, cold drizzle, and finally a hail storm. After a miserable, nearly sleepless night in the highlands, they found a welcome rest at the home of a Honduran supporter of Sandino in the town of Jacaleapa. There Beals became ill with influenza. Because of the possibility of detection by unfriendly government agents and fears of disloyal contacts, however, the party continued through Danlí. Leading their horses on foot, they negotiated narrow trails flanked by "colossal cliffs" as they approached the Honduras-Nicaragua boundary.[21]

After crossing the Honduras-Nicaragua border secretly to avoid customs inspection, the party added a few more rebels as escorts and began to search for Sandino in northwestern Nicaragua. Beals's first destination was the rebel camp at El Chipote, a mountain surrounded by tropical vegetation at its base. Unknown to Beals and his companions, the Marines had organized an expedition to attack El Chipote, and Sandino, judging the odds to be against him, had withdrawn to avoid battle.[22] This unexpected turn of events complicated Beals's plans. It left him with a choice between abandonment of the search or pursuit of Sandino through the jungle. He chose the latter and sent a note by runner to Sandino, requesting an interview. In replying, Sandino suggested a meeting in El Remango.[23] Beals, Siquieros, and the others plunged into the jungle to keep this appointment. Instead of El Remango, Sandino stopped in San Rafael del Norte; an exhausted, but triumphant, Beals hurried there for the interview.[24]

The meeting with Sandino took place before sunrise on the morning of February 3 in San Rafael del Norte. With only two hours of sleep, Beals was "red-eyed and shaky" but eager to complete his mission. In the course of the interview, he found Sandino to be an admirable character, "utterly without vices, with an unequivocal sense of justice, [and] a keen eye for the welfare of the humblest soldier."[25] Sandino insisted that he was fighting because of the presence of foreign troops and that as soon as they left, he would lay down his arms. He disavowed any political ambitions and said that he preferred his humble occupation of mechanic to a career in public service.[26] He felt his struggle was eminently patriotic; he was fighting to "defend not only Liberals, but all Nicaraguans, since all are betrayed by their present government."[27] In reply to frequently heard charges, he protested that his men were not plunderers of innocent civilians. In San Rafael, he gave strict orders against looting. Beals found that local shopkeepers attested to the effectiveness of this directive.[28]

On military affairs, Beals was skeptical of Sandino's version of the fighting, although he was duly impressed with his guerrilla tactics. Sandino relied on his army's mobility and the geography of central Nicaragua to confound the slower moving Marines, who had to rely on lines of communication and supply with Managua and Leon. Sandino's men lived off the land and utilized an effective intelligence network to stay one step ahead of the Marines.[29] It appeared to Beals that these tactics were successful for Sandino, but a rebel list of battles and Marine casualties invited some doubts. Beals described this list by the statement: "His conclusions are as exaggerated as the Marines, perhaps more so."[30]

Sandino's comments on the motives of the United States in Central America offered insight into the rebel leader's justification for his resistance. To him, the U.S. government's claim that the Marines were sent to protect American lives and property was an excuse. What the United States really wanted, according to Sandino, was the continuance of economic and territorial concessions made by previous Nicaraguan regimes. Sandino specified the Bryan-Chamorro Treaty as a case in which Nicaragua surrendered sovereignty over a future isthmian canal in exchange for $3 million. With a bit of overstatement, Sandino added that this sum was "not enough for each Nicaraguan citizen to buy a soda cracker and a sardine." He condemned this arrangement because "the deliberations regarding this sale were made by a fake congress behind closed doors guarded by Conservative party troops backed up by Yankee bayonets." An unnamed Sandinista told Beals that United States influence opened concessions to New York bankers for railroad construction, which resulted in excessive transportation costs for coffee planters in central Nicaragua. In Sandino's estimation, "eighteen years of American meddling in Nicaragua have plunged the country deeper into economic misery."[31]

In addition to his military tactics and anti-imperialist ideology, Sandino's personality was an important factor in his leadership. An incident involving Beals's guide Santos Siquieros was indicative of Sandino's authority as a commander. As Beals prepared to leave San Rafael, Siquieros came to him greatly upset. The cause of his anxiety was a growing fear that Sandino planned to shoot him. Beals tried to allay this fear, but the brave, haughty Siquieros was afraid for his life. From this experience, Beals "sensed an uncanny power of domination in Sandino, something subtle, devious, but not at all obvious." Six months later, Sandino had Siquieros shot as a traitor because the rebels had discovered documents on him that indicated his intention of deserting to the Marines.[32]

A few days after Beals departed Sandino's camp, he arrived in Managua to begin work on his articles for *The Nation*. The return trip proved costly when Beals's horse panicked and threw him onto some rocks. The resulting injury to his lower back was to be painful for several years.[33] In spite of this injury and accumulated fatigue, Beals began work on a series of articles on a rented typewriter in the Hotel Lupones.[34] To heighten the effect of immediacy, he sent the first three of them by telegraph directly to Freda Kirchwey in New York. He transmitted the first of these on February 10, 1928 and the next two on February 18 and 27. These three articles required twenty-seven pages for telegraph transmission, even after Beals extracted most of the prepositions and many of the verbs (which were later inserted by the editors).[35] Beals mailed manuscripts of all the articles to New York on or before February 19. For "security" reasons, he sent rough drafts of the entire series to his mother in Berkeley, California, who in turn, mailed them to *The Nation*'s editorial offices.[36]

### The Central American Response

Within a week after he left Sandino's camp, Beals became a public figure throughout Central America—the object of unsolicited advice and praise and also of criticism and government intimidation. The reaction to Beals and his reporting illuminates the impact of the United States intervention and the resulting Sandinista movement in the region. As a foreign journalist, Beals became a part of the story he covered, a situation not uncommon for reporters at work on controversial topics.

Liberal José María Moncada, a former general, wrote to Beals on February 12, and offered advice on what to investigate and how to interpret the findings. Moncada disliked Sandino. The primary reason for this attitude centered around the Tipitapa agreement signed by Moncada and Henry Stimson in May 1927. Moncada agreed to disband the Liberal army under the threat of "forcible disarmament" of his troops by the United States military. Sandino was the only officer who refused to accept the agreement, which, according to Moncada, he had earlier promised to support.[37] In his letter to Beals, Moncada sought to discredit Salomón de la Selva, a Sandino partisan and self-proclaimed labor leader, who had recently published an article highly favorable to the rebels in *The Nation*. Moncada accused de la Selva of accepting money from Conservatives and supporting the Chamorro government. He insisted that de la Selva, who had his headquarters in Washington, did not represent the workers of Nicaragua and was not qualified to make public statements on Nicaraguan affairs. Finally, Moncada claimed that the Marines were needed in Nicaragua to maintain the peace between Liberals and Conservatives.[39]

Two of Nicaragua's major newspapers found Beals a welcome source of new information. While Managua's Conservative paper *La Noticia* shared Moncada's distress with the activities of Salomón de la Selva in far-off Washington, its Liberal rival *La Prensa* showed greater concern for the threat of violence in the Nicaraguan capital.[40] On February 12, *La Prensa* mistakenly reported that Sandino told Beals that an armed uprising in Managua would come within a few weeks.[41] Two days later, Beals clarified this story. Sandino did not mean that his men might lead the revolt, but that "political disturbances" were likely under the instigation of Managuan leaders.[42] In a calmer mood, *La Noticia* praised Beals for impartiality in his efforts to hear all sides of the Sandino issue. According to *La Noticia*, Beals's attitude contrasted with that of Salomón de la Selva who had spread "lies and slanders" in his recent article in *The Nation*.[43] Beals cultivated good relations with local journalists. Both the Liberal and the Conservative papers held him in esteem when he left Nicaragua.

By March 3, Beals was in liberal Costa Rica, where he received a warm reception from outspokenly pro-Sandino groups. Roy T. Davis of the United States legation there wrote to the State Department in Washington that Beals had several interviews with the local press and that "a few Costa Ricans who are rabid anti-Americans visited him at his hotel."[44] *La Nueva Prensa* of San José deplored the recent incarceration by Honduran police of Beals's former guide Santos Siquieros. The paper asserted that the United States diplomatic representatives in Honduras had exerted pressure on local authorities to carry out that action, which caused the "humiliation of the small Central American governments under the iron boot of Uncle Sam."[45] In interviews published by *La Nueva Prensa* and *La Tribuna*, Beals insisted that Sandino was a patriot, not a bandit as many United States officials claimed.[46]

The warmth of his Costa Rican reception was offset by unfriendly exchanges involving officials in Honduras and El Salvador. In a letter from the owner of the Hotel Roma in Tegucigalpa where he stayed on his way into Nicaragua, Beals learned that the police of that city wanted to see him. Beals sent a collect telegram to the chief of police in which he offered to pass through Tegucigalpa on his way to Mexico to settle any unfinished business. The police paid for the telegram but did not reply.[47] Beals's account of the inspection and confiscation of possessions by customs agents in La Unión provoked a response from the Salvadorean minister to Costa Rica. He explained that his country was under martial law at the time, and that now Beals or any other foreigner could travel through El Salvador without fear of involuntary searches. The minister did not mention the confiscations. Beals retorted that he intended to limit his visits to "more civilized countries like Costa Rica."[48]

On March 11, Beals left the hospitality of Costa Rica to return to Mexico, traveling part of the way on board the steamer *Corinto*. The voyage up the Pacific coast, however, was marred for him by an altercation with the Guatemalan government. Beals wanted to disembark at the port of San José, Guatemala, and continue overland to Mexico. President Lázaro Chacón, however, ordered that he be forbidden to enter the country. Chacón was not especially concerned about

Beals's interview with Sandino; he deeply resented Beals's statement in a *Current History* article that the late President Manuel Orellana was of Negro ancestry.[49] Chacón and Orellana had been childhood friends, and the former considered this comment to be a personal affront.[50]

Inconvenienced, angry and unsure of the causes for his rejection by Guatemala, Beals fired off a letter of protest to the *Diario de Guatemala*.[51] Openly sympathetic to Sandino, the *Diario* deplored the treatment of Beals and called him "a friend of the Latin American countries . . . who has recently made known in the United States, Mexico and Central America the true situation of those who fight with Sandino and the ideals of the hero of the Segovias." Another Guatemalan paper *El Mundo* took issue with the *Diario's* defense of Beals and charged that after his 1926 trip to Central America he "wrote a series of calumnies and indecencies against Guatemala."[52] United States Minister Arthur Geissler complied with his duty to assist an American citizen and cleared the way for his entry on March 24, three days after the controversy arose.[53] A week later, Beals reached Mexico City; his arduous journey behind him.[54]

## Beals and the State Department

Beals's portrait of Sandino as a sincere Nicaraguan patriot caused the American State Department considerable displeasure, but little surprise. Aware of Beals's writings on the Mexican revolution, State Department officials maintained an interest in his Central American travels. On January 30, Jefferson Caffery in San Salvador reported to Washington that the local police chief had informed him "that one Carleton Beals, alleged American citizen, Sandino's courier in Central America, is now in Tegucigalpa."[55] Charles Eberhardt in Managua wired the State Department that mail intended for Beals was intercepted (by persons and methods not explained) in Chinandaga. The packet reportedly contained letters of introduction from Leonardo Vacasey, an associate of Zepeda in Mexico City, to three Nicaraguans, two of them "prominent liberals," and seven hundred dollars in bank drafts. (There is no indication

that the State Department people thought this money was payment from Sandino supporters. Perhaps they felt this report
was insufficiently substantiated to justify further action.[56])

Misinformation from Honduran law enforcement agents
confused the picture, but a second intercepted letter clarified
Beals's intentions. On February 4, the State Department representative in Honduras George Summerlin heard from local officials that Beals had left Tugucigalpa "under cover" and moved
to the north through the province of Comayagua, in the general direction of Guatemala.[57] This report contradicted previous intelligence supplied to the State Department and was
quickly discredited. Jefferson Caffery, on the same day, reported the interception of a second letter to Beals by Colonel
Leitzelar, chief of police in San Salvador. The letter was from
Zepeda to Froylan Turcios and introduced Beals "as a friend of
Sandino."[58]

Meetings between Beals and the United States diplomatic
and military representatives were inevitable after he left Sandino and took up temporary residence in Managua. His first
visit from American officialdom on February 8 was by a young
officer from military intelligence, who in Beals's words, "started to brow-beat me, till I put him in his place."[59] The officer
insisted that Beals report to the United States legation in Managua which he did, but at his own convenience, two days later.
He found the legation to be "flabbergasted" at his account of
the visit with Sandino, but he also observed that "they have
gone out of their way to be obliging."[60] He characterized Minister Eberhardt as friendly, but somewhat reserved. Dana
Munro was "studious," but had "acquired the air of an apologist."[61] General Frank R. McCoy, sent by the Department of
State to supervise the Nicaraguan election, was distinctly different—"one of those iron-willed, super-logical, single-track
types whose stern jaw carries not an ounce of compromise."[62]

General McCoy was greatly concerned about a letter sent
to Sandino by Admiral David F. Sellers, commander of United
States military operations in Nicaragua. A Marine pilot
dropped the letter while on an air raid against Sandino's
troops, just prior to Beals's interview with the rebel chief. Un-

known to McCoy and other American officials, Beals had both the letter and Sandino's reply. He decided not to release them, however, for fear of prosecution under the Logan Act, a century-old law which prohibited the participation of an unauthorized private citizen in negotiations between the United States and a foreign government. Beals informally told McCoy the nature of Sandino's reply and then sent the documents to *The Nation's* editors, who published them in the March 21 issue as news items, thereby circumventing the Logan Act.[63] With these letters, Beals sent two additional messages from Sandino, one for the United States Senate and the other for the Sixth Inter-American Conference to be held in Havana.[64]

The purposes of Admiral Sellers's letter were to encourage Sandino to accept the Stimson-Moncada agreement and to determine his conditions for a cessation of the fighting. In very pointed terms, Sandino replied that he did not recognize the Stimson-Moncada agreement and that his army intended to fight to achieve the following:

The immediate withdrawal of the invading forces [of the United States] from our territory; the substitution for the president of some Nicaraguan citizen not a candidate for the presidency; and the supervision of the coming elections by Latin American representatives instead of American marines.[65]

A few days after he wrote this reply, Sandino led his troops south towards the small city of Matagalpa to continue his guerrilla campaign.[66]

The State Department collected much information about Beals's actions in Central America. Caffery's report on January 30 that he was a "courier" for Sandino was premature. On March 2, however, Eberhardt telegraphed the details of the Beals-McCoy conversation to Washington with the conclusion that "Sandino gave Beals the letter to deliver but . . . he failed to deliver it fearing to involve himself in difficulties."[67] Apparently, Beals avoided involvement in such difficulties, since the State Department dropped its interest in his role as messenger.

The State Department had a special sensitivity to the spread of Beals's articles throughout the Spanish-speaking nations and instructed its agents to monitor newspaper coverage in their respective localities. Many of the articles appeared in translation directly from *The Nation,* particularly in Central America and Mexico; but the prime outlet for them in Spanish was *El Sol* of Madrid.[68] Ogden Hammond of the United States embassy in Madrid conscientiously sent translations of these articles to Washington.[69] Jefferson Caffery sent a translation of an editorial comment that appeared in *El Día,* a Salvadorean paper. This editorial was indicative of the attitude that worried the State Department most. It called Beals a respected journalist, whose work helped to illuminate "the imperialistic policy of Mr. Coolidge in the countries of the Central American Isthmus."[70]

The State Department developed an abiding curiosity in Beals's connections with the All-American Anti-Imperialist League, a leftist propaganda organization with a base of operations in Mexico City. The success of his publications on Sandino alerted the consul general in Mexico City Alexander W. Weddell, who knew of Beals in Mexico. Under the subject "Beals, Carleton, Anti-American Activities of," Weddell filed an interview extracted from the April 17, 1928 issue of *El Libertador,* the newspaper published by the league. In this article, Beals discussed atrocities in Nicaragua: "After the European War it was easy to talk about the atrocities committed on both sides. The same happens in Nicaragua. In truth war is impossible without atrocities."[71]

In his report, Weddell detailed Beals's role as speaker in a mass meeting in Mexico City, where a collection was taken for Sandino by some of his Mexican sympathizers.[72] A later report by the consul general discussed his connections with Diego Rivera, the radical Mexican muralist and editor of *El Libertador.* It was based largely on the evidence that Beals's name appeared in "certain issues of this scurrilous sheet."[73] Weddell qualified as one of the State Department's most diligent observers of Beals's activities.

In summary, the relationship between Beals and the State Department, while friendly in some individual cases, was generally hostile. Beals entered Nicaragua secretly to interview

Sandino and then wrote critical articles about United States policy in that nation. The State Department responded by monitoring his movements and amassing a file on him, in part under the heading "Anti-American Activities." The department's receipt of Beals's intercepted mail from Salvadorean officials constituted complicity in an unethical, dubious, and perhaps illegal, act. The acceptance of the Vacasey letter and the bank drafts by Eberhardt and Caffery added apparently falsified material to the file on Beals. To the State Department, Beals was an adversary, a member of the outspokenly critical American press, whose unique reporting on Nicaragua had a significant influence both at home and abroad.

### Balance Sheet

Beals's expedition to Central America was one of the high points of his career in journalism. It lasted nearly three months, and in that time, made him the most widely recognized North American reporter on the Sandino movement. His previous work in Mexico brought him much public notice. The controversial nature of the Nicaraguan situation and the dramatic circumstances surrounding his interview, however, captured the attention of a broad spectrum of readers in the Americas and Europe; yet, this episode was not without its negative aspects. Beals's health suffered, particularly as a result of his fall from the horse; the tension of more than eleven weeks of constant travel, much of it in unfriendly territory, left him emotionally drained. Finances, however, proved to be the least expected problem.

The question of money was a source of irritation. Beals departed Mexico City with reasonably good financial arrangements. *The Nation* was to wire him money for expenses at regular intervals; and at the conclusion of the venture, he was to receive his salary. He also had an agreement with Kenneth Durant of the Russian news agency Tass to write some material for him, in exchange for a small fee.[74] However, the gap from his first payment of $500 from *The Nation* on January 6 until his second payment of $250 on February 29 was seven weeks.[75] It was during this time that he made the most hazardous part of the journey and lost many of his personal belongings.[76]

On his return to Mexico City, he and *The Nation* engaged in an extensive correspondence on the matter of compensation, a discussion which was never concluded to Beals's satisfaction. Kirchwey wrote Beals on March 30 that *The Nation* was working on the problem. She suggested that he might cover some of his expenses by a lecture tour in the United States, in the wake of the rise in his popularity.[77] Beals was not happy with this proposal, and it remained for Lewis Gannet, the treasurer of *The Nation*, to make the concluding offer.[78] In his statement, he listed $1130.21 for expenses ($1330.21 minus $200.00 from Tass) and $1200.00 as twelve-weeks salary, for a total of $2330.31 Gannett's tone was apologetic; he pointed out that *The Nation* was not a wealthy publication.[79] Beals did not complain about this settlement. Four years later, however, he wrote to Ernest Gruening that the medical expenses resulting from his injury cost him more than his payments from *The Nation*. "From any corporation I could have received proper indemnization, but as I admire the liberal and noble principles of *The Nation*, I have never even told them about it [the injury] in fact no one except you now."[80]

Although Beals's papers contain no detailed record of the finances of his Central American trip, it is clear that he made little, if any, profit. It is also clear that he felt that his expense account and salary were not sufficient for the inconveniences, danger, and injuries he endured. From his experience, it appears that reporting on the turbulent events in Central America of the 1920s for a liberal journal in the United States was not a lucrative occupation and involved fiscal as well as physical risks.

**The Long View: Conclusions**

The reactions of subsequent writers to Beals's published work on Sandino offer interesting testimony of the continuance of the controversy surrounding events in Nicaragua in the late 1920s. In the 1930s, opinion divided along partisan lines. In his polemic against Sandino, Anastasio Somoza, head of the national police force who arranged the rebel leader's assassination and later became dictator of Nicaragua, dismissed Beals's writings because they were, in his estimation, based on a superficial knowledge of Nicaraguan affairs.[81] Writers who took a pro-Sandino stance, however, held a different point of view. Gustavo Alemán and Ramón de Belausteguigoitia regarded Beals's publications as reliable.[82]

The next generation of students of the Sandino movement were mostly scholars from the United States. They also tended to disagree, both on Sandino and Beals. Writing in 1951, Joseph Baylen saw Sandino more as a patriot than a bandit and stressed Beals's role in revealing his exploits to the public in the United States.[83] Seven years later in his doctoral dissertation, Charles E. Frazier found Beals's description of Sandino's revolutionary aims in *The Nation* to be "the best" on that subject.[84] William Kammen, who characterized United States policy in Nicaragua as well intentioned, but awkward, and Sandino's resistance to the intervention as of questionable benefit for Nicaragua, saw only slight value in Beals's work.[85] Neill Macauley in his military history of Sandino's operations, however, quoted heavily from the characterization of General McCoy in *Banana Gold*.[86] In general, critics of Sandino have seen little worth in Beals's publications; while those more sympathetic to the rebel leader have held the opposite point of view.

Beals had a much deeper interest than simply describing Sandino's response to the American intervention. He saw the conflict between Sandino and the United States as one phase of the struggle between the nations of Latin America and the imperialism of their neighbor to the north. He was concerned about the expansion of what he called "the machinery of American intervention," operated by well-paid middle-level bureaucrats. This machinery often developed powers of self-propagation and a propensity to involve itself in local partisan politics.[87] Beals saw similarities between American imperialists and their arch-enemies, American Communists. Both were "dogmatic, earnest, sincere, sentimental;" both strove for the implantation of an idea on a people by force; and neither had a grasp on the reality in which they labored. Nonetheless, it was easy to distinguish the imperialist from the Communist on the question of racial bigotry. The imperialist "does not analyze his own deeper motives nor does he see the contradiction between his faith in democracy and his fervent belief in his own race superiority." An example of this inconsistency was General McCoy, who planned for democratic elections in Nicaragua, and at the same time, argued that only dictatorship could save Nicaragua from disaster.[88]

Beals's opinions on United States imperialism and Sandino's revolution against it were obvious throughout his writings, yet he was also able to detect subtleties at variance with his own ideological perspective. While he concluded that the United States intervention in Nicaragua was wrong, he did not engage in blanket condemnation of the Americans involved. In an interview with the Costa Rican newspaper *La Nueva Prensa,* he stated that many of the Americans treated the Nicaraguans with respect.[89] In spite of his expression of confidence in the future of Sandino's movement in an article in *The Nation,* in a less sanguine moment he privately predicted that its defeat was inevitable.[90] This interpretation coincided with his doubts about Sandino's account of his military success against the Marines. In short, Beals's perceptions were sufficiently open to accept facts and judgments that did not agree with his personal predilections.

Beals was aware of the limits of the influence of the press in its criticisms of United States policy in Latin America. In a letter to his father, he revealed a sense of futility:

I have no illusions and know that I am swimming against the current for the next two hundred years or so, but there is some zest even in that, and a convenient feeling of irony. About the only effects my warblings will have, as well as those of others similarly minded, I presume, will be to put the brakes on the mad process, so that it proceeds with more decorum, and perhaps thus saves us from some of the future disasters that such a course will inevitably bring to us.[91]

Beals's pessimism was not overstated, and the impact of such writing on government policy seemed temporary at best. High ranking U.S. diplomatic officials, including Secretary of

State Frank Kellogg, were deeply disturbed by the vitality of the anti-imperialist movement in Latin America and the United States.[92] They saw Beals as a prime contributor to this cause. Although it is difficult to gauge public opinion on the general issue of imperialism, the quantity of published writing on the subject was quite large, and the opponents of U.S. policy in the Caribbean were numerous.[93] After his 1928 account of Sandinismo, Beals stood at the fore of these opponents whose influence, however, was short-lived.

# ♦ 6 ♦

# Disillusionment

Beals returned to Mexico from Nicaragua as something of a hero among leftists in Latin America and the United States. The edge of his triumph was blunted, however, by a series of unfortunate events in Mexico that began with the assassination of President-elect Alvaro Obregón in July 1928. In the next three years, Mexico's insecure leaders seemed to drift to the right; and the ever ambitious generals once more became restless. Beals described these difficulties in his publications. At the same time, he experienced personal troubles that included the murder of a close friend, his arrest by Mexico's military intelligence on an entirely separate matter, and his second unsuccessful marriage. Both Beals and his adopted homeland were plagued by problems that cast grave doubts about their immediate futures.

## Murder of a Friend

Beals's most profound shock in these years was the murder of Julio Antonio Mella, a Cuban Communist, who had taken up residence in Mexico City in the mid-1920s. Beals knew Mella well and admired his defiance of the Cuban dictator Gerardo Machado, who had forced the young Communist into exile. On the night of January 10, 1929, Mella, accompanied by Tina

Modotti, was shot down on the corner of Abraham González and Morelos streets in the heart of Mexico City by unknown assailants. Modotti was not harmed. She, along with Beals, Diego Rivera and Frances Toor, rushed to the Red Cross Hospital, where Mella died within a few hours. The Mexico City daily *Universal* reported that Mella's deathbed statement implicated the Machado government in the attack.[1]

The Mexico City press reported the Mella murder in sensational terms. Both major dailies *Excelsior* and *Universal* attempted to implicate Modotti as a conspirator in Mella's murder. They discussed Modotti's previous affairs with other men and recent relationship with Mella as evidence of immorality and implied that the murder may have been a crime of jealous passion. *Excelsior* published a letter from Modotti to Mexican artist Xavier Guerrero and another more recent letter from her to Mella, both of which contained emotional declarations of affection. Although *Excelsior* insisted that the publication of these letters was relevant to the investigation of Mella's death, the logical connection between Modotti's past love affairs and the murder was never clearly established.[2]

Another possibility was that Mella's death was a political assassination, resulting from the struggle between the Machado government and exiled Cuban radicals. Central to this theory was the testimony of Manuel Flores and David Malpica, both attendants at the Red Cross Hospital. They claimed Mella told them shortly before his death that his attackers had acted on instructions from the Cuban embassy in Mexico City.[3] The Mexico City police arrested José Magrinat, a Cuban living in Mexico, whom *Universal* described as "a kind of adventurer," who carried "various wounds on his body" as a result of previous risky endeavors.[4] Modotti, however, was not cleared in this hypothesis. The press reported the possibility that she was in league with Magrinat and had led Mella to the fatal ambush.[5]

Carleton Beals was drawn into the case in two ways. First, the press speculated that a gun Beals loaned to Modotti sometime before the crime might be the murder weapon. The newspapers soon dropped this notion, and presumably, the police did also.[6] Beals's second involvement was more important. He, Diego Rivera and other friends of Modotti urged Police Chief Valente Quintana to drop the case against her and concentrate on links to the Machado government. Nine years later in his autobiography, Beals openly accused Quintana of connivance in the Mella murder. He also claimed that the police engaged in a smear campaign against Modotti to divert attention from one of Quintana's friends who was involved in the murder.[7]

The identity of Mella's murderer (or murderers) remained unclear. The police eventually released Magrinat for lack of evidence. Neither the police, the press nor Modotti's friends ever clarified her role in the case. Her biographer Mildred Constantine concluded that even though "damage had been done" to her reputation, "her name had finally been cleared," presumably because she was not indicted.[8] In response to a letter from Modotti, Edward Weston wrote in his diary that "she has maintained and proved her innocence."[9] However, L. F. Bustamante concluded in 1942, soon after Modotti's death, that she carried a secret with her to her grave. Was she involved in Mella's murder, and if so, in what way? Diego Rivera's firm insistence that Modotti was innocent did not convince Bustamante.[10] For his part, Beals was certain that both Mella and Modotti were victims of the Machado dictatorship and Quintana's corrupt police department.[11] Beals's anguish over this affair stayed with him for several years, and in 1933, supplied part of the motivation for his condemnatory investigation of Machado's government.[12]

Mella's death and Modotti's ordeal marked the disintegration of the leftist community in Mexico City. Undoubtedly, other factors such as the conservative trend in Mexican politics, which made the intellectual climate less hospitable, played a part in the group's dissolution. Also, some individuals in the group needed a change of scene to stimulate their creative instincts. Beals saw the essential diversity of the group as the primary cause of its demise. In 1931, he wrote that many members of the community "have jumped up to their necks in politics or have discovered a new creed, or a new technique, and have gone their separate ways."[13] Whatever the causes, Beals lost touch with many of his friends and associates who had made Mexico City their temporary home in the 1920s.

## Assassination and Aftermath

On July 17, 1928, President-elect Alvaro Obregón fell victim to an assassin's bullet. His death created a quandary for Mexico's other political strongman Plutarco Elías Calles. (The two had alternated in the presidency with Obregón in power from 1920 to 1924; and Calles, from 1924 to 1928.) Obregón's expected return to office in 1928 would have enabled the two to continue this system, and at the same time, to abide by the constitution's prohibition of two consecutive terms. Obregón's death and Calles's ineligibility in 1928, however, threw Mexican politics into a state of confusion for the next five years. Undoubtedly, Calles held on to much power, but his relationship with the next three presidents remains unclear. These three men had limited authority and were unable to dominate Mexican politics as Obregón and Calles had done from 1920 to 1928. From Obregón's death until 1934, the revolution seemed to falter. As Beals and other observers noted, the government followed more conservative policies than in the early and middle 1920s.

Obregón's assassination grew out of hostile feelings that surrounded Mexico's church-state controversy. Ironically, Calles, not Obregón, was the architect of the government's anticlerical policies from 1926 to 1929. The Calles administration required all priests to register with the government, prohibited political activity by priests and imposed nonreligious education in church schools. The responses to these and other regulations by the Catholic church and its faithful followers were instantaneous and highly disruptive. Priests went on strike by refusing to say Mass or perform any religious service. In central and western Mexico, the peasants were deeply disturbed by what they perceived to be the government's demonic campaign against the church. These peasants fought a civil war against the government, a struggle which threatened the very existence of the Calles regime.[14] Other Catholics resisted in less dramatic ways; but a few, like the small cell of fanatics around the charismatic female leader Mother Conchita and her loyal assistant José Leon Toral also resorted to extreme methods. Their hatred for the Mexican government fermented for nearly three years. Finally, on July 17, 1928, Toral struck down Alvaro Obregón.

Obregón's assassination deeply distressed Beals. He felt that Obregón offered the possibility of a revival of the agrarian reform program that Calles had virtually abandoned. Threats to Obregón's life early in the 1928 election campaign endangered the promise of revolutionary resurgence. Beals noticed that the open, relaxed style of Obregón's first presidency had given way to apprehension and uncertainty. Four right-wing extremists disabled the presidential limousine and nearly killed Obregón in a frightening, but futile, hit-and-run attack. Beals examined the car soon after the attempt and concluded that the bullets had passed only a few inches from Obregón's head.[15] Obregón's death confirmed the worst of Beals' suspicions and placed the future of the revolution in doubt.

Beals learned of the assassination when he heard a newsboy shout from a streetcorner near his apartment, "Obergón murdered!" He attended the trial of Toral, who had been captured at the scene of the assassination. Beals described Toral as "a pale neurasthenic, but completely calm, his sunken eyes glowing with a strange fire." Toral was one of a group of right-wing Catholics led by Mother Conchita, who exercised an apparently extrasensory influence over her spiritual underlings. Beals interviewed her and found her to be "a large, horse-faced woman, not overly physically attractive, yet in few women have I sensed greater, more potent sex appeal. There was something diabolic in her physical magnetism." The Mexican authorities convicted Toral of murder and executed him. Mother Conchita was convicted of conspiracy and given a twenty-year sentence. In spite of his great disappointment with Obregón's death, Beals was fascinated by Toral's and Mother Conchita's fanatical commitment to the Catholic church.[16]

Calles faced the national crisis squarely, and in Beals' eyes, effectively. In September 1928, Calles strode into the Chamber of Deputies to face not only the unsettled legislators, but also the ambitious military officer corps. His speech was a masterful mixture of cajolery and intimidation. To the civilian politicians, he put himself in the role of commander of the army, capable of enforcing his rule by force. To the army, he gave a lecture on civics, which included a denunciation of militarism in politics. To the Obregonistas present, many of whom suspected that he played a part in Obregón's assassination, Calles showed unbending determination to hold his position in the revolutionary elite. At the end of the speech, his audience rose to its feet and rewarded him with applause. Only Aurelio Manrique, an irreconcilable Obregonista, refused to be moved and hissed "out a virulent and sinister 'farsante [liar].'" Beals interpreted Calles's speech as a "turning point" in the struggle between orderly civilian rule and the threat of militaristic adventurism.[17]

Beals's praise of Calles reached it high point in early 1929. In a lengthy analysis for *Current History,* Beals portrayed Calles as a "statesman" weathering the storms of factionalism and militarism to lead the revolution into a promising new era. He cited accomplishments in land reform, agrarian credit, rural education, irrigation and public health—all of which seemed to offer the hope of an improved life for the lower classes.[18] But Calles's greatest achievement, according to Beals, was the establishment of civilian control over the military. The dreary record of military-led revolts of the previous decade was not to be repeated while Calles held power.[19]

Beals's enthusiasm for Calles cooled later in 1929 as the Mexican government began to drift to the right. A central character in this trend was Pascual Ortiz Rubio, the successful presidential candidate of the newly formed P.N.R. (National Revolutionary party). This political organization, created by Calles and his followers, nominated Ortiz Rubio and then carried him to an easy victory on November 17, 1929. Beals studied the P.N.R.'s campaign against the Anti-re-election party's candidate José Vasconcelos. He wrote that Ortiz Rubio's victory meant "the close of the revolutionary epoch, [and] the crystallization of a regime based on the liberal postulate of the 1917 Constitution of Queretaro." Beals hypothesized that Ortiz Rubio would maintain the laws limiting foreign economic penetration, but restrict domestic reform. In short, he concluded that "the Mexican regime has reached the middle of the road."[20]

In his description of the 1929 campaign, Beals included a few remarks on the Vasconcelos candidacy. Beals saw Vasconcelos's appeal as too narrow, reaching only rightest Catholic groups, conservative student organizations and women's clubs. Vasconcelos was unable to organize these diverse groups into a political machine, and therefore, lagged far behind the larger, more efficient PNR. Beals predicted that the Communist party candidate Pedro Rodríguez Triana would poll more votes than Vasconcelos, whose electioneering methods were a reversion to "the old-style personalism."[21]

Beals's analysis of the Vasconcelos campaign brought heated rebuttals from the defeated candidate's camp. A perplexed Bruce Bliven, editor of the *New Republic,* wrote Beals on February 5, 1930 that he had on his desk "quite a mass of material from friends of Vasconcelos." They claimed that their candidate campaigned under death threats much of the time, and that in a fair election, he would have won easily. Bliven asked Beals for a letter "not for publication, saying how much truth there is in these allegations."[22] Beals replied that there was some truth in the claims of the Vasconcelistas, but that "the matter is not worth going into now." He stated that some local military commanders violated election laws, but these violations occurred on both sides. Beals was more concerned about the righward drift of the Ortiz Rubio government than about the complaints of the Vasconcelistas.[23]

A few months later, Vasconcelos wrote a bitter denunciation of U.S. press coverage of his campaign, that appeared in *Repertorio Americano,* a Costa Rican journal. He accused Beals of deliberately falsifying his account of the 1929 election by his failure to emphasize that most of the "fourteen million" Mexicans who voted for the Anti-re-election party were not included in the final count. Vasconcelos also accused Beals of neglecting the attempt to assassinate him and the widespread violence directed against his supporters.[24] Beals replied that the number 14 million was a gross exaggeration; and that while there was violence in the campaign, both sides seemed to be equally guilty of incitement.[25]

Vasconcelos's complaints indicated that Beals's journalistic evaluations carried considerable weight in Mexico. Almost all of Beals's writing appeared in periodicals or books published in the United States; but Mexican leaders were aware that the U.S. press, especially the liberal wing, paid much attention to Mexican affairs. They also realized the image of Mexico that appeared in these liberal publications had diplomatic and political ramifications mainly because of the tenuous state of U.S.-Mexican relations and because of the frequency of Mexico as a topic in U.S. politics. Beals's central role in the dissemination of information and opinion on Mexican affairs in the United States made him an important figure in politics as well as journalism.

## Under Arrest

A few minutes before noon on Friday February 14, 1930, plain clothes agents of the Mexican military police arrested Beals in his apartment, thrust him into a waiting car and carried him to the office of the commanding general of the valley of Mexico. Beals knew the reputation of the commanding general Eulogio Ortiz, who was notorious for his brutal treatment of political prisoners. Mexico City was alive with tension in the wake of the unsuccessful assassination attempt by a right-wing fanatic against President Pascual Ortiz Rubio on his inauguration day. Many officials, including General Ortiz, mistakenly assumed that Communists had been involved in the plot. Beals, known to be a friend of prominent Communists such as Diego Rivera and the late Julio Mella, had become critical of the Mexican government's drift to the right in recent months. Apparently, General Ortiz leaped to the conclusion that Beals was, in some way, a threat to the national interest.

Beals's arrest had the elements of a dramatic confrontation.

The military police agents informed Beals that he was to accompany them to the office of General Ortiz. Beals refused and suggested that they carry him to the U.S. embassy instead. The agents rejected this proposal and informed Beals that he had no choice in the matter. Beals hurriedly wrote a note for a friend in a nearby apartment. The agents asked for the note, and on his refusal to relinquish it, took it from him by force. On their way out of the apartment building, the military police found the main door locked. They demanded Beals give them the key to open it; he refused. They attempted to shove the door open but failed. After some frustrating moments, they located a maid who opened the door for them.[26]

Once on the street, the agents moved Beals in the direction of their car. Miss Morrell, an American woman who lived in the same apartment building and knew Beals, happened to be washing her hair on the roof. She saw the agents taking Beals to their car and called out:

"Where are you going?"

"They are taking me to the military," Beals replied. "Phone the embassy."

The agents "shoved" Beals "violently" into their car and left. The neighbor notified the U.S. embassy of Beals's predicament.[27]

Beals's treatment in Ortiz's office did nothing to allay his growing fears. After Beals arrived, the military police stashed him in a toilet for nearly ten minutes until General Ortiz was available. In the meantime, officers searched Beals and relieved him of his address book and immigration papers. Beals then faced an angry General Ortiz who confronted the hapless reporter with some documents that, at least to the general's satisfaction, implicated him in serious antigovernment activities. One document was a copy of a letter from Beals to Bruce Bliven (probably the letter of February 10, 1930, in which Beals criticized unnamed Mexican military commanders for "high-handed" acts against the Vasconcelistas and also complained of the Ortiz Rubio government's move to the right) and the other was "a mutilated fragment of a news telegram." Ortiz asked Beals if he had written them. Beals replied in the affirmative. Ortiz became visibly angry, threatened Beals with deportation and cursed him in vile language. He ordered his prisoner to a jail cell, that Beals later described as "filthy" and populated with "five very disreputable persons." Beals remained in the cell for more than six hours without food or water or access to a bathroom.[28]

Officials in the U.S. embassy soon came to Beals's aid. Herschel Johnson, chargé d'affairs, received Miss Morrell's phone call about noon. He ordered the staff to contact the civilian police. After these inquiries brought no positive results, Chargé Johnson asked Colonel Gordon Johnston, the military attaché, to approach the Mexican military. Johnston discovered that Beals was in Ortiz's custody and arranged a 5:30 P.M. meeting with the general, who explained that Beals was "in close arrest" and "incommunicado." Ortiz displayed the two documents as evidence against Beals, but he was unable to specify a charge of criminal activity. Johnston convinced Ortiz to release Beals in his custody as military attaché of the U.S. embassy. Beals's ordeal ended early that evening following the Johnston-Ortiz agreement.[29]

Both Johnson and Johnston concluded that Ortiz had insufficient evidence to justify Beals's arrest. Johnston noted that Ortiz thought Beals was "connected with . . . communistic action" but could not support that assumption.[30] In his report to the State Department, Johnson suggested that Ortiz intended to deport Beals, which

. . . would be a mistake from the viewpoint of Mexico, as Beals whatever his political opinions may be, is not an enemy of Mexico nor of its government. He has moreover a considerable audience particularly among a group of people in the United States disposed to be friendly to Mexico. He is thus in a position to do Mexico considerable injury in public opinion and his expulsion from Mexico would serve no useful purpose.[31]

The potential for harm to Mexican-U.S. relations was understood in the Mexican Foreign Relations Ministry. The Mexican embassy in Washington expressed concern that Beals's arrest would cause an adverse reaction among left-of-center journalists in the United States. The embassy's report mentioned that Beals's friend Charles Wilson threatened to lead "an editorial campaign against our [Mexican] government in protest against . . . Beals's arrest." The report also included copies of articles from the Associated Press, *The New York Times* and the *Washington Post* that seemed to offer support for Wilson's "editorial campaign." Mexican diplomats were clearly worried about the U.S. press response to Beals's incarceration.[32]

On Monday February 17, Beals and Colonel Johnston went to the office of Colonel Hernández Chazaro, private secretary to President Ortiz Rubio to discuss the arrest. Chazaro's attitude was friendly and almost apologetic. He said that Beals's arrest came as a result of "zealous efforts" by Ortiz "to perform his duties creditably" in the wake of the attempt to assassinate Ortiz Rubio. He asked Beals not to make judgments about the new administration until it had been in power for a considerable length of time. Beals replied that his arrest "had been decidedly unpleasant," but in no way, diminished his affection and admiration for Mexico. Beals also explained the content of his article in the *New Republic* (which he believed to be unpublished at the time) about the Mexican government's restrictions on the Communist party. Beals said the article was written in "a critical spirit, but not necessarily in an unfriendly spirit." The meeting was pleasant, and apparently, satisfied all parties involved.[33]

In the course of the meeting, Chazaro phoned General Ortiz and ordered him to cease his investigation of Beals. Nearly a decade later, Beals wrote a colorful, and perhaps partially fictional, version of the telephone conversation, in which he recalled Chazaro's angry words to Ortiz: " 'Then get this. The President orders you to lay off Beals . . . And if you forget what I've told you, you'll regret it the rest of your life.' " Then Chazaro turned to Beals and Johnston and said in "a soft voice, 'Kindly pardon my language. But it is the only language he understands.' "[34]

The exact cause for General Ortiz's arrest of Beals remains unclear. The available evidence, however, indicates that the two intercepted pieces of Beals's correspondence were the most important factors. Beals's letter to Bliven contained two especially provocative passages, one of which accused some unnamed military commanders of "destroying free suffrage" in the November election. The other passage condemned the new government for "using the attempted assassination of Ortiz Rubio to persecute all of its political enemies."[35] The second document was a "mutilated fragment of a news telegram" in which Beals described the detention and search of a Russian diplomat by Mexican government agents. Beals claimed that the version in Ortiz's hands was incomplete because it omitted his account of statements by Mexican officials that refuted the Soviet charges.[36]

There is the possibility that Beals's article "Mexico and the Communists" angered Ortiz. (Only indirect evidence exists, however, to show that the general was aware of it.) The article contained sharp attacks on Ortiz and Valente Quintana, who was, by then, head of Mexico's secret service. Beals accused Ortiz of "arbitrary" and "brutal" actions and implied that Quintana was involved in the murder of Julio Mella. This article appeared in the February 17 edition of the *New Republic*, which was on the newsstand by February 12.[37] The Mexican embassy in Washington notified the ministry of foreign relations in Mexico City of the appearance of Beals's article on February 12, two days before his arrest.[38] There is no indication, however, that Ortiz saw the article before he ordered Beals's arrest.

Soon after his arrest, Beals wrote to Bruce Bliven of the *New Republic* about the incident. Beals complained that he had received no correspondence for about a week before his arrest and concluded that the Mexican government was tampering with his mail.[39] Bliven's reply reinforced some of Beals's assumptions. Bliven had not received the letter of February 10, although the February 18 letter did reach him.[40]

Beals launched a personal inquiry into the possible role of the Mexican post office in the interception of his mail. In a written response, the Mexican Director General of the Mails Arturo M. Elías (a relative of former President Calles) insisted that Beals's " . . . mail at no time has been tampered with"; but he also stated that he had ordered an investigation.[41] In late

April, Beals sent Elías a strongly worded letter, in which he listed more than ten pieces of mail that either had failed to reach his apartment or had failed to reach the intended destination.[42] Elías sensed the anger in Beals's letter and replied sternly that "this department refuses to accept the grave charges made in your letter, unless fully substantiated."[43] In some cases, Beals could have shown that his letters never reached the parties to whom they were addressed. He could not prove, however, that the Mexican post office, or any branch of the Mexican government, actually siezed his mail. After another letter of protest to Elías, Beals gave up this quest.[44] Apparently, Elías never made public the results of his investigation.

Beals's note of thanks to the U.S. State Department for the assistance it rendered during this affair suggested a distinct contrast with the middle and late 1920s, when Beals and U.S. diplomats usually were bitter enemies. The State Department and the Mexican Ministry of Foreign Relations both revealed an appreciation of Beals's importance as a commentator on Mexican affairs. The internal correspondance of the two governments showed that, at least among middle-level diplomats, Beals was a writer to be read, and from the Mexican point of view, to be treated with respect.

## The Revolution Falters

Beals's rising prestige as a writer made his negative judgments on the Mexican government in the early 1930s especially noticeable. His writing in the 1920s often praised the work of revolutionary administrations and damned the threats of interference that emanated from Washington. In these years, the U.S. State Department accused Beals of being a paid publicist for the Mexican government. In 1930, however, Beals took refuge in the protective services offered by American diplomats in Mexico City to escape the clutches of Mexican authorities. This reversal in Beals's adversarial relationships grew out of policy changes in the two governments. (His arrest, however, may have contributed to his outspoken rejection of Mexican leaders.) The Mexican government moved steadily to the right after the assassination of Obregón. At roughly the same time, President Herbert Hoover made a calculated effort to win support among the Latin American nations—Mexico was one of the leading beneficiaries of this new friendliness, through the capable ministrations of Ambassador Dwight Morrow.[45] Beals found little cause for complaint in this new policy, but much to criticize on the domestic scene in Mexico.

Beals's criticisms were couched in harsh terms, including a charge of "fascist tactics" against the nation's political leaders. While he never defined the term in a strict academic sense, Beals held the impression that fascism involved an elite-controlled government with little or no concern for social reform, but with an intense drive to eliminate political opposition. As early as 1923, he detected a tendency towards fascism among widely scattered, and generally unorganized, segments of Mexico's population. In 1929 and 1930, he saw evidence of increased centralization under Calles and also growing intolerance of press criticism. Weighing the results of the election of 1929, he predicted a decided shift to the right under President-elect Pascual Ortiz Rubio. By 1931, Beals saw serious evidence of fascism present at the upper levels of the new national revolutionary party (Partido Nacional Revolucionario or PNR). With the active support of Calles, the top echelon of the PNR was clearly the most powerful group in Mexican politics. There were virtually no challengers inside or outside the party.[46] Beals also saw the expanding military influence in the PNR.[47] In his judgment, the Calles-PNR organization had "betrayed the original purposes of the revolution." In a pessimistic appraisal, Beals insisted that "Mexico has washed her hands of the revolution" by the abandonment of "Indianism, communal landholding and proletarian doctrine, in favor of the old economic doctrines of Europe and Díaz."[48]

Beals's criticisms of Mexico's leadership and his defense of the revolution's original goals were affirmed by his Mexican friend Luis Quintanilla. In spite of close ties to Emilio Portes Gil, Mexico's diplomatic representative in France, and President Ortiz Rubio, Quintanilla praised *Mexican Maze* as typical of its author's "unpardonable weakness of telling THE TRUTH." He expressed confidence in Beals's "love for Mexico," his "revolutionary values" and "the seriousness of his investigations."[49]

### Escape into History

Beals seemed to encounter unhappiness everywhere he turned. In addition to his disappointments related to the troubled state of the revolution, he suffered through his second unsuccessful marriage. Allen Dawson, a U.S. diplomat, testified to the hastiness of Beals's decision to marry. He wrote to the bridegroom that he was "as surprised as most of your friends but, knowing your excellent taste, do not hesitate to congratulate you."[50] The congratulations were misplaced, for Beals's marriage to Betty Daniels ended in divorce in less than a year.[51]

Only in his writing did Beals find some measure of success. The publication of *Mexican Maze* in 1931 and *Banana Gold* in 1932 enhanced his reputation as a leftist commentator on Latin America.[52] In 1932 and 1933, he entered a period of calm in his life. Supported by a Guggenheim Fellowship, he wrote a biography of Porfirio Díaz, the dictator of Mexico from 1876 to 1910 and the nemesis of the revolution. For most of this period, Beals rented a picturesque house in the pleasant Mexico City suburb of Coyoacán, where he resumed a busy social life. In some ways, it was reminiscent of his activities in the middle and late 1920s.[53] His version of the life of Díaz was an affirmation of his faith in the early revolution and the struggles of Madero, Villa, Zapata and Obregón. Díaz was a distant, authoritarian figure who presided over the looting of his nation by foreign powers and the exploitation of the poor by the wealthy. Beals's critics generally praised the biography, with the exception of its undocumented conversations among principal characters—a novelistic device that resembled popular, more than scholarly, history. Although *Porfirio Díaz* was a typical liberal-leftist interpretation of the dictatorship, Beals's audacity in taking on such a monumental subject was noteworthy.[54]

The publication of *Porfirio Díaz* marked the end of a decade in which Beals wrote four books and several dozen shorter pieces on Mexico. The revolution of the 1920s gave Beals the subject matter on which he established himself as a professional journalist. His identification with Mexico and his favorable view of its revolution were shaken by events from 1928 to 1932. The Obregón assassination removed the one political leader that, to Beals, was committed to social reform. The apparent involvement of some Mexican authorities in the Mella murder was another source of dismay. Beals's heavy-handed incarceration by Mexican military police must have reinforced his growing disappointment with the government's movement to the right. Nonetheless, *Mexican Maze* and *Porfirio Díaz* indicated that Beals had not lost faith in the revolution; in his perception, the government had betrayed the revolution.

# • 7 •

# Cuba

Beals's next major undertaking was an exposé of the dictatorship of Gerardo Machado in Cuba. In spite of his many years spent in close proximity to civil strife and ugly violence, Beals was appalled by what he found in Cuba during his visit from early September to mid-October of 1932. Beals had arranged appointments with Clemente Vázquez Bello, President of the Cuban Senate and an ally of Machado, and Leopoldo Freyre de Andrade, an opponent of Machado. On September 27, 1932, both men were brutally murdered, apparently victims of the terrorist war raging between the dictator and his enemies.[1] Beals was unable to interview either man before his death; their murders gave him a quick initiation into the bloody processes of Cuban politics.

Beals arrived in Havana thirty-four years after U.S. troops invaded Cuba to take part in the liberation of the island from Spanish rule. What became known as the Spanish-American War was only the last chapter in Cuba's fight for independence. On the verge of victory before the U.S. entered, Cuban patriots were frustrated by the presence of a U.S. military governor for three years after the end of the war. The Platt Amendment, dictated to the new Cuban government by Secretary of State Elihu Root in 1903, provided for U.S. intervention in Cuba at any time that Washington deemed necessary. Cuba's hard-won independence suffered severe limitations, while American influence in the new nation knew few bounds.

The Machado government began under relatively good conditions and rode the crest of prosperity for five years, only to be dashed on the rocks of economic disaster in the early 1930s. Machado won the presidential election of 1924, when material growth and political stability seemed possible for the first time in the brief history of the Cuban nation. Although free of military intervention in the 1920s, Cuba's economy was dependent on the huge North American sugar market. While the Coolidge prosperity continued, Cuba's economy boomed. Machado used tax revenues to build highways, schools and hospitals; but he also suppressed leftist labor and student movements. When the U.S. economy collapsed in 1929, the Cuban economy fell even further. In these troubled times, university students joined Communists and workers to protest Machado's increasingly stubborn resistance to appeals for the government to deal with the depression. At the time of Beals's arrival, Machado faced hostility, exacerbated by his own heavy-handed authoritarian tactics.[2] The ever-growing opposition came from a group of young, college-educated, middle-class leftists, who seemed to increase their agitation in direct proportion to Machado's use of repression. In October 1931, many of these leftists organized the ABC, an anti-Machado political party, which used terrorist tactics and radical propaganda against the dictatorship. It gained more adherents within the peace-loving middle class as Machado's fight to hold power became increasingly desperate.[3]

To Beals and most foreign observers, Machado was easily recognizable as the evil tyrant; the potential leftist hero was more difficult to locate. The ABC was full of possible candidates, but it was not the only organized opposition to Machado. The Student Directory, which was first organized by students from the University of Havana in 1925, continued to have influence into the 1930s.[3] The Cuban Communist party was also active and contributed to the general confusion that existed at the left end of the political spectrum.[4] These three organizations, along with other anti-Machado groups, attempted to maintain separate identities, in their effort to over-throw the common enemy Machado.

The U.S. government, for more than thirty years the self-appointed arbiter of Cuban politics, watched the Cuban situation with growing concern. The destabilization of the Machado regime in the early 1930s ended five years of political calm and economic expansion, in which U.S. diplomats and business-men took much satisfaction. Machado had been a businessman before entering politics, and his relations with U.S. companies operating in Cuba were good. The U.S. State Department re-lied on Machado to maintain order; and as Machado's political power weakened, U.S. diplomats and businessmen saw Cuba sliding back into chaos. By the last part of 1932, the outlook for Machado was dismal; but President Hoover was determined to avoid military intervention, which had been so costly for the United States in Nicaragua. Both he and his successor Franklin D. Roosevelt chose to rely on diplomats, not soldiers, to achieve their goals in Cuba.[5]

## The Crusade

When Beals left Havana for New York in mid-October, he was convinced that the reading public in the United States should know the real nature of the Machado dictatorship. He also intended to use all of the journalistic influence at his command to convince the State Department to abandon Machado in his time of trouble. Beals's first public statements on Cuban affairs appeared in *La Prensa,* a Spanish language newspaper published in New York City. In this interview, Beals insisted that Machado had no support among the Cuban people, a fact ignored by U.S. Ambassador Harry F. Guggenheim, who continued actively to support this unpopular government.[6] Beal's first attack on Machado and Guggenheim did not cause much of a sensation in the United States, but it did attract the attention of a number of anti-Machado Cubans living in exile in New York and Washington. Many of these exiles wanted to publicize the brutal side of the Machado government to the U.S. public and saw Beals as a valuable ally in this effort.[7]

One such exile Octavio Seigle wrote Beals a remarkable letter in which he detailed some of Machado's abuses of justice. Seigle was a member of the Cuban Patriotic League, an anti-Machado propaganda organization based in the United States.[8] He accused Machado and his henchmen of eighteen murders and included detailed information on most of these assassinations. He gave examples of Machado's use of illegal arrest and imprisonment, and of the government's suppression of opposition newspapers.[9] One item in the letter that must have stood out for Beals was Seigle's account of the murder of Julio Antonio Mella, Beals's friend from his Mexico City days. Seigle claimed that "the assassins were sent from Cuba and took refuge in the Cuban embassy" in Mexico City. One of them, presumably José Magrinat, was "recently judged and condemned in Mexico." Seigle added that Valente Quintana, the Mexico City police chief, was involved in the murder plot. All of these statements were in accord with Beals's view of the Mella murder.[10]

Appearing in a new left-wing journal *Common Sense*, Beals's first publication on Machado's Cuba was a wholesale condemnation of the dictator and U. S. Ambassador Guggenheim. Beals insisted that Machado, called "president of a thousand murders" by the Cuban people, was possessed by a "neurosis of bloody grandeur." Repulsed by Machado's violent excesses, Beals's anger carried over to color his assessment of Guggenheim, who at least to Beals, was openly cooperative with Machado. On May 20, 1930, less than twenty-four hours after the Cuban army fired into an anti-Machado political meeting, killing and wounding many, Guggenheim appeared with Machado in public, thereby showing support for his government. Citing some of the murders listed by Seigle (with no mention of the source) and Mella's assassination in Mexico City, Beals deplored Guggenheim's failure to speak out against Machado's use of violence to eliminate his opposition. Beals also accused Guggenheim of allowing Cuban policemen to stand guard inside the entrance to the American embassy, thereby giving them access to the switchboard and the message center. Beals's conclusion was a sweeping, if somewhat awkwardly phrased, indictment of U.S. policy toward the dictator-ship: "Cuba today lies in economic, social and political ruins under the heel of a small clique of murderous officials main-tained in office by the good offices of Ambassador Guggen-heim".[11]

Machado's administration promptly censored Beals's arti-cle in Cuba. *The New York Times* reported that Machado's min-ions confiscated 126 copies of the December 29, 1932 issue of *Common Sense* and arrested the owner of the local news service that attempted to sell the periodical.[12] Editor of *Common Sense* Alfred Bingham dashed off a strongly worded letter of protest to Secretary of State Stimson, but the State Department took no action, mainly on the grounds that the case fell within the jurisdiction of the Cuban courts.[13]

The confiscation of *Common Sense* only increased Beals's determination to publicize the evils of Machado's government. Fernando Ortiz, an exiled Cuban scholar living in the United States, reinforced this conviction. Beals first met Ortiz in mid-October 1932 at the New York City apartment of Laurence Dug-gan, a respected young expert on Latin American affairs.[14] For six months, Beals in New York and Ortiz in Washington ex-changed correspondence on events in Cuba and policy changes in Washington.[15] Ortiz had gained an international reputation as an anthropologist in the 1910s. He became a political activist in the next decade, initially to protest political corruption and later to oppose Machado.[16]

Ortiz worked for the Cuban-American Friendship Council, an organization ostensibly intended to promote better relations between the two countries. Actually, it was an anti-Machado propaganda organ; it claimed the only terms on which har-mony might be reached was the complete withdrawal of U.S. support for Machado.[17] Ortiz wanted to contact influential peo-ple in the United States in the fields of publishing politics. Beals was able to help him with introductions to Bruce Bliven of the *New Republic* and Ernest Gruening of *The Nation*. In a letter to Beals, Ortiz described a conversation with Gruening, who was friendly "although on [Ambassador] Guggenheim's side."[18]

Ortiz expressed opinions about American scholars and reporters who wrote on Cuba and Cuban-U.S. relations. In addition to his compliments on Beals's writing, Ortiz lauded the work of Harry Elmer Barnes, the Columbia University historian and editor of the Vanguard Press series of anti-imperialist studies. He was disappointed by Hubert Herring, who had announced his opposition to Machado, "but without any suggestion as to what should be done and avoiding any adverse criticism of Guggenheim's policies." Ortiz berated George Cox of the *Christian Science Monitor*, who talked with the Cuban-American Friendship Council and then went on to Cuba, where he wrote a series of pro-Machado articles.[19] Occasionally, Ortiz unburdened himself of his concerns and doubts about U.S. policy in Cuba. In April 1933, in a bleak mood soon after Franklin Roosevelt's inauguration, he wrote "Roosevelt is helping Machado and . . . all hope for justice is lost."[20]

Through the summer of 1933, Beals immersed himself in a study of the sordid nature of Cuban politics. He found much support for his dislike of Machado and Guggenheim in his discussions and correspondence with Siegle and Ortiz, his initial judgment of Machado, however, came from the vividly painful memory of the death of Julio Mella. Beals plunged into one of the most intense and unrewarding imbroglios of his career: his attempt to link the patrician Guggenheim with the despotic Machado and drive them both from power.

### The Guggenheim Affair

Beals's writing on Cuba reflected his emotional involvement with some of the personalities and events he described. Many observers shared his abhorrence of Machado, his sharp attacks on Ambassador Guggenheim, however, surprised, and even angered, some of his colleagues. At times, his customary advocacy approach to journalism acquired an irrational air. In later years, Beals attempted to block out these experiences as indicated by his omission of any mention of Guggenheim or of the downfall of Machado in the second volume of his autobiography.[21] Apparently, this time was a difficult and painful period for him.

Beals was not the first U.S. journalist to criticize Machado. As early as May 1929, *The Nation* editorialized against Machado's repression of student and labor opposition. Six months later, it called for the U.S. to apply diplomatic pressure against the Cuban dictator.[22] In May 1931, Ernest Gruening condemned Machado's authoritarian government but complimented Ambassador Guggenheim's handling of a complex situation.[23] By 1931, many commentators in the United States openly opposed Machado, a position that was duly noted by the State Department.[24]

Before the publication of Beals's articles in *Common Sense*, Guggenheim read his interview in *La Prensa* and moved to defend himself in a cautious and indirect way. He requested that a friend Jacob Billikopf try to convince Beals to withdraw the articles. Although he admitted that some of Beals's accusations were correct, Guggenheim claimed that they created a distorted picture because the author did not place them in their full context. For example, he admitted that there were two Cuban policemen stationed in the U.S. embassy; but he insisted that the presence of locally recruited guards was routine in many U.S. diplomatic establishments. He pointedly denied that these guards determined who might see the ambassador. They were "no more than messengers." Guggenheim asked Billikopf to convey "to Mr. Beals the absurdity of some of the personal charges" that could only harm the delicate nature of U.S.-Cuban relations.[25]

Billikopf asked Ernest Gruening to intercede in the affair. He frankly urged Gruening

. . . to use your influence with Carleton Beals not to publish his article or articles until such time as he has had an opportunity to discuss the matter with Mr. Guggenheim, or, at least, give [sic] the ambassador a chance to review the story and present whatever factual data Carleton Beals may wish. It would seem that Fair Play [Billikopf's capitalization] demands this, and I am sure that Beals, who is regarded in this country—and justly so—as one of the greatest interpreters of Latin American relations, will not want to make statements that will be subject to modifications or reinterpretations.[26]

Gruening opened the way for an exchange of letters between Billikopf and Beals. Beals wrote first and his letter was set in sharply moralistic tones:

Ambassador Guggenheim . . . has become involved in a very iniquitous situation. This, I take it, is due to the peculiar position of the American embassy in Cuba and is concerned with the whole American policy in that island. I take it . . . that . . . you approve of Mr. Guggenheim's activities with relation to Machado, the opposition, and American interests in Cuba. I intend to discuss those activities fully, and I can see no harm in doing so. The situation of Cuba is so grievous that no decent man can stand by at this time without doing his utmost in behalf of that unfortunate people.

Beals closed his letter with the suggestion that Billikopf jumped to the defense of Guggenheim because of that family's healthy contributions to Jewish charities, (Billikopf was head of the Federation of Jewish Charities of Philadelphia.)[27]

Billikopf's rejoinder was conciliatory, lengthy, impressive and unheeded. He attempted to play on Beals's leftist sympathies by describing Gruening, Leland Jenks, Hubert Herring and other left-of-center scholars as friendly to Guggenheim.[28] Beals rejected this approach, as well as the efforts of Herring to defend Guggenheim.[29] Beals's response to Herring revealed the depth of his personal involvement in the Machado-Guggenheim dispute:

If you had stood over the dead body of my friend Julio Antonio Mella, as I did, and had seen the life go out of him because of foul assassins, as now has been conclusively disclosed, sent by Machado personally; if you had blundered into the Freyre de Andrade home in Havana, and had seen three of the finest men one could meet anywhere in the world, lying in pools of blood; then perhaps you would appreciate my impatience at you for worrying about Guggenheim, when there is something vital to worry about.[30]

Beals, Ortiz, Siegle and other anti-Machado writers and publicists were convinced of Guggenheim's connivance with Machado. The historical record, however, does not support this position. Guggenheim wrote an account of his years as ambassador in which he disputed the "propaganda" campaign against him. He claimed that the embassy did intercede to encourage fair trials for imprisoned members of the Machado opposition and that he offered no comfort or support to the dictatorship.[31] A generation later, historians Robert Freeman Smith and Jules Robert Benjamin found in State Department records evidence that Guggenheim suggested to Washington a complete break with Machado, in order to pressure him into compromising with his opposition.[32]

Beals mistook Guggenheim's failure to condemn Machado for tacit support, this false assumption probably arose from two main factors: The first was Beals's aversion toward dictators and his affinity for the anti-dictatorial Left in Cuba and throughout all Latin America. On the Machado-Guggenheim liaison, he found ready support from Cuban leftists Octavio Siegle and Fernando Ortiz. The second factor was his lingering outrage over the murder of Julio Mella, that he blamed on Machado. He vented much of his pent-up frustration on Guggenheim, who seemed to support Machado against public accusations in similar cases.

### The Crime of Cuba

Beals's book *The Crime of Cuba* appeared in early September 1933, barely two weeks after Machado fell from power. The subsequent political instability in Cuba gave the island nation a prominent place in U.S. news. It also gave Beals's book some topical interest, although it was outdated, in part, because he wrote it before Machado's overthrow. The title came from Beals's conversation with Miguel de Araunuz, a Cuban mathematics professor, who was forced to take irregular employment as a baker after being barred from teaching by Machado's persecution.[33] For Beals the word "crime" carried two distinct, but related, meanings. One meant the evil nature of Cuba's recent despotic governments; the second, the imperialistic presence of the United States, which made the life of the Cuban masses even more woeful. Beals's aim was to publicize these conditions and arouse sympathy for the unfortunate people of Cuba, who were exploited from within by tyranny and from without by imperialism.

Lippincott's managing editor J. Jefferson Jones was highly pleased by the manuscript (except for the possibility of a libel suit by Guggenheim). He felt that Cuba would be "the next high spot in public affairs" and that Beals's work had the chance to become the "book of the hour." Proof of Beals's dedication to this project came from his rejection of an offer by Covici Friede to write a book on Venezuela. He also accepted Jones's advice concerning revisions to avoid court action by Guggenheim. Jones cautioned that the phrase "publicly, Guggenheim collaborated with Machado" and the paragraph that followed might be libelous.[34] Through a series of questions that made clear the author's assumptions without any direct accusations, Beals suggested a Guggenheim-Machado connection in the published version.[35]

Beals and Jones were fortunate to secure the services of a talented young photographer Walker Evans to illustrate the book. Evans went to Cuba for a month from mid-May to mid-June 1933. Soon after his return, he wrote Beals that "the old butcher [Machado] seems firmly in, still, for some time to come." He named some of Beals's Cuban friends who helped him with his photography, especially Jose Ántonio Fernández de Castro, a Cuban journalist, and J. D. Phillips, a reporter stationed in Cuba by *The New York Times*.[36] His photographic essay captured the lower classes of Havana in a stark, but spontaneous, style that conveyed the grim, dirty reality of the urban tropics. Two pictures seemed to stand out: one was of a mother with her three young children sprawled, partially clothed in a closed, unfriendly doorway; the second, of a bleak interior patio complete with flaking walls and grimy garbage cans.[37]

Evan's photographs complimented the first ninety-two pages of Beals's text especially well. This part of the book was a subjective interpretation of Cuba's ethnic, social and cultural ambience. His use of the first person in his descriptive passages seemed more like fiction than journalism, but it did convey a vivid picture of Cuban life in the 1930s. "Fela" was an octoroon who used her physical charms to coax drinks, dances and money from male American tourists. Beals created an overly dramatic and perhaps exaggerated word-picture of Fela as a symbol of Cuba's heterogeneous ethnic composition. He claimed that "her grape-snug skin covered over a complex heritage" more African than Spanish, and full of the cultural contradictions that seemed to underlie the instabilities of Cuban society.[38]

The character of the Cuban male concerned Beals, especially his *choteo*, the tendency "to take nothing seriously, to toss everything nonchalently to the winds." Beals analyzed choteo, a hybrid of Spanish and African influences, as a kind of protective mask behind which the male hid his most sensitive feelings. The Mexican, by contrast, allowed his inner feelings to the surface, but

the Cuban prefers ordinarily to appear flippant, to show disrespect, to ignore surrounding persons, ideas and objects . . . Choteo demands that the user be 'agin' all things without considering their intrinsic values, a sinister ingenuity to prove that nothing is worthy of respect. Patriotism, the home, culture, bring a sarcastic, often pointless remark, "sheer romanticism." Even though the speaker think differently it behooves him to deride—a socially obligatory approach.[39]

Beals's fascination with the Cuban people contrasted with his outrage at the role of U.S. imperialism in recent Cuban history. After the U.S. victory in the so-called Spanish-American War, Cuba began to feel the full weight of the twin yokes of American imperialism: business enterprise and diplomatic intimidation. Business worked for "the largest profits possible without regard for the welfare of the Cuban people," and diplomats strove "to maintain the status quo, the insure stability often regardless of the wishes of the Cuban people."[40] The Platt Amendment, the legal rationalization for U.S. interference in Cuban affairs, was the symbol and the implementing device of imperialism. Beals saw this unwarranted involvement was a cause of Cuba's political and economic problems, that seemed to deepen with the passage of time. U.S. domination was so pervasive that the Cuban government became a minion of foreign, i.e. mostly U.S., interests, at the expense of the Cuban masses. Under these conditions, "the government merely placates the people or batters them into submission. As our interests and those of the Cuban people are largely antithetical, the people are more often battered than placated."[41]

The United States chose the wealthy and the powerful in Cuban society as allies, thereby ignoring the poor and the weak. From the early years of Cuban independence, American diplomats sought out "the Tories, the respectable Cubans, the people who had looked with apprehension on a free Cuba" as partners in the creation of a new government.[42] An over-riding fear of revolution and its resultant instability led the United States to cooperate with dictators, who usually were a source of stability through strong-arm methods. According to Beals, these policies placed the United States on the side of conservative tyrants and in opposition to the forces of reform and democracy. This policy of convenience in Cuba favored "tyranny, corruption and American capitalists at the expense of human liberty."[43]

U.S. imperialism in Cuba involved sugar more than any other part of the economy. The expansion of Cuban sugar production in the late nineteenth century was heavily dependent on the U.S. domestic market for consumption, on U.S. banks for capital and on U.S. entrepreneurs for the development of the necessary transportation and industrial infrastructures. Beals deplored this increasing dependence in the first third of the twentieth century, particularly the Chadbourne Plan of 1930, under which U.S. bankers, in agreement with Machado, limited the production of Cuban sugar. In theory, this was to raise sugar prices; but there was no firm commitment to restrict production elsewhere.[44] Beals also aimed a barb at William H. Woodin, Roosevelt's new secretary of the treasury, who had "intimate connections" with several U.S. firms that operated in Cuba with official favoritism from Machado.[45]

Woodin replied to Beals's accusations indirectly through a United Press correspondent who relayed this information to Jones at Lippincott. According to Jones's paraphrase, Woodin stated:

I have no more interest in Machado than I have in John Doe. I've met him a few times, once in New York when Jimmy Walker gave a dinner in his honor. That is the extent of our relationship. I own a few hundred shares of Consolidated Railroads of Cuba, but I wouldn't call that a financial interest.[46]

Historians Hugh Thomas and Robert Freeman Smith disagreed. Bearing out the general thrust of Beals's argument, they described Woodin as the holder of "extensive investments" in Cuba in the Machado years.

Beals's prescient summation of the effects of America's foul deeds in Cuba was full of the colorful prose typical of much of his writing. The United States consistently pursued

a policy which has helped drive her [Cuba] to despair and ruin, and which if not checked will drive her ere long to the folly of a bloody revolution, costly in Marines, property and international good-will. Beneath the tropical opulence of Cuba, hidden in the tangled jungle of her present cruel political tyranny, are the fangs of bitter discontent. Cuba, unless a remedy is soon found, will be reaped to the holocaust of civil war.[48]

If U.S. imperialism was the ultimate cause of Cuba's sad condition, the dictator Machado was the most immediate and visible cause. A native of Santa Clara province, Machado was a cattle thief, who became a political opportunist and climbed the ladder to success in the turbulent years after independence.[49] Once in power, he heaped money and other favors on the Cuban military to cement his position. Beals contrasted this largess with the paucity of funds for public schools and colleges, many of which closed in the Machado years.[50] Beals blamed the dictatorship for the terrorism that engulfed Cuba in the early 1930s, while he exhonorated the ABC and other dissident groups for using similar tactics. In Beals's estimation, the repressive nature of the Machado regime made terrorism a necessary part of the opposition's struggle to oust the dictator.[51]

Beals held to his anti-Guggenheim line, in spite of the barrage of objections from Billikopf, Gruening, Herring and others. Beals restated his earlier complaints about Cuban policemen in the U.S. embassy and Guggenheim's refusal to help anti-Machado politicians, who were harassed, persecuted and sometimes murdered by agents of the dictatorship. Beals stressed that Guggenheim allowed Machado to use his (Guggenheim's) name and the embassy in a propaganda effort to convince Cubans, and foreigners alike, that the U.S. supported the current government.[52]

Beals's *Crime of Cuba* was the last major salvo in the lengthy press bombardment of Machado. Only two weeks before the book went on sale, rebels forced the dictator out of office. The *Crime of Cuba* had no influence on this revolt, but Beals's earlier articles in *Common Sense* and other periodicals were an important part of the anti-Machado movement in the United States. While it is difficult to measure the effects of publicity campaigns on public opinion and government policy, one historian reached the following conclusion:

If they [anti-Machado writers] did not stir up public opinion in the United States to the point where popular pressure would force direct action by the Government, they at least damaged the reputation of the regime to the point that no great concern would be raised if the United States stood by while Machado's enemies overthrew him. It can be stated with confidence that any sympathy which may have existed in this country for Machado and his government was smothered and negated by the propaganda campaign waged by his detractors.[53]

Although most reviewers expressed reservations about the book because of the carelessness of detail, few disputed Beals's central contentions about the twin evils of dictatorship and imperialism. Ernest Gruening in *Books* blamed Beals's errors on his haste to publish the book before Machado fell from power and out of the public limelight.[54] Samuel Guy Inman brought up a familiar criticism—Beals's penchant for "literary effects" at the loss of "logical presentation" and "historical accuracy."[55] Leland Jenks, author of the widely acclaimed *Our Cuban Colony*, was more enthusiastic about Beals's interpretations. He observed that *The Crime of Cuba* was "based, as the reviewer can testify, upon accurate use of the best sources."[56]

Beals received a mixture of congratulations and admonitions from Cuban readers of his book. Ramón Grau San Martín was president of Cuba at the time he wrote Beals to comment on the book. Grau, expressing an attitude typical of the reform movement then in power in Cuba, praised Beals as a friend of Cuba, who stood firmly against "those who seek to destroy all national ideals for ill-advised reasons of personal profit."[57] Another admirer of the book was Jorge Mañach, a leading member of the ABC.[58] In contrast, Beals received an anonymous, threatening letter in broken English when he returned to Cuba in December 1933:

We are friend of the U.S. and we love to be under the Enmienda [Amendment] Platt, that prevents us to kill each other, as it would happen if President Roosevelt rid himself of this Enmienda. . . . Please, GO TO HELL and deliver us from your presence, and sail very soon; if you DON'T act so we are afraid we will have to shoot-gun you.[59]

Damning criticism came in a private letter from Ernest Gruening. The review by Gruening in *Books* was much more favorable than his letter, which tersely rebuked Beals for his treatment of Guggenheim. Gruening insisted that "Guggenheim's assignment was to get along with Machado. He might have resigned after he found that he couldn't stop the killings . . . . But after all, resigning is very frequently merely running away." Gruening contradicted Beals's assertion that Guggenheim used the ambassadorship to protect his own financial interests. In reply to Beals' indictment of Guggenheim, he argued that "you have not the facts to bolster up the conclusion—at least they do not appear in your book." Gruening implied that Beals should have confronted Guggenheim personally with the charges contained in the articles and the book. Beals's marginal notes on the letter indicate his complete disagreement with the points raised by Gruening.[60]

### The Crime Continued

Machado's departure did not bring stability to Cuba. The various left-wing factions seemed to coalesce briefly behind

Ramón Grau San Martín, who served as president for four tumultuous months in late 1933. The ultimate arbiters in Cuban politics, however, were the U.S. State Department and Sergeant Fulgencio Batista of the Cuban army. Ambassador Welles described Grau's comprehensive economic and social reforms as unrealistic and irresponsible, and thereby discredited the new administration in the eyes of the State Department. The calculating and ambitious Batista, who had pushed the officer corps out of the way on his climb to the top of the army, lost little time in engineering the overthrow of Grau. American diplomats hailed Batista as the military strongman with the aptitude for stabilizing Cuba; Batista, the power behind the scene, looked to Washington for recognition of his new puppet government, which came on January 22, 1934, only a week after Grau resigned.

Beals thought Guggenheim's replacement Sumner Welles was not only as guilty as Guggenheim for this involvement in Cuban politics but was also one of the instigators of the fall of Grau's administration. Writing just before Grau's resignation, Beals accused Welles of attempting "to create a government subservient to Washington . . . [and] to forge a reactionary bloc to confound the present Cuban government and crush all the Cuban aspirations." Beals felt that the overthrow of Machado resulted from a genuine social revolution led by leftists, but that Grau was only a figurehead president, dependent on Batista for military support. According to Beals, Welles's connivance in Cuban politics tended only to make a bad situation worse. He was pleased by Welles's departure from Havana on December 22, 1933.[61]

For the next year, Beals was busy on matters outside Cuba; but he kept a careful watch on the Cuban cauldron. About a month after he left Cuba in January 1934, Ruby Hart Phillips, wife of *The New York Times* correspondent, wrote to Beals of the growing authority of Batista behind the puppet presidency of Carlos Mendieta. Cuba was beset by strikes, leftist agitation and threats of military revolt. Mendieta gave the impression of weakness under such pressure that Phillips speculated about the likelihood of another U.S. intervention to try to end the unrest.[62]

The seemingly endless debate in the U.S. on how best to save Cuba continued with Beals's scathing review of *Problems of the New Cuba*, a book of academic essays on recent trends in the island nation. Beals lambasted the book as timid, inept and useless. His most severe criticism went to Ernest Gruening's chapter on public utilities, which contained, in Beals's words, "company propaganda without due analysis." Beals claimed that Gruening presented a white-wash of Machado's personal investments in public utilities and of the overall irresponsibility of the industry's excessively high rates that were charged for low-quality service. Other essays bogged down on currency reform, debt settlements and half-hearted land reform, with only scattered mention of what Beals thought were the main "problems": U.S. political and economic domination.[63]

Beals's next target was Batista's secret police organization. In an unusual role as a newspaper syndicate's correspondent, Beals gave a detailed account of the machinegun murders of two Cuban civilians at the hands of Cuba's secret police. A third man Pedro Cala was seriously wounded in the same incident but lived to identify the agents of the secret police.[64] Ambassador Jefferson Caffery, disturbed by Beals's article, complained of its inaccuracy in a letter to the editor of the North American Newspaper Alliance. He insisted that no one had been murdered in Cuba in the fashion described by Beals.[65] The author replied that the article was correct and that Caffery was "a very partisan apologist for the Batista-Mendieta regime."[66]

Ruby Phillips sent Beals more ammunition to use against Caffery. In a letter on May 2, 1935, she related that her husband was pressured by the ambassador to cease publication of any articles that might picture the current Cuban government in a bad light. Phillips bluntly rejected Caffery's dictum. He accused the ambassador of placing the defense of the Roosevelt's Cuban policy ahead of the issues of brutality and corruption under the Batista-Mendieta regime.[67] Beals included charges of attempted censorship against Caffery in a letter published in *The Nation,* but did not mention his sources, probably to protect the Phillipses, who remained in Havana.[68]

Beals received aid in his battle against Caffery from The International Committee for Political Prisoners, a liberal group that protested the internment of political activists by repressive governments. The committee released a statement that accused Caffery of "helping to maintain 'a reign of terror' under the Mendieta government." The committee labeled Caffery "a close friend of Batista who viewed his job in Cuba as that of a 'colonial administrator.'" Beals signed this release along with Arthur Garfield Hays, Oswald Garrison Villard, Lewis Gannett and Bruce Bliven.[69]

Beals continued his criticism of the Batista-Caffery duo with the publication of two articles in July and August of 1935. He identified Batista as Cuba's "new Machado," who came to power with the help of Welles and Caffery. As a reward for his aid in destabilizing Cuban politics and inadvertently opening the way for Batista, Welles was promoted from the embassy in Cuba to the desk of under-secretary for Latin American affairs in Washington. Caffery carried on by bringing Batista to the fore of the military authority in Cuban politics. Eventually, the ambitious ex-sergeant, who had taken over the army by revolution, took over the government with astute political infighting and substantial boosts from Caffery. In response to Caffery's comment that he was only an observer in this process, Beals exclaimed that the ambassador was "as much an observer as was Baer in his last fight with Carnera."[70]

Beals talked with Batista on at least two occasions and was impressed by his "energy, audacity and ability." He found Batista's main weakness to be his ignorance of social and economic matters, a result of his inability to bring himself out of the narrow-minded militarism that affected many Latin American soldiers who had pushed their way into the uncertain world of politics in the 1930s. Beals saw Batista's domination as an outgrowth "of the tragic weakness of the Cuban people who are worse off than their forbears under Spanish rule" and as "a symbol of the hypocrisy of Roosevelt's New Deal in Latin America."[71]

During the summer of 1935, Beals cooperated with poet-playwright Clifford Odets and fellow leftist Conrad Komorowski in the publication of an avidly anti-Batista pamphlet "Rifle Rule in Cuba."[72] Ruby Phillips wrote Beals about the misfortunes of the "Odets Commission," a group of well-intentioned, anti-imperialist intellectuals that failed to gain entry into Cuba because, according to Phillips, it trumpeted its blatant hostility towards the Batista government so loudly, that the dictator had little choice but to block their unwanted visit.[73] Odets described the detention of his group by the Cuban government with considerably less amusement than Phillips. Beals was not a part of this venture, but later contributed another stinging denunciation of Caffery and Batista to the committee's pamphlet. Judging from Beals's letters, Komorowski did most of the editorial work for this publication, which seemed to have little impact either on the general public or on leftist intellectuals.[74]

Beals's interpretation of the Batista-Welles-Caffery period was much closer to the findings of recent historical research than his writing on Machado and Guggenheim. Although they disagreed on the extent to which this policy was justifiable, the two major works on this period found U.S. diplomats in collusion with Batista and other political factions.[75] Beals was more accurate in his assessment of events after Machado's overthrow because of the dimunition of his emotional ties to the central characters on the Cuban stage. His personal hatred of Machado probably clouded his judgments on Guggenheim, but his dislike of Batista, Welles and Caffery was based on journalistic observation.

The publication of *The Crime of Cuba* and related articles, with all of the bitter controversy that surrounded them, did not hurt Beals's image as a crusader of the antidictatorial, anti-imperialist Left; but they did cost him his personal friendships. His relations with Ernest Gruening and Hubert Herring were never the same again. This episode must have hurt Beals. From his point of view, he acted to avenge the murder of one friend

Julio Antonio Mella; and in so doing, he alienated two others—Gruening and Herring. His omission of any of these matters in his autobiography and his willingness to comment on them only indirectly in interviews testify to the depth of his feelings about these people and these times.

The complexities of Cuba were enough of a problem for the outside observer, but the presence of emotionally wrenching memories made objective journalism an even more difficult enterprise. Mella's murder predisposed Beals to an extreme anti-Machado position, which was reinforced by Cubans Fernando Ortiz and Octavio Siegle. Beals's attacks on Machado and Guggenheim in *The Crime of Cuba* would have caused even more controversy if the dictator had not fallen from power two weeks before the book appeared. For all of its prejudgmental flaws, however, Beals's writing on Cuba gave the U.S. public the opportunity to read a forceful indictment of a tropical dictatorship and a scathing denunciation of the complicity of U.S. diplomatic and business interests with that authoritarian regime.

# • 8 •

## Into the Establishment

A fiercely independent leftist, Beals became a well-known expert on Latin American affairs in the 1930s and thus, moved as close to the center of the publishing business as his combative, free-spirited nature would allow. His earlier work brought him public notice for short periods of time, but as the Mexican revolution, Sandinista raids and Machadista atrocities lost the spotlight, the demand for Beals's writing suffered cyclical declines. By the mid-1930s, however, the cumulative effect of a dozen books and over one-hundred periodical articles made him an author of considerable importance. Radio news commentator Lowell Thomas asked him in 1934 "to send me a line now and then and I'll be delighted to tell the folks where you are and what you are up to."[1] In the same year, the University of Missouri School of Journalism selected *The Crime of Cuba* as one of the forty most important books of 1932–1933.[2] Four years later, the *Time*'s review of his book *The Coming Struggle for Latin America* described Beals as "the best informed . . . living writer on Latin America."[3]

Beals's acceptance by important people and institutions brought him into the journalistic establishment, but Lippincott and other publishers knew only too well that his name on a book cover did not guarantee its financial success. Beals's name in the 1930s was something less than a "household word," but it was widely and readily recognized among journalists, academicians, literary figures and politicians, particularly those interested in Latin America. For several years, Beals was able to bask in this type of acclaim, although he did not enjoy the financial rewards that one might expect for such a prominent writer.

Beals's leftist convictions seemed to moderate in the mid-1930s. In this way, he was no different than other leftists in the U.S. Most intellectuals, however, were preoccupied with the New Deal. Since Beals seldom wrote on U.S. politics, his ideas do not fit easily into the general pattern of leftist thought in these years.[4] There was a close correlation, however, between the achievements of President Roosevelt's domestic policies and his Good Neighbor Policy in Latin America (with the exception of U.S. machinations in Cuba). Beals seldom criticized either of these liberal programs, and at least temporarily, saw a bright future for the Western Hemisphere, both north and south of the Rio Grande.

## A New Life

While Beals's journalistic reputation was rising, his personal life underwent abrupt changes. His separation from Betty Daniels Beals ended in an April 1934 divorce, which was followed five months later by his marriage to Blanca Rosa Leyva y Arguedas, an attractive young Peruvian he met on his trip to her country earlier in the year. These rather sudden decisions took many of his friends by surprise. Soon after she heard of the divorce, Frances Toor complained of Beals's "silence" and insisted that he write her more often.[5] Even though the marriage took place in Mexico City, his private papers contain no notes or letters of congratulation, which suggests that he did not inform his friends in Mexico City or the United States. Personal letters dated soon after the ceremony from Earle James and Bailey Diffie gave no indication that either of the writers, both friends of Beals, knew of the marriage.[6] This marriage was his third and it is not unreasonable to assume that memories of his past unhappiness caused him to avoid the awkwardness of confronting old friends with a new bride.[7]

In the weeks preceeding the marriage, Beals's spontaneous life-style and his winning ways with women met a formidable challenge in Leyva's ever-present chaperon, her sister Seyna. This Latin custom was common among families of aristocratic heritage, but even the *simpático* Beals had difficulty dealing with it. A letter from his mother reflected some of his unhappiness with the situation:

It seemed as tho[ugh] one could not be so natural and intimate with another virtual stranger present, no matter how lovely they [sic] may be. You seemed a bit sad and disheartened in your letter of May 23. I hope you have no regrets over the recent legal action [divorce from Bettie] and that you will be a bit slow in again encumbering yourself.[8]

In spite of his mother's advice, Beals continued with his plans for marriage. An unexpected complication arose when Leyva and her sister arrived in their Mexico City hotel in August 1934 accompanied by the hapless Beals who was arrested by Mexico City police. They apparently assumed that he had entered the room of his *novia* and her chaperon without their permission. U.S. Ambassador Josephus Daniels acted quickly to secure Beals's release.[9] The manager of the hotel apologized for the hasty and unwarranted action, but the damage was done.[10] The incident brought press attention; unfounded rumors that Beals was involved in some dispute with the Mexican authorities similar to the 1930 affair flew in Mexico City and New York.[11] Finally in September, the couple was married in a quiet ceremony in Mexico City.

## Peru

In Peru, Beals not only met his third wife; he also studied her country and its problems. From December 1933 to April 1934, he observed Peruvian politics and culture in Lima, several provincial cities and some remote mountain areas. He was particularly sensitive to the currents of left-wing populism that seemed to run beneath the artificially calm surface imposed by the military dictatorship. Only seven months before Beals's arrival, a fanatical of APRA (Popular Revolutionary Alliance of America) member had assassinated President Luis Sánchez Cerro. Sánchez Cerro's violent death was the climax of a bitter struggle between his supporters—an unusual coalition of the urban poor, the military and some members of the Peruvian upper class—and APRA, a rival party headed by the intellectual Víctor Raúl Haya de la Torre, who appealed to university students as well as to the Peruvian lower class, especially the urban laborers.[12] Although the death of Sánchez Cerro doomed his political party, the clash between these two populist movements caused disorder in Peruvian politics. The military took control of the government and managed to restore order through authoritarian tactics, which included the arrest or expulsion of many Apristas in late 1934.[13]

The political instability of the early 1930s was caused, at least in part, by the emergence of Peru's urban masses onto the national political scene. From Spanish colonial times, an elite of landowners, who collaborated with or controlled the political leaders in Lima, Peru. From 1915 to 1930, Peruvian cities experienced rapid growth as a result of heightened overseas demand for Peruvian exports and increased foreign investment in the nation's economy. By contrast, the rural areas were isolated from this prosperity and continued to have a low standard of living. Urban growth attracted thousands of these peasants so that by 1931, approximately 40 percent of the residents of Lima were migrants from rural areas. Many of their newly found jobs disappeared, however, in the economic collapse of the early 1930s.[14] By 1934, Peru's urban lower class suffered from the dislocation produced by recent migration and the unemployment caused by economic depression. Although it was not in power, under such conditions, Haya's APRA, found much fertile ground for expansion in the cities; it also looked to the countryside for additional support from the peasantry.[15]

Beals was also concerned about conditions outside Lima, where the majority of Peruvians lived in centuries-old political, economic and cultural patterns that remained relatively un-changed. It was the relationship between leftist intellectuals and the common people of rural Peru that interested him most.

Beals's arrival in Lima marked the beginning of his intensive study of Peru. He relied on the advice of *The New York Times* editor Lester Markel concerning topics that might interest the press in the United States.[16] His main source of advice on Peru, however, was Ben Ossa of the Latin American Press Syndicate, who furnished a lengthy reading list of Peruvian authors.[17] Because of his international reputation, Beals was able to inter-view highly placed APRA officials, including Víctor Raúl Haya de la Torre. On April 21, 1934, *Acción Aprista*, the party news-paper, described Beals as "an indefatigable student of American reality, an anti-imperialist from a typically imperialist nation."[18]

While the leftists were not in power in Peru, they exerted considerable influence. Beals gave much attention in his writing to these leftists, whom he believed to be the harbingers of a fundamental social revolution against the long-entrenched coastal aristocracy. Beals was relatively certain that APRA and its sympathizers would eventually dominate Peru by means of such a revolution.[19]

In Peru as in Mexico, Beals found art to be a significant aspect of the revolutionary culture. Perhaps the most outstand-ing artist was José Sabogal who illustrated Beals's book *Fire on the Andes*. Beals observed that although Sabogal did not evince the emotionalism of Rivera or Orozco, his work, nevertheless, was revolutionary in content. Sabogal borrowed from native art to the extent that "more than anyone else in politics, literature or music . . . [he] has discovered Peru in all its historical, geo-graphical and ethnic variations."[20]

In general, Beals found Peru's best writers to be social com-mentators and social theorists, not novelists as in Mexico. Out-standing in this group was the recently deceased Marxist intel-lectual José Carlos Mariátegui. Beals accepted his analysis of Peru's agrarian problem, which reflected Mariátegui's basic as-sumption that the peasants must be freed from exploitation by the *gamonales* (Peru's landowning aristocracy) if Peru was to make meaningful social progress.[21] Beals also quoted Mariátegui on the old problem of regionalism, which continued to divide Peru. Simply to champion decentralization was insufficient, for "as Mariátegui has stated, 'Federalism does not appear in our history as popular revindication, but rather a revindication of gamonalismo and its clientele.' "[22]

The central figure in Peru's revolutionary culture was Haya de la Torre. Beals first met Haya in 1923 in Mexico City, where the young Peruvian associated with a cosmopolitan group of leftists. Beals observed the deterioration of Haya's relationship with Julio Mella, the ill-fated Cuban exile, whose ardent communism turned the two radicals into enemies.[23] Haya maintained a course independent of international communism. Beals found him to have a populist outlook designed to appeal to the masses of Peru, with slight regard for Marxist-Leninist dogma.[24]

Haya's interest in the Indian and *mestizo* peasantry was reflected in his writing and speeches. He advocated a variety of economic, educational and cultural approaches for the improvement of rural Peru, including the promotion of agricultural development and the establishment of rural schools. Haya's Aprista party used Indian names as party symbols in their political pronouncements. His plans for rural cooperatives were based on his conception of the communal organization of the Inca empire.[25]

Although his sympathies were clearly with Haya and his party, Beals was critical of the diverse nature of APRA. Although APRA drew its membership from disparate sources, including workers, peasants, intellectuals and Peru's small middle class, Beals found the party to be mainly a middle class movement. Its "program is comprehensive, too comprehensive. It is opportunistic, bureaucratic, hybrid. It is based on petty bourgeois reforms with slight collectivist tendencies."[26]

A young Aprista Luis Alberto Sánchez challenged Beals's critique of the party in a friendly, but disputatious, letter. Sánchez professed great respect for Beals's writing on Peru; he, however, disputed Beals's "middle class" categorization of APRA and claimed that its members were mostly workers or *campesinos*. Nonetheless, his general reaction to *Fire on the Andes* was positive; and he urged Beals to find a publisher for a Spanish translation.[27]

Beals befriended a young Peruvian novelist Ciro Alegría, whose experience testified to the dangers of involvement in the Aprista movement in the early 1930s. When Beals first met Alegría, he was a twenty-seven year old political radical and journalist. He had recently completed his first novel *La serpiente de oro*, a portrayal of the struggle for existence by the Indians in the Marañón Valley of eastern Peru. Alegría was a native of that region; but af fifteen, he had left his home for secondary and college education at Trujillo, a small city in northern Peru. While in college, he took part in the ill-fated 1931 Aprista rebellion against the fraudulent election of Luis Sánchez Cerro. For the next two years, he spent most of his time in jail. Released under the general amnesty proclaimed by the moderate Peruvian government in late 1933, Alegría went into exile in Santiago, Chile, rather than face the risk of incarceration under a new wave of anti-APRA repression.[28]

While in exile in Santiago, Alegría secured Beals's help in an attempt to find an English translator for *La serpiente de oro*. Alegría wrote to Beals that his novel was well received in Spanish South America. Beals agreed it was a superior work of fiction, that sympathetically presented the plight of the Indian. Beals was able to convince his agent Max Leiber to try to find a translator and a publisher. The entire project fell apart in 1937, when Alegría found the translation by Alice Roberts Koch far below his expectations.[29] The 1941 translation of his novel *El mundo es ancho y ajeno* by Harriet de Onís was published as *Broad and Alien is the World* by Farrar and Rinehart. It led to international recognition of Alegría's skill as a novelist. Two years later, Farrar and Rinehart published Onís's translation of his first novel, *The Golden Serpent*. Although few direct results came from Beals's support, his assessment of Alegría's talent was confirmed by the Peruvian's later success.[30]

Sabogal, Alegría, Mariátegui and Haya de la Torre all expressed, in their various media, a sense of spiritual wholeness within the mixed cultural heritage of Peru. Beals, sensitive to the importance of ritual, symbol and myth among the common folk of Peru, insisted that these Peruvian savants were leading their people to a cohesive national culture based on the melding of Quechua and Spanish traditions. Their "visions of rebirth" anticipated a new period in Peruvian history: "Only in politics and economics does Peru remain colonial and backwards. Soon it will, it must heed the message of its creative minds. That day Peru will at last be born into the world of valid independent nations."[31]

Since Beals was usually sensitive to criticism, the negative comments of Philip Ainsworth Means on *Fire on the Andes* in the *Saturday Review of Literature* elicited an equally caustic rebuttal from the author. Means accused Beals of reporting that distorted the Peruvian past and present for the sake of radical ideology. Means asserted that since "Russia is rapidly paling to a pretty pink, he [Beals] goes to Peru in quest of the tumult and chaos his soul loves."[32] Beals's letter to the editor of the *Saturday Review* placed Means in the category of a "rancid" reactionary:

By his defense of Lima's pleasantly decadent Creole society and all its moss-back feudal creeds and exploitation of the people of the Sierra who comprise 70 percent of the country's population, Means merely reveals himself to be a rancid Bourbon, a kisser of the toes of aristocracy, a sacred institution chest-pounder.[33]

## Back to Mexico

Beals left Peru for Mexico in April, 1934 to deal with the problem of his divorce from Betty and to make arrangements for his September wedding to Blanca. His correspondence from mid-1934 to early 1935 suggests that he had little contact with his old friends in Mexico City. Frances Toor wrote him that Diego Rivera was "painting watercolors furiously," and that he and Bertram Wolfe had recently completed their pictorial and prose collaboration *Portrait of Mexico*. She went on to write that Moisés Sáenz, who had accepted the position of Mexican minister to Peru, did so in spite of bad health and that Frank Tannenbaum was touring Mexico "in his usual bloated condition over the great success of his recent books." Toor urged him to rejoin this social and cultural whirl; but the old comraderie of the 1920s never revived, at least as far as Beals was concerned.[34]

The years 1934–1935 were crucial for the Mexican revolution, and Beals's personal preoccupations did not inhibit his journalistic instincts. The disruption of the revolution that he described in the early 1930s was corrected, to some extent, by interim President Abelardo Rodríguez (1931–1934), a wealthy, ostensibly conservative businessman from Sonora, who was surprisingly open to leftist reforms. A young, relatively unknown politician and ex-army officer Lázaro Cárdenas was elected in 1934 to succeed Rodríguez. He had the support of Plutarco Elías Calles, who still held much power, although he remained in the background. Cárdenas, who proved to be a clever and effective leader in his own right, managed to take control of the presidency and the P.N.R. from Calles by 1935. Cárdenas then used his power to institute a number of large-scale reforms designed to benefit the rural and urban masses. While Cárdenas was not the radical that many foreign observers thought him to be (he encouraged private capital for industrialization), he allowed several leftist movements and programs to flourish under his presidency—enough to make Mexico in the middle and late 1930s an exciting environment for liberal and leftist writers.

Beals enjoyed a friendly relationship with Ambassador Josephus Daniels, one of the key figures in U.S.-Mexican relations in the 1930s. Beals met Daniels in December 1934, and exchanged pleasantries with him several times over the next two weeks.[35] The two had in common their experiences in journalism and shared similar populist and liberal opinions on most issues. Daniels knew very little of Mexico, however; and many veteran observers, especially those who remembered that the North Carolinian had been Secretary of the Navy in 1914 when U.S. Marines occupied Veracruz, considered his selection by Roosevelt for the ambassadorship to be a mistake.

Daniels overcame the handicap of this background with his open, friendly personality and his easy-going style of diplomacy, which charmed Mexican officials and the usually skeptical Beals.[36]

It was Daniels's misfortune to become embroiled in Mexico's highly disruptive church-state controversy. The end of the Cristero revolt in 1929 was only a temporary cessation of the crisis. In 1932, faithful Catholics mounted a large celebration on the four-hundredth anniversary of the appearance of the Virgin of Guadalupe; at the same time, Narciso Bassols, an avowed Marxist and Rodríguez's minister of education, launched a campaign against religious education in Catholic schools. These issues were only background noise for the explosion which occurred during the fall of 1934: the government's enforcement of socialist education for private as well as public schools. The adoption of this new policy was indicative of the widespread interest in Marxist ideas during the depression years among Mexican intellectuals. [37]

Daniels innocently stumbled into the controversy by his use of a quote from Calles's famous (for conservatives, infamous) Guadalajara speech, in which the then power-behind-the-presidency stated, "We must now enter and take possession of the mind of childhood, the mind of youth." Daniels gave this quotation in his speech before Hubert Herring's annual seminar on Latin American affairs (with Beals present) and placed it in the broad context of Mexico's ongoing program of social reform through education. He intended his remarks as an endorsement of universal education, a typical populist position, but Catholic enemies of Mexico's socialist pedagogy saw them as an endorsement of anticlericalism. Within a few weeks, Catholic newspapers and periodicals on both sides of the border issued ringing denunciations of Daniels's unfortunate quotation and his unintentional approval of socialist education. U.S. Catholics soon called for Daniels's resignation and threatened to make his work in Mexico an issue in the 1936 presidential election. [38]

Favorably impressed by Daniels's work in Mexico, Beals came to the ambassador's defense. At a meeting of the prestigious Foreign Policy Association in Boston on February 16, 1935, he termed Daniels's speech "a simple straight-forward talk, sympathetic to the Mexican people, which emphasized his faith in democracy and education." [39]

Both Daniels and Beals knew that socialist education posed a complex problem in U.S.-Mexican relations. Beals was an adamant opponent of any effort by the United States to use intimidation to eradicate the radical approach in education, but he also recognized that this policy was not well suited for Mexico. As an indication of his balanced approach to these issues, Beals wrote a severe critique of the government's plan to institute socialist education in public and private primary and secondary schools:

Socialist education has been made obligatory in the schools. What for? To make misfits for a capitalist society? Who will teach the new doctrines? There are not half a dozen real Marxian scholars in all Mexico, and several of these have been persecuted. Socialists, Communists, labor leaders are to be found in the Islas Marías prison—sent there without trial. The instruction proposed 'will fight to form the solidarity necessary for the progressive socialization of the means of economic production.' Yet in practice the government has rapidly been receding from such socialization. In agriculture it has attempted to change from a policy of collectivism to that of the inalienable family patrimony.

Beals called the founders of socialist education "millionaire socialists, knight-errant Marxian capitalists."[40]

In his 1937 book, *America South*, Beals wrote an account of Cárdenas's removal of Calles that pictured the young president-elect as an astute politician dedicated to social and economic change. Beals seemed more confident about Mexico's leftist reforms in general than he had been about socialist education in 1935:

Mexico, more than any other Latin American country, is attempting to found a nation based on economic freedom for workers and peasants through semicommunal landholding, co-operative enterprise and gradual collectivization, banking for the poeple instead of for speculators, a great new experiment in education, democracy and collectivization.[41]

Beals's praise of the Cárdenas administration in Mexico and optimistic assessment of APRA in Peru was reminiscent of his writing on the Obregón and Calles governments in Mexico in the early and middle 1920s. In the 1930s, however, the historical circumstances were different. Cárdenas, the left-wing populist, held power in Mexico at the same time that Franklin Roosevelt's New Deal inundated Washington. Beals, at least temporarily, was a member of the liberal-leftist establishment in the United States. He and his third wife, Blanca, purchased a cottage on the Connecticut coast and prepared to enjoy what they believed would be the calm, secure life-style of a prominent and successful journalist.

1 Tina Modotti made this portrait of
Beals in 1926 in Mexico City.
CBC Photographs.

2 Beals (front row, center) had a moustache in 1924 when he served briefly as an English teacher at the Colonia del Vallejo public school in a poor neighborhood in northern Mexico City. He is pictured here with his fellow teachers. CBC Photographs.

3 Beals took this photograph of Plutarco Elías Calles in late 1923 when the soon-to-be president was leading government forces against a rebellion. Author's collection.

4 Diego Rivera with an unidentified woman. Rivera and Beals were close friends from the 1920s until the Trotsky hearings of 1937. Author's collection.

5 Frances Toor in Mexico about 1928. She and Beals corresponded periodically until her death in 1956. Author's collection.

6 Part of the group that accompanied Beals on his expedition into Nicaragua in early 1928 to interview Sandino. Author's collection.

7 Beals (on the right) in Sandino's camp with unidentified Sandinista. Author's collection.

8 United States Marines march through a Nicaraguan city (probably Managua) in 1928. Author's collection.

9 Beals's confident smile in the 1940 back-cover picture for *Pan America* gave no hint of his personal turmoil in the aftermath of the Trotsky hearings. Author's collection.

10 Beals in his schoolhouse-study in 1973. Author's collection.

## • 9 •

# On Revolution and Imperialism

Settled in his Connecticut cottage, Beals began to write articles and books that gave a broad assessment of Latin America and the role of the United States in hemispheric affairs. His absence from Latin America deprived him of the firsthand experiences that were the basis for much of his earlier work; it apparently encouraged him to try for an Olympian view of the tumultuous events he had covered over the previous fifteen years. Such an exercise is fraught with perils, especially for a journalist accustomed to activity "in the field" for so many years, but Beals had always exhibited a penchant for sweeping generalizations grounded in his own unique ideological outlook.

Although his residence in Connecticut placed him between Boston and New York, two centers of leftist ferment in the 1930s, Beals was intellectually more distant from his radical and liberal colleagues in the United States than he had been in the 1920s. He directed most of his attention to Latin America and its problems in the depression decade. When he placed these problems in an international context, Beals cast the United States and the administration of Franklin D. Roosevelt (admired by many leftists) in the role of villain. The internal economic and social disarray of the Latin American nations bore some resemblance to the domestic scene in the United States; but for historical and cultural reasons, Beals saw very little similarity. Beals did share with American leftists the search for the ideal society as an alternative to the apparently failed system of capitalism. Unlike most of his colleagues north of the Rio Grande who engaged in national introspection, Beals sought most of his answers in Latin America; therefore, his focus on the issues of backwardness, revolution, and economic nationalism did not readily fit into the pattern of leftist thought in the United States.

## Conservatism and Backwardness

The publication of *America South* in 1937 was the result of his "departure on a new tangent."[1] In this book, Beals attempted to define the fundamental problems that blocked the way to economic progress in Latin America. While his conclusions on these troublesome issues were not unique among those who studied Latin American affairs in the 1930s, it is necessary to explore these ideas briefly in order to understand his positions on revolution and imperialism.

Beals defined conservatism as opposition to reforms intended to benefit the masses. He isolated three main groups as its sources of strength: the army, the estate owners and the churchmen. He could find nothing good to say about the first group. Soon after leading the struggle for independence in their respective countries, according to Beals, the military "as a ruling-class institution . . . destroyed all liberty in a crass fight for the spoils" of victory. The tradition of selfish, irresponsible leadership continued into the twentieth century as sergeants, captains and generals continued to build systems of personal loyalties based on corruption and intimidation. Not only was the military a cause for political disorder and graft, it also retained, and even amplified, the tendency toward cruelty in the treatment of the defeated, which was so prominent in the post-conquest society of Spanish America. The military often mobilized itself to protect its privileged position but showed little interest in "national loyalty or civic responsibility." Possessing weapons and a semblance of organization, the military was often an effective force against reform.[2]

Beals's second element in conservatism, the landowners, often traced their land titles back to the colonial period. For obvious reasons, they had no tolerance for any liberal scheme that included the redistribution of property from the wealthy to the poor. Even in the twentieth century, wealth in Latin America was measured in land, not in stocks or bonds. Beals sided with the poor peasants, who were the landowners' chief source of labor and who received little compensation in return for their work. Beals used geographer Mark Jefferson's evaluation of the Argentine *estancia* where: "methods are universally backward. Large land-holding is more an aristocratic obsession than an economic obligation. Great areas and cheap labor obviate the necessity of using up-to-date methods and machinery."[3]

His third bastion of conservatism, the Catholic church, was less culpable in Beals's assessment of Latin American backwardness than the military or the landowners. He excused some of the actions of the church against the Indian population at the time of the conquest because cruelty was endemic to those times; he did not excuse the political and psychological impact of the church in the twentieth century. The imperious moral authority of the church in the past "rested upon the monarch and upon the priest. One had a right to trick these two, just as a child temporarily slips from under patriarchal authority." The pervasive influence of the historical church helped to open the way for trickery, bribery and other venalities that weakened the fiber of civic life in the twentieth century. Those weaknesses plus the ceaseless conflict between church and state in national politics made the role of religious institutions injurious to the political health of contemporary Latin America.

As a governing institution, the church provided assistance in stern colonial control, and it has since provided unity, and at times, promoted popular acceptance of governmental authority; but as in our own large cities, politics are hideously corrupt. The church has failed to imbue public officials with a spirit of honesty, and nowhere is thieving from the public treasury more an accepted and tolerated practice. In addition, the church has invariably supported the most reactionary regimes, those opposed to progress and popular liberty.[4]

To Beals, the power of the unholy trinity of churchman, landlord and general had to be destroyed if the common people of Latin America were to have a chance to better themselves. Even though the church had operated schools for four centuries, there was massive illiteracy. Even though the landlords prospered and the military instituted authoritarian regimes, there was economic backwardness and political chaos. Beals believed that reformist governments must defeat, or at least subdue, the three conservative elements by replacing church schools with universal public education, by breaking up the big estates and by placing the generals in a tight harness to remove them from politics. Beals praised movements such as Haya de la Torre's APRA and the left wing of Mexico's P.N.R. because they advocated these types of reform.[5]

Although Beals detested the social roots of Latin American conservatism, he recognized that they were not the only causes of illiteracy, poverty and instability. He addressed the larger issue of "Why Latin American Backwardness" in a provocative, but delicately written, chapter in *America South*. Almost all of his sources for this chapter were Latin Americans, whom he shielded in anonymity, probably because their statements were highly critical of their homelands.

The opinions that Beals assembled were far from uniform. They did include, however, most of what might be called the various "schools of thought" on the causes of Latin American backwardness. A Mexican *mestizo* blamed the Spanish who imposed their values on the conquered Indians, values that included "'the idea that honest labor is degrading, fanaticism, the subjection of women [and] political absolutism.'" A Peruvian *criollo* disagreed with this assessment. He pointed to Costa Rica and Argentina as paragons of progress because they were without a doleful, unresponsive Indian population. Another Peruvian saw the worst of both the European and Indian worlds in the combination of Spanish and Indian fatalism. He called it "'a dreadful composite weighting down all initiative'" in many fields, including economic endeavor. A Guatemalan poet and a Chilean doctor faulted not the region's social and cultural background but a more mundane factor—the presence of endemic diseases in most Latin American countries, which drained the general population of its vitality and took a high toll in terms of individual life.[6]

Beals attempted to synthesize these explanations and came up with three general categories of causation: European history, American geography and international economics. The Spanish and Portuguese carried the vestiges of European feudalism to America and imposed them on the native population that survived the conquest. This imperial imposition included a rigid class system and nearly impenetrable class barriers, that virtually eliminated any chance of peaceful social or economic mobility. The land held many resources in abundance; but the rugged mountain ranges blocked trade, and thereby, held back commercial and industrial expansion. Although the climate in tropical areas was usually pleasant, it presented a constant threat of diseases, like malaria and yellow fever. It was, however, the last category—international economics—on which Beals placed his greatest emphasis. He argued that the United States and other industrialized nations siphoned off valuable resources, kept the profits gained in the process and left Latin America with only a minimal return.[7]

### On the Ambiguities of Revolution: Mexico and Peru

One possible solution to the problems of backwardness and conservative domination was revolution. In his usage of this word, Beals did not mean a simple coup d'etat in which one political faction replaced another; but rather he meant a widespread rising of the disadvantaged against the powerful, with subsequent social and economic reforms to benefit the former. Beals usually praised such movements, often citing the Mexican revolution as an example. His praise was not unqualified, however, because he saw potentially harmful trends in the revolutionary changes directed against the traditional ways of life among the peasant population. Beals, the prorevolutionary journalist, thus, became a critic of certain revolutionary policies—a position that few of his readers (whether conservative, moderate, or leftist) seemed to understand.

Much of Beals's writing has relevance to the more recent work of social scientists and historians, particularly on the topic of social change in the Third World. Of course, Beals did not use the terminology developed by social scientists after 1950; but he did address some of the same issues that are prominent in the literature of modernization. One example concerns the problems associated with rapid modernization in peasant societies, a subject of much disagreement among social scientists. Many investigators of this subject assumed that modernization through the diffusion of new technology, market economies, and literacy to the local level axiomatically meant a better way of life for the people.[8] In the 1960s and 1970s, however, many scholars began to question the validity of this and related assumptions.[9] The purpose of this section is to explore Beals's precursive studies on this issue in Mexico in the late 1920s and Peru in the 1930s.

Beals lived in Mexico for most of the decade from 1923 to 1933 and was fascinated by the interplay of politics and social change that centered around the revolutionary government. Presidents Obregón and Calles sought to achieve political stability and economic prosperity through the enactment of reforms, that included the distribution of land to peasants, promotion of new agricultural techniques, and expansion of public education. Virtually all of these programs were conceived and carried out from Mexico City, under the watchful supervision of Obregón, Calles and other members of the political elite.[10]

Beals studied the interaction of revolutionary change which originated in Mexico City and the native conservatism that emanated from the countryside. In his view, a modern agricultural economy with crop rotation, tractors, specialized products and a market system would overwhelm the quiet, isolated, largely subsistence village economies, that were intimately attached to the past.[11] He also concluded that this heritage was, to an extent, superior to the rapidly expanding, modern industrial civilization. Beals distinguished between the sympathetic cultural elite, who appreciated the Indian past, and the aggressive political elite, who pushed for rapid change. The social and economic reforms fostered by Obregón and Calles threatened Indian-mestizo culture. Beals struggled in his writing to reconcile the conflict between the way of life of the rural masses and the revolutionary goals of the political leaders.

Beals saw a need for certain types of economic and social improvements in rural Mexico. He believed that the *campesino* must be taught to apply new scientific methods to village agriculture. The division of large estates into peasant-operated collective farms was essential; but in the last analysis, agrarian reform had to result in the "modernization of the *ejido* system." By "modernization," Beals meant that literate and informed peasant farmers would use irrigation, dry farming, crop rotation and other advanced techniques.[12] The food requirements of a rapidly expanding urban population demanded that such changes be implemented quickly.[13] At the end of the decade, however, Beals found that the peasants still lacked the basics in knowledge as well as land, and government support to achieve these purposes.[14]

Although he felt changes were imperative, Beals sensed a danger in the expansion of the governments' social and economic programs into rural Mexico. Beals cited the disruptive changes promoted by the government of Porfirio Díaz (1876–1910), which he felt acted to weaken the premodern unity of the nonmaterialist, often mystical, native values.[15] In the revolution, he saw a direct conflict between the largely Indian culture of the masses and the European and North American culture of the nation's elite groups. He further suggested that this conflict was the latest stage in the centuries-old contest between the natives and the foreign conquerors, which spanned the time from the Spanish conquest to the twentieth century.[16] In the village of Tepotzlán, the natives faced the challenge of an

. . . alien culture that ruffles their inner harmony and sullenly struggles for its place. And the freshly seared scars of revolution! These brusque, uprooting factors are well concealed, but bit by bit the stoic, stark independence of the inhabitants is becoming darkly overcast. In the brimming cup of their normal unaffected lives whirls the backwash of the tempest of the changing world. They feel subtly, uncomprehendingly, the tug of these conflicting influences; yet they little realize how much they are puppets of grotesque, gigantic forces. . . .[17]

This cultural conflict had its economic and political counterparts. The cities of Mexico grew during the 1920s, largely because of the expansion of industry and commerce. Labor unions prospered in these years under favorable government policies, while the peasants endured a low standard of living and experienced many problems in building cohesive organizations. In 1927, Beals pointed to a split between workers and peasants in that

. . . the tendency is for Mexican labor to become identified with the process of industrialization, seeking its gains in rapid economic expansion and at the expense of continued low rural standards, hence, the inevitable continuation of the cleavage between labor and peasant movements. Industry and the native industrial worker thus became identified with the western European invasion that began four centuries ago under Cortez. The peasant movement may ultimately be caught up in the same current; at present, it is more closely linked with the great indigenous race surge of the Mexican people.[18]

In Beals's estimation, the Catholic church was too reactionary and too weak to help resolve this conflict. According to Beals, the church retained an "invisible empire" among the peasants, even though it failed to comprehend the significance of the rise of Indianism in Mexico.[19] Although Beals underestimated the peasants' willingness to stand and fight against the government's anticlerical campaign (1926–1929), his assessment of the internal weaknesses of the church was more realistic.[20] The hierarchy was too distant from the rural parishes to understand their problems.[21]

In Beals's opinion, the government was the institution most capable of ameliorating the conflict between tradition and modernity for the rural masses. While he occasionally praised the actions of political leaders in areas such as rural education, he found much to criticize elsewhere.[22] The revolutionary government's use of coercion against the Yaqui Indians to subdue their defiant nature was a prime example of the government's willingness to destroy or weaken local native culture for the sake of national unity.[23] Beals was particularly wary of "the antique instrument of social control, the Army, which if it can be used for modernization can also be used for oppression." Such devices offered the possibility of a unified national culture, but at a very high cost to the Indian and mestizo peasants.[24]

For Beals, Mexican anthropologist Manuel Gamio offered the preferred solution. From studies of the people of the valley of Teotihuacán, Gamio concluded that the local village community and its internal coherence should be preserved within the modernization process. The survival of these traditional values might soften the often painful transition from isolated rural communities to integrated parts of a commercial and industrial society. Beals was deeply impressed by Gamio's implementation of these ideas in Teotihuacán and saw promise in his early work in Oaxaca. Much to Beals's disgust, Gamio lost his position in the ministry of education in 1925 as a result of a personality clash; it was a serious loss to the revolution.[25]

In spite of many adverse factors, Beals maintained a persistant optimism. He saw Indian-mestizo culture as active, not passive, in its confrontation with the elite-promoted modernization. Beals saw signs of a cultural synthesis, rather than a continued conflict, based on the merger of European and North American industrialism with native traditions. He, however, did not specify the content of the cultural synthesis nor the means by which it might appear. In a representative statement, he insisted that "the native culture is wrapping its arms about the newest industrialism, modifying its methods of work. . . ." His metaphor indicated the presence of a vague belief, rather than a complete certainty.[26] It is worth noting, however, that he held to this belief, in spite of his understanding of the many conflicts involved in revolutionary change in the countryside.

In Peru, the position of the revolutionary political elite was more tenuous than its counterpart in Mexico because of the

dominant position of a firmly entrenched conservative aristocracy. APRA was the center of revolutionary politics in Peru
during the 1930s, and its antipathy toward the aristocracy was
well known.[27] Beals saw less obvious, but potentially important, sources of discord between the APRA leadership and the
peasants. While this type of conflict was not as clearly deline-
ated as it had been in his writing on the political elite and the
masses in Mexico, it was prominent in his analysis of the Peruvian situation.

Beals felt that the Indian and mestizo masses of Peru, like
those of Mexico, had preserved many valuable traditions, in
spite of the inroads made by modern commercial civilization.
He was impressed by their seemingly unplanned, almost in-
stinctual, ability to live in harmony with nature. The center of
Indian life was the *ayullu* or community social organization,
which furnished guidance and direction for family life, economic pursuits and local government. In spite of generations of
exploitation and disruption by the European aristocracy, *ayullu*
survived as a source of stability in rural Peru. To Beals, this was
an accomplishment of great importance.[28]

Beals found that APRA and the Indian-mestizo peoples
had a common enemy in the coastal aristocracy, that continued
to control the government, in spite of the Aprista's attempts to
gain power. In Mexico, the revolution swept aside the landowning upper class; but in Peru, the *gamonales* remained in
command. To Beals, they were an arrogant, racist and parasitic
lot, who blocked APRA and held the Indians and mestizos in
servile conditions. Under the legal system enforced by this aristocracy, the Indians and mestizos were not full citizens. In
Beals's words,

. . . they are rounded up like animals for the army and for labor on
the large haciendas; they frequently lose their lands; they are mer-
cilessly exploited. Their relation to the Peruvian state is one of
onerous obligation, not of rights.[29]

In Peru as in Mexico, Beals denounced such cruel exploitation of the masses; but he also recognized that well-meaning
reforms, if enacted abruptly, might bring harmful effects.[30] Al-

though there is some disagreement among historians concerning Haya's sincerity in calling for land reform, there is little doubt that he stood for commercial and technical innovations in the rural areas.[31] Nonetheless, the natives' emotional attachment to the soil and to the old style of cultivation made innovation difficult. Beals cited the study of rural Peru made by Mexican educator Moisés Sáenz, who concluded that the land was of such importance to the peasant that he could not see it as "property" subject to sale or transfer. Land was a part of the natural environment that, in the indigenous mind, could not be changed in any way without causing great harm. With such an outlook, the natives perceived land reform and agricultural modernization as threats to a deeply ingrained, almost religious, devotion to the old ways.[32] Beals, however, did not see this conflict in the simplistic terms of primitive versus modern. To him, Indian Peru was "a world of weird beauty and potential greatness." Beals warned, "Let not the makers and masters of machines sneer or feel too superior."[33]

Beals found potential for additional problems in APRA's relationship with the peasantry. He felt that the party attempted to include too many social groups—both urban and rural. Haya sought to make the rural masses one of the three sources of support for APRA, along with intellectuals and the middle class.[34] By implication, this approach had limited utility for the Peruvian peasants. Beals also decried Haya's personal domination of the party, in which he appeared to be "perhaps too much of a God" to the lower echelon membership. In spite of these tendencies, Beals admitted that "Aprismo must be recognized as the most vital popular force in Peru."[35]

As with Mexico, Beals saw a possible reconciliation of materialistic European civilization with the traditional, mystical aspects of Indian civilization. He posited the appearance of:

. . . an organic evolution out of native culture and traditions, the fusing of elements long warring in open contradiction. It involves, especially among socialization compounded of modern needs, colonial institutions and ancient indigenous experiences—all embraced in theories of democracy, Marxian economics and Fascist force—

mass rhythms obeying vital life forces, new social concepts, and determinate aesthetic and ideological forms.[36]

## A Leftist Critique of Revolution

Although Beals gained wide recognition as an anti-imperialist and as a defender of revolutionary causes, these ideological positions did not necessarily lead him to accept the policies of the leftist government of Mexico or of Peru's Aprista party. Some of his critics accused him of blindly sympathizing with revolutionaries—an accusation substantially negated by a close reading of his publications and private correspondence. Beals found fault with the authoritarian political leaders of Mexico and the personalistic Aprista movement in Peru. He expressed grave doubts about the effects of revolutionary change on the Indian and mestizo peoples.

Beals's immersion in the questions surrounding the conflict of tradition and change in Latin America tended to pull him away from many of the central issues in U.S. intellectual circles of the 1930s. On at least one major issue, i.e. the attempt to reconcile the well-being of the individual with that of the community, however, Beals had concerns very close to those of his North American colleagues. John Dewey, V. F. Calverton, and Max Eastman addressed this problem from several perspectives within the boundaries of leftist ideology. In general, they agreed that the doctrine of rugged individualism died with the onset of the depression. On the question of which form of community (or collectivism) was appropriate for the United States, there was much uncertainty and no concensus.[37] By contrast, Beals in his observations of Indian-mestizo traditions in Mexico and Peru, generally accepted the positions of Mexicans Gamio and Sáenz and Peruvians Haya de la Torre and Mariategui. They believed the village community provided a deeply rooted indigenous institution, around which the rural population could coalesce and, in the process, revive their ancient pre-Marxist forms of collectivism.[38]

One of Beals's most penetrating insights involved the ambiguities of elite-led revolutionary change among the rural masses of Mexico and Peru. While he did not systematically analyze these contradictions in a manner that would satisfy the modern social scientist, he did recognize and emphasize them in his writing. Combining findings of contemporaries like Gamio and Sáenz with his own personal experiences in the backlands, Beals developed an understanding of the peasant point of view. He was not unique among North Americans in this accomplishment; certainly Robert Redfield, Frank Tannenbaum and Stuart Chase appreciated this perspective in Mexico.[39] Beals, however, added some provocative generalizations that pointed out the potentially disruptive effects of the reforms initiated by revolutionary political elites.

Beals's struggle with the conflict between revolutionary change and peasant traditionalism was a genuine dilemma for him. If pressed to place him on one of the many sides of the issue, one could conclude that he held an essentially prorevolutionary position, tempered by a strong dose of populism. Beals hoped for a gradual, benevolent transition from tradition to modernity of the type advocated by Gamio. He never completely lost faith in the long-term benefits of social revolution. Beals felt, however, that a benevolent transition might lessen the pain of social and economic change for the peasantry, as well as do as little damage as possible to their lives.

## Good Will, Good Neighbors and Imperialism

If social revolution was not a panacea for Latin America, neither were the "good will" efforts of diplomats, businessmen, academicians and assorted other do-gooders from the United States. Franklin D. Roosevelt's Good Neighbor Policy of the 1930s marked the high point of this trend in U.S.-Latin American relations; its origins, however, dated from the 1920s, when college professors, journalists and business promotors criss-crossed the hemisphere, spreading their messages of international amity. Beals called these promotions of hemispheric harmony "the Good-Will Racket" and showed no mercy in his commentary on its many manifestations.

"The Good-Will Racket" was facilitated by the rapid improvement in cable communications between the U.S. and Latin America during and immediately following World War I.[40] As underwater lines reached the major cities of the hemisphere, the flow of information between U.S. and Latin American business, political and cultural centers increased. U.S. entrepreneurs moved into Latin American communications rapidly, in direct competition with previously established European firms. Beals observed that the competitive fires of U.S. capitalism were stoked by individuals like James S. Carson, who charged that European companies used " 'publicity in the guise of news throughout a large area in an effort to discredit American merchants.' " By the early 1920s, the U.S. overcame this disadvantage and began to use its own publicity weapons against its weaker European rivals.[41]

Foremost among the "Good-Will Racketeers" were promoters like Carson, who moved from the Associated Press in the 1930s to an executive position with the American and Foreign Power Company, an international corporation with investments from Cuba to Chile. John L. Merrill, president of All-American Cables, joined Carson and other U.S. business executives to form the Pan-American Society, a public relations organization intended to extoll, throughout Latin America, the benefits of U.S. business expansion in the hemisphere. The Pan-American Society and its sister institution the Council (or Committee) on Inter-American Relations brought forth many pleasantly vapid generalities like Carson's 1933 comments: "I am a believer in Pan-Americanism and I fully appreciate the value of intangibles such as good-will and mutual understanding. They are the very life-blood of the Pan-American movement. . . ."[42]

Another "Good-Will Racketeer" was economist Walter Kemmerer, a proselytizer for the gold standard in Latin America, especially in Colombia. He was a much sought-after economic consultant among Latin American governments; but his advice, according to Beals, was of more benefit for U.S. private businesses than the struggling Latin American economics.

Kemmerer was a gold-standard die-hard. He wanted currencies in Latin America kept high and stable as the rock of Gibraltar, regardless of the international trade situation, the price level, or anything else. This was, and is, our official desire. It enables Latin American countries to buy American goods and pay American debts. It helps prevent them from developing an independent economy. In short, Mr. Kemmerer's sound financial ideas were tied to the apron string of New York financial interests. He was the wizard of South American finance. He helped dictators put their abused revenue sources in order, so they could squeeze out more funds to pay more debts, buy more munitions, and pay their police forces to keep the people down and avoid revolution. He was hailed by Wall Street and . . . by the dictators of a continent and a half as a wonder-worker.[43]

The Carnegie Endowment for International Peace, which Beals regarded as a hotbed of inter-American activity, ran the gamut from serious proimperialist propaganda to frivolous inter-American tours. He saw the endowment's publication of Dana Munro's *The Five Republics of Central America* as the promulgation of an "interventionist" tract. Samuel Flagg Bemis was the endowment's traveling representative in Latin America for a time, Beals felt his appointment was consistent with the endowment's goals, since Beals, even then, was "a rather official-minded authority on Latin American diplomacy." Beals belittled the endowment-sponsored 17,000 mile tour by five female activists from the United States as a "fluffy-sleeved mockery" of international relations. Their purpose was to encourage the Latin American nations to sign peace and arbitration treaties, which according to Beals, would have no effect on hemispheric relations, whether signed or unsigned.[44]

Beals did praise some workers for hemispheric harmony. He described Eyler Simpson as "a fine and conscientious student," whose "remarkable study of the Mexican agrarian question *The Ejido: Mexico's Way Out*" appeared in 1937.[45] Beals also praised Protestant missionary Samuel Guy Inman as an outspoken opponent of U.S. intervention and as a defender of national independence in the region. Inman "has not hesitated to denounce unsavory business and diplomatic practices in the most courageous terms." The Committee on Cooperation in Latin America, the coalition of missionary organizations that Inman represented, gained in financial resources and cultural influence as a result of his work.[46] Another ebullient missionary was Hubert Herring, head of the Committee on Cultural Relations with Latin America, a branch of the Congregational churches. Although Beals often made fun of Herring's undying enthusiasm in the promotion of cultural seminars, he also recognized their importance in influencing many leaders in the U.S. to take a more understanding view of Mexico in the troubled 1920s.[47] Beals noted with pleasure the growth of studies of imperialism, pioneered by Parker Moon and Harry Elmer Barnes and exemplified by Bailey Diffie's *Puerto Rico* and by Leland Jenks's *Our Cuban Colony*, both of which roundly condemned U.S. domination of these two Caribbean islands.[48]

Beals believed the rapid improvement in telegraphic communication lines that tied Latin America to the U.S. made possible "the Good-Will Racket." It was his conviction that the content of newspapers, magazines, pamphlets and books fed by this system was heavily biased in favor of the U.S. business community and its goals for expansion in Latin America. This revolution in communications was exploited to the fullest by U.S. private enterprise; there was little or no consideration for allowing Latin American views to flow north in a fair exchange. With the exception of a few anti-imperialists, Beals found that the good-will types offered only excuses for U.S. political and economic domination of the hemisphere.

Roosevelt's Good Neighbor Policy was similar to the "Good-Will Racket." On the surface, it seemed to offer much of great benefit to Latin America; but in Beals's analysis, it failed to live up to its high sounding goals and actually disguised the continued expansion of U.S. power. Beals was favorably impressed by the Good Neighbor Policy in its early stages. He was an open admirer of Ambassador Josephus Daniels in Mexico. Like many enemies of U.S. imperialism, Beals was pleased to hear of the apparent disavowel of military intervention in Latin America by the Roosevelt government.[49] In Beals's later writing, however, he exposed these evidences of good neighborliness as only fragments of the story. In part, they were a public relations smokescreen that momentarily hid the administration's real intentions.

Like many policies of President Franklin D. Roosevelt's administration, the Good Neighbor Policy contained several apparent inconsistencies. Although Secretary of State Cordell Hull, the chief proponent of economic recovery through international free trade, was the main target of Beals's attacks, he seemed to have very little influence in administration decisions in 1933 and 1934. In 1935, Roosevelt, however, changed his approach and assumed a more active role in world affairs. He unleashed Hull on the Latin American nations to mold the hemisphere's economic patterns to fit the overall aims of the United States.

The brunt of Beals's criticism was directed against Hull's promotion of free trade between Latin America and the United States. Hull, aided by Under-Secretary Sumner Welles, busily engaged in the negotiation of a series of treaties, which were intended to lower tariff barriers in the hemisphere, and thereby, promote international trade. Beals argued that this policy was not only unrealistic, but also harmful, for the Latin American nations. Following the ideas of Parker Moon and other students of imperialism, Beals insisted that the juxtaposition of an industrialized power, like the United States, with many relatively poor agricultural and mining nations, such as existed in Latin America, meant that free trade would inevitably drain the weaker nations of raw products and currency for the benefit of the larger nation.[50]

Beals cited the dramatic speech given by J. M. Puig Casauranc, Mexico's representative at the seventh inter-American conference at Montevideo in 1933, to rebut the Hull-Welles line that free trade meant prosperity. Puig pointed out that nations exporting raw products were unable to earn enough to pay for their imported manufactured goods. This unfavorable balance of trade usually forced the poorer nations to pay for their imports through the loss of national metallic reserves or through a further extension of credit. Either remedy weakened an already unstable economy and made recovery from the worldwide depression even less likely. Puig Casauranc joined other anti-imperialists in his conclusion that trade between industrial and nonindustrial nations inevitably weakened the latter. His comments at the Montevideo conference gained considerable support among the Latin American delegates. Nonetheless, Secretary of State Hull was able to prevent the passage of any meaningful resolution that would have reduced the burden of the debtor nations.[51]

Beals summarized Puig Casauranc's case in blunt language:

What Hull and Welles are really demanding of the Latin American countries—which are the ones that above all others should resort to proper tariffs, and protective currency and quota and exchange rates—is that for the sake of American merchants they do not try to achieve economic freedom, do not try to build up new industries, but remain dutiful little colonies under Uncle Sam's tutelage.[52]

In reaching for an historical perspective on the free trade issue, Beals placed the Latin American nations in the roles of small, but growing, Davids under the aegis of a British Goliath in the nineteenth century and a U.S. Goliath in more recent decades:

The political institutions of Latin American were born of free trade, as a result of the effort to break through Spanish imperial monopoly. The result was independence and open markets for British, later American, goods.
But gradually Latin America began to emerge from its colonial status. New laboring and industrial and middle classes are emerging. They demand, now, as Earl K. James puts it, 'a positive State, to control and create new wealth, not merely to act as a policeman.'
Latin America had to begin a new struggle, not for political independence, but for economic independence. Economic nationalism was born, just as it was much earlier in the United States. Mr. Hull may not know it, but the free market in Latin America began actually to disappear in 1900—over a third of a century ago. It has been disappearing almost entirely since the World War. It has now disappeared.
And yet Mr. Hull wishes us now to follow the pattern of ideas he gathered sometime before the Spanish-American War. He is imposing them on us now. He is thereby merely moving in a shadowy

world of unreality—except that strange shapes therein have hard corners on which our country needlessly barks its shins.[53]

For Beals, U.S. free trade and free trade propaganda had no place in Latin America. The "Good-Will Racket" and the Good Neighbor Policy seemed intended to wedge Latin America into the capitalist mold with its boom-bust cycles, unrealistic debt policies and unfair exchanges between industrial and nonindustrial nations—all omens of the unequal relationship under economic imperialism. Roosevelt, Hull and Welles abandoned the military interventions of the early twentieth century for the subtle, but even more debilitating, policies of economic exploitation.

### Economic Nationalism to the Rescue

In his inquiries into the meaning of the Good Neighbor Policy and the causes of backwardness in Latin America, Beals emphasized the international economic system. Although never a doctrinaire Marxist (but an admirer of Engels's *Socialism: Utopian and Scientific*), Beals found that the normal commercial relationships between Latin America and the industrial nations enervated the former to the benefit of the latter. More recent studies by social scientists use the word "dependency" to describe this unequal economic exchange. Beals did not deduce his assertions on the debilities of the Latin American economies from Marxist theory or from dependency theory; he used his own observations to reach (and, at times, to jump to) conclusions by means of inductive reasoning. That his conclusions resemble, in a general sense, the conclusions of some neo-Marxists and dependency theorists testifies more to the nature of the historical problems under study, than to the concepts employed to study the problems.

Many journalists were jolted into an appreciation of economics in the 1930s by the catastrophic worldwide depression. The 1920s were a period of expansion and optimism, but the 1930s proved to be a time of contraction and pessimism. Beals observed that easy credit in the international loan market for

Latin America, typical of the 1920s, ended because of the sharp decline of capital available in European and U.S. banks. As the industrialized economies collapsed, they curtailed their imports of raw products, a tendency which in turn strangled the export-oriented nations of Latin America. In this dismal context, Beals saw one relatively bright ray of hope—the rise of economic nationalism in nonindustrialized countries. Through this policy, the Latin American nations attempted to revitalize their economies by protective tariffs and government programs, which provided insulation from the vicissitudes of the international market.[54]

Beals insisted that planning was essential to economic nationalism. The Mexicans were leaders in this field. Their comprehensive Six Year Plan of 1934 provided for the diversification of agriculture and industry to reduce dependence on foreign economies. Other Latin American nations seemed likely to follow the Mexican example. Beals understood that economic planning was not simply an emergency, stopgap measure, but instead, constituted a reasonable method for dealing with the problems of economic underdevelopment. It, therefore, was likely to become a permanent fixture for many nations in the region.[55]

Beals agreed with most Latin American economic planners that industrialization should be their main objective. In spite of his doubts about the effects of commercial and industrial expansion in the countryside, Beals recognized that the security and well-being of the Latin American nations were closely tied to their ability to supply their own domestic markets with manufactured goods, and thereby, reduce or eliminate dependence on foreign industry. His old friend Frank Tannenbaum disagreed with this thesis. Tannenbaum reasoned that the absence of natural resources, technical expertise and capital in Latin America was simply too much to overcome. He believed that emphasis should be placed on small industry, with limited capital and technological requirements, rather than on the herculean challenge of copying the modern industrial establishments of the United States and western Europe. The traditional pottery, weaving and leather industries were examples of the type of enterprise that might benefit the area.[56] Beals accused Tannenbaum of passive acceptance of economic imperialism, which Beals felt was a ". . . comforting doctrine for the United States, for we should like to think of those countries as minor dependencies from which we could extract raw supplies and sell the finished products."[57]

A serious impediment to industrial growth was the onerous burden of foreign debt, that pressed down heavily on the Latin American economies. Beals insisted that the creditor nations, primarily the United States, should scale down these debts to bring amortization within the realm of possibility. Many of the debts were incurred in the "golden age" of relatively easy credit and were unrealistic extravagances at their inception. In the depression-ridden 1930s, the terms of these loans were even more unrealistic. Full repayment would drain Latin America of desperately needed investment capital.[58]

Beals's customary skepticism gave in to a vague optimism about the future of Latin America. At the center of his belief in industrialization was a belief in the serendipitous effects of technological change. He cited the discovery of petroleum as an energy source in industry and transportation and the consequent benefits for the Mexican economy. He forecast the exploitation of the great hydro-electric potential of the Andes and pointed out the changes in population patterns that airconditioning might bring to the tropical areas, like the Amazon Basin.[59] He offered only a few concrete rebuttals to Tannenbaum's pessimism; but perhaps his position was more an outgrowth of his absorption of the attitudes of aggressive economic nationalists in Latin America, than a cool appraisal of the realities of the situation.

To Beals, it was a question of *how,* not *if.* Because Latin American industrialization lagged behind the United States, western Europe and Russia, the latecomers had a chance to study alternatives. Beals favored uniquely designed programs to fit the needs of the Latin American nations and opposed efforts to copy the U.S. system, which was too wasteful, and the Russian system, which was too oppressive. Beals again cited Mexico's Six Year Plan for its exemplary innovations that set standards for the 1930s, a time of "effervesence, experiment and new development" in Latin American economics.[60]

The central villainy of international capitalism, for Beals, was its harmful effects on the economic history of nations like Peru. He cited the sad story of the Peruvian national debt to show the disasterous results of the interlocking of a fragile economy with the large machinery of international economics. Peru's political elite readily borrowed from British bankers in the middle 1800s, without any regard for the limited ability of the economy to yield the tax revenues to retire these debts. National indebtedness (mostly in British-held bonds) increased in spurts in the last half of the nineteenth century. It was further complicated by the material losses incurred by Chile's victory in the War of the Pacific (1879–1883). In 1893, the Peruvian government made an agreement with W. R. Grace, a United States-based corporation, to consolidate this huge debt. In exchange, the corporation wanted extensive economic privileges in the utilization of the nation's resources and transportation system. British pre-eminence in Peru continued to decline during World War I. Peru's exports boomed and U.S. bankers scrambled to finance this expansion, and at the same time, push aside their British rivals. The mania for loans from U.S. sources continued under President Augusto Leguía in the 1920s. This unsound financial structure, based on foreign credit, collapsed in the 1930s, leaving the hapless nation with a huge debt, far beyond its capacity to repay.[61]

The most potent corrective for rapacious international capitalism was not simply nationalism, but nationalization—the outright expulsion of a foreign corporation and the takeover of its property by the national government. A dramatic example occurred in Mexico on March 18, 1938. President Lázaro Cárdenas ordered the seizure of all foreign petroleum holdings. This executive act ended what had been a major international controversy for several months. Beals wrote an article for *Current History* that went to press only a few days before Cárdenas's action. In the article, he persuasively argued for Mexican economic nationalism and noted that in the two previous decades the U.S. employed armed intervention, coercion, the Big Stick, diplomatic pressure [and] friendship, but whatever the methods . . . Mexican nationalism is all the more militant today; the efforts to eliminate foreign control of natural resources [is] more determined than ever before.[62]

Beals mentioned some of the laws recently enacted to regulate foreign businesses, especially the 1936 Expropriations Law, which laid much of the foundation for the nationalization of March 18.[63]

Beals railed against the efforts of the U.S. oil companies to block Mexican oil workers' demand for higher wages, a movement that precipiated the crisis. He gave a prescient summary of Mexico's rising nationalist sentiment. He saw it largely as an outgrowth of

. . . the veiled diplomatic warnings of Under-Secretary of State Sumner Welles by various diplomatic protests concerning tariffs and against her [Mexico's] awards of higher wages in the oil industry. Mexico has been greatly angered by the increasing anti-Mexican propaganda put out by American petroleum and mining companies, which she feels is likely to bring about our previous traditional policy of coercion and meddling.

Whatever the merit or lack of merit in attempting to protect certain American property rights in Mexico, our recent use of diplomatic pressure to try to prevent the Mexican workers from increasing their wages makes Mexico more than ever convinced of the righteousness of her nationalistic program. She feels that her measures to control corporate wealth and elevate living standards are very similar to our own New Deal and have even more justification because the so-called "economic royalists" are aliens.[64]

Mexico's nationalization of its oil resources was to Beals a logical extension of the anti-imperialist position. Foreign business operated in its own self-interest to maximize profits. The extraction of raw materials, which resulted in great profits at a relatively small cost in wages and taxes, seldom met the requirements of broadly based economic growth within the Latin American countries. Beals adamantly favored the promotion of economic development through the government's assertion of its authority—using nationalization, if necessary—against foreign businesses. Like most economic nationalists in Latin America, Beals saw government action, not private initiative, as the most practical means to guide national economic development.[65]

## Conclusion

Beals's presentation of Latin America's problems for the reading public in the United States was comparable, in some ways, to the work of such writers as Hubert Herring, Frank Tannenbaum, Robert Redfield, John T. Whitaker and Archibald MacLeish; but his conclusions were unique in at least two ways.[66] His questioning of the effects of revolutionary socio-economic change in rural areas revealed a willingness to challenge some of the implicit assumptions of the Latin American Left. His critique of the "Good-Will Racket" and the Good Neighbor Policy placed the handiwork of many U.S. liberals in a highly unflattering light. At the same time, it reiterated one of Beals's favorite themes: the continued presence of the seemingly incurable disease of imperialism in the Western Hemisphere. Beals joined MacLeish and a few other U.S. writers in explaining the rise of economic nationalism in Latin America. They gave readers in the U.S. the opportunity to understand the case against international capitalism—a point of view no doubt unpopular even in those depression-ridden times. None of these theses was propounded to win friends or to secure a niche in the intellectual or publishing establishments. Beals depended to a large extent on his income from the sale of his books, yet he seldom compromised his ideological convictions for the prospects of larger sales.

His influence on U.S. government policy makers is difficult to assess. Beals, the subject of considerable concern within the States Department in the 1920s, seemed to generate little controversy in the 1930s. Several State Department officials noted his travels in Latin American and read his publications, particularly *The Coming Struggle*.[67] There apparently were no reactions against his criticisms of Hull's free trade ideas, however, that could compare with the extreme hostility of Alexander Weddell and his associates in the Coolidge State Department in the 1920s.

In the late 1930s, when many leftists found positions in New Deal agencies, private corporations or organized labor, Beals retained his independent status as a freelance journalist. His ideology was consistent with this professional position. His books and articles were the products of a singular approach to journalism. Beals catered neither to Marxism, liberalism, nor capitalism, but rather drew from the wellsprings of an intuitive populism, and usually sided with the meek and the lowly against the haughty and the powerful.[68] This approach made Beals's writing unusual; and it left him isolated, even from his journalistic and academic colleagues of the Left.

Unlike most U.S. writers on Latin America, Beals was aware of the mystical element of the Indian world. This dimension was an important component in Beals's condemnation of the spread of the techno-industrial civilization of the United States and western Europe into Latin America. Like his contemporary Waldo Frank, Beals admired the essential unity of life in the native villages and their unspoiled, holistic perception of existence. The segmented, regimented, time-obsessed quality of a middle-class, industrial society seemed as repulsive to him as the rigid, dogmatic, authoritarian orientation of communism. Beals's populistic sympathies were reinforced by his fear that the harmony of native life might deteriorate before the onslaught of movies, Fords, and the market economy.[69]

# The Trotsky Affair

One of the most painful episodes in Carleton Beals's life began soon after Blanca and he arrived in Berkeley, California in early March 1937 to visit his family. The transcontinental trip by car was broken by previously arranged speaking engagements in Norman, Oklahoma; Galveston and Denton, Texas; and San Francisco, which earned Carleton $356.26.[1] Nowhere along the way did they encounter any hint of the trouble that lay ahead. A casual letter to his old friend Victor Calverton written on March 15 indicated that Beals and his wife intended to stay in Berkeley until early April.[2]

## The Call of the Left

The controversy that soon ensnared Beals centered around Leon Trotsky, the Communist leader driven into exile from Russia in 1929. Much of the non-Stalinist Left wanted to clear Trotsky of the alleged charges heaped upon him in absentia by the Moscow Trials of the mid-1930s. Beals's friend Benjamin Stolberg was active in the creation of the American Committee for the Defense of Leon Trotsky. He urged Beals on March 12 to join the organization to help disprove the charges from Moscow that Trotsky had betrayed the Russian Revolution.[3] One week later the Trotsky committee secretary George Novak, on the advice of Stolberg, asked Beals to serve on the commission of inquiry, a select group of prominent leftists who were "to hold formal hearings to take Trotsky's testimony and to examine the documentary evidence in his possession." The commission met in Mexico City, where Trotsky had at last found a haven after years of international wandering. Novak and Stolberg consulted with John Dewey, also a member of the commission, and this trio agreed that Beals's "training, [his] known integrity, and [his] obvious nonpartisanship" qualified him to be a member.[4]

Beals did not respond immediately; on March 25, Stolberg sent him a telegram which read:

Could not reach you long distance/Dewey very much wants you with him in Mexico/he also postponed lectures at new school for one month/committee can wire you immediately two hundred fifty dollars and another two hundred fifty if necessary to compensate loss of time/can you and Blanca drive to Mexicocity direct to be there at most two weeks/we leave April second by train/Chamberlain and Adamic joined Commission/all this confidential/wire collect immediately love Blanca=
    Ben.[5]

Beals submitted to these urgent requests and departed for Mexico City by car with his wife. On April 5, he and Blanca intercepted the commission at Laredo, Texas. There Beals exchanged greetings with Dewey for the first time since the formation of the commission. He and Blanca then continued their trip to Mexico City by car, while Dewey, Stolberg, and the other organizers enjoyed the camaraderie of the remainder of their trip by rail.[6]

Beals took his judicial responsibility quite seriously. In a letter to Victor Calverton written in Mexico City on April 8, Beals asked Calverton to postpone the publication in the *Modern Monthly* of his answers to a questionnaire that mentioned the "Moscow Trials" "in order not to prejudice me and the work of the commission" in the public eye. Beals was concerned that the commission of inquiry be above reproach and free of any implication of premature judgment.[7] Calverton readily complied with his request.[8]

Trotsky's arrival in Mexico was but the final stage of an eight-year odyssey, that had taken him from the Turkish island of Prinkipo to France and then to Norway. For Trotsky, Mexico promised a more receptive environment than the previous stops on his international pilgrimage.[9] His travels, his isolation, and the weight of the charges made against him in the Moscow Trials took their toll, leaving him exhausted and often depressed. In January 1937, he accepted Diego Rivera's invitation to take up residence in Mexico, an offer reinforced by President Cárdenas's extension of friendly greetings to the tired revolutionary. Trotsky and his wife Natalya received a warm reception from George Novak and Frida Kahlo, Rivera's wife, when they landed in Tampico on January 9, 1937. In Mexico, he might, at last, have the chance to assemble the evidence necessary to refute the Stalinist charges against him.[10]

The commission of inquiry came to Mexico City with the generally understood purpose of giving Trotsky a forum in which he could respond to the Moscow Trials. The commission's five members were all leftists of some repute in intellectual circles. Columbia University philosopher John Dewey served as chairman and was the best known member. Suzanne La Follette was an editor and art critic in her own right, although she shared some of the fame brought to her family name by her uncle Robert, the former Senator from Wisconsin. Otto Ruehle was a German historian and biographer of Karl Marx, who chose exile to escape the excesses of Hitler's Germany. Ben Stolberg, from the United States, was a specialist in labor organization and its history.[11]

Of his four fellow commissioners, Beals knew Stolberg and Dewey from earlier meetings. The latter visited Mexico in the mid-1920s and knew Beals slightly.[12] Beals was closer to Stolberg, whom he first met in New York in the early 1930s, where the two were members of the left-of-center literary scene.[13] Neither Stolberg nor Dewey had been in close contact with Beals in the months immediately preceeding the Trotsky hearing; there is no evidence to suggest that he met either La Folette or Ruehle before the quintet assembled in Mexico City.

Beals came to Mexico City with considerably different expectations than at least three of its other members. Dewey, Stolberg and La Follette were aware of the furor their plans for the Trotsky hearing had raised among leftists in the United States. Communists loyal to Stalinist Russia vehemently condemned the commission, while other leftists were repulsed by the Moscow Trials and saw Trotsky "as a tragic, maligned figure," who deserved an opportunity to defend himself.[14] Beals was not affiliated with any Socialist or Communist organization and had little or no involvement in the controversy, until Stolberg and Novak recruited him for the Mexico City hearings. Of the five, Beals had the least personal commitment to the pro-Trotsky movement, a fact that the other Commissioners soon discovered, much to their displeasure.

### The Hearing

An inconspicuous little house in Coyoacán, a quiet suburb where Beals lived in the early 1930s, became the location for a gathering of internationally known intellectuals, writers and activists who played a major role in the ever-widening divisions within world communism. Diego Rivera, the owner of the house, had opened it to Trotsky and his entourage as a temporary residence; the commissioners agreed to meet there to simplify security arrangements. The house, in a general state of disrepair as evinced by its crumbling walls, offered a humble setting for one of the twentieth century's most famous revolutionaries—Leon Trotsky, "the prophet" of the Russian Revolution of 1917. There was a depressing air about the house and about the entire event. Beals noticed the front of the house "with double entrance doors, guarded by the police who frisk all comers" and "the gloomy reception room with all the street windows bricked up." Beals remembered the remarks of one commissioner who confessed " 'I want to weep' . . . as we pass[ed] out on to the frowzy street, 'to think of him [Trotsky] being here.' "[15]

Before the opening of the commission of inquiry's twelfth session Beals resigned his seat, an act that resulted from intense discord between Beals and the other four members. The main source of disagreement was Beals's determination to ask Trotsky unfriendly and often embarrassing questions. Students of the Trotsky hearings have generally condemned Beals's interrogations as improper and harmful to the purposes of the commission. Trotsky's biographer Issac Deutscher accused Beals of "a pro-Stalinist bias"; Trotsky, himself, thought Beals was a Russian agent.[16] These accusations, however, did not take into account the entire story of Beals's work on the commission.

From the earliest information available to him about the hearing, the independent-minded Beals had formed an entirely different perspective on his responsibilities than did the other commissioners. Novak's March 19 letter to Beals stressed "integrity" and "nonpartisanship" as characteristics that guided the organizers in their selection of members.[17] In his description of the commision's role, John Dewey's statement at the opening session reinforced this impression. It was

solely an investigatory body, to take Mr. Trotsky's testimony on the accusations made against him in the confessions of the Moscow defendants; to accept such documents as he had to submit in his own defense; and to report to the full Commission on the basis of this evidence our decision whether or not Mr. Trotsky has a case warranting further investigation.[18]

Novak's use of the words "integrity" and "nonpartisanship" and Dewey's statements about "testimony," "documents" and "evidence" helped to create the impression that the commission intended to conduct an impartial investigation. Beals, who was the last person to join the commission, perhaps applied a more literal interpretation to these words than the other members. Because of the previous work on the hearing, the first four members understood its function as the provision of an opportunity for Trotsky to reply to the charges made in the Moscow Trials.

Beals's first pointed question concerned Trotsky's personal archives. He asked if all of Trotsky's archives were in Mexico City. When the reply was negative, Beals probed more deeply: "What was the basis of your selection of material which you thought would be of interest to this commission?"[19] Trotsky responded that he had "all the necessary documents" and that by these

documents I can prove, first, that the concrete premises of proofs and evidence [of the Stalinist indictments against him] are false, are frameups; and secondly, that politically they are impossible. There is a certain gradation of my proofs from the political to the philosophical.[20]

Beals's followup question was more unfriendly:

I believe that in the courts of the United States a defendant is considered innocent until found guilty. At least that is the theory. Whereas, the courts of Russia proceed a little differently. A defendant is considered guilty until he proves himself innocent. For the purpose of this line of questioning, I am considering you guilty, and therefore I would like to ask you what assurance the commission would have in examining your archives that you have not destroyed that which was unfavorable to yourself.[21]

Trotsky used his integrity as his chief defense against Beals's implications. He replied:

. . . my aim is not to convince the commission by the documents which I have allegedly destroyed, but by the documents which remain in my archives. I will prove to the commission that the man who wrote from year to year those thousands of letters, those hundreds of articles, and those dozens of books and had those friends and those enemies, that this man could not commit the crimes of the indictment. It is the most genuine evidence I have.[22]

Beals then posed another embarrassing question for Trotsky. By the 1917 Treaty of Brest-Litovsk, Lenin and Trotsky surrendered a portion of Russia to Germany, in order to stabilize the new and still uncertain Bolshevik government. Beals asked if this treaty might indicate that Trotsky was a German agent. Trotsky replied that this concession was made to Germany to protect the opportunity to implant socialism in Russia. Beals followed with the hypothetical question: if Trotsky had the opportunity, would he sacrifice more Russian territory to bring himself and his concept of socialism to power. Trotsky responded, somewhat tangentially, "that the only way possible to materialize the ideas of socialism is to win the masses and to educate the masses."[23]

These exchanges between Beals and Trotsky indicated that the two men had entirely different expectations for the hearings. Beals was coldly objective and asked unfriendly, accusatory questions. Trotsky apparently saw the hearings as a chance for personal vindication and usually answered in terms of his own ideology or, as with the question on his archives, in terms of his moral character.

Beals soon was aware that the other four commissioners shared Trotsky's view of the purpose of the hearings. The second session adjourned after the Beals-Trotsky exchange; the other commissioners apprised Beals of their distress with his hostile questions. Stolberg led the others in their approach to Beals. They agreed that most of his questions were "necessary," but implored him to "refer to matters of fact only"; they insisted that the "questions about Brest-Litovsk were entirely out of place." A few weeks after the hearings, Beals vituperatively described the attitude of the other four commissioners toward Trotsky as "an air of hushed adoration for the master."[24] By the time Beals wrote these words, he was trying to defend himself against the attacks of the pro-Trotsky forces. His dismay at the way in which the other commissioners seemed to cater to Trotsky, however, helps to explain some of his disruptive actions after the first session.

The third session began with more hostilities—this time between Beals and the commission's lawyer John Finerty, on the possibility of Trotsky's extradition from Mexico to Russia. Beals claimed that such extradition was impossible because no diplomatic relations existed between the two countries. Dewey's opening statement held that extradition was possible, and Finerty defended this position against Beals.[25]

Not far beneath Beals's cold exterior was the feeling that he was the outsider on the commission. There was an underlying feeling of alienation in Beals's reply to Finerty on the commission's extradition position: "I wish also to get on the record that I was here when this [preliminary] report was drawn up and was not consulted."[26] Later, Beals wrote that he was personally offended by what he perceived as the exclusionary tactics of the other commissioners. He placed most of the blame on Dewey, who released the preliminary report to the press and who

leaped to his feet to declare that I had arrived in Mexico City after the commission's statement had been prepared and that there had been no opportunity to show it to me. The truth was that I had been in Mexico, in touch with the commission, two days before the opening session, during which time the Dewey statement had been given to the press.[27]

Beals may have jumbled the facts about the weekend meeting and Dewey's statement, but there is no doubt that he was deeply hurt because he was not invited. The other commissioners' failure to communicate their plans to Beals before the sessions began may have been a slight oversight from their point of view. (There is no evidence on this point.) For Beals, it was an affront. After an exhausting journey of over 2,000 miles by car, he probably expected a warm reception in Mexico City, or at least, admission to the inner workings of the commission. He received neither.

At the fourth session, Dewey apologized to Beals:

As chairman of this preliminary commission of inquiry, I am, of course, responsible for the conduct of its internal affairs. I wish first to say that Mr. Beals—that he was in the city the day of the final draft of the opening address read by me at the first session. April 10th, is entirely correct. My remark this morning that he was not here to be consulted referred to the previous days in which the other members of the commission were conferring together about the material to be contained in the opening address. I am sure that if we had had the benefit of Mr. Beals's counsel, that address would have benefited.

Mr. Beals's statement this morning was the first knowledge I had that he had not seen the opening document. I do not say this to excuse myself, but because I accept fully the fact that it was the responsibility of the chairman to make sure that he had seen the document and approved or disapproved its contents. I mention the fact, then, simply formally to acknowledge that responsibility and formally to record my regret that it was not satisfactorily fulfilled.[28]

Beals responded to Dewey's apology by affirming his basic agreement with the other commissioners on most issues; he also announced, however, that he would continue to express "independent opinions" and "constructive suggestions." Trotsky's lawyer Albert Goldman restated Finerty's argument about the possibilities of extradition, to which Beals made no reply.[29]

Beals was relatively quiet for the next three sessions, but mention of the Spanish civil war led him to touch on another sensitive area. Beals asked Trotsky if the Spanish Communists should support the liberal government against the forces of Fascist Francisco Franco. Trotsky seemed to sidestep the question; but Stolberg, following Beals' lead, restated it in a way to urge a direct response: "We have a civil war in Spain. Surely a purely orthodox or puristic position does not answer the problem. With whom would you side at the present time in Spain?"[30]

Trotsky answered that Communists should support the government but not join it: "Every Trotskyite in Spain must be a good soldier, on the side of the Left. . . . While we defended Kerensky (in Russia in 1917) against Kornilov, we did not enter his government."[31]

Beals saw an inconsistency in Trotsky's position and attacked. He argued that the Communists' refusal to join the liberal government would insure victory for Franco and another victory for fascism. Trotsky clung to his theoretical distinction between fighting in support of a government and becoming a part of that government. He argued that the Spanish peasants had to be educated as to their true class interests, if communism was to succeed in Spain.[32]

That Stolberg joined Beals in questioning Trotsky on the Spanish civil war was an indication of some reconciliation—at least between Stolberg and Beals. Beals's pursuit of Trotsky's ideological refinements as applied to Spain was similar to their exchanges on the Brest-Litovsk Treaty and the theoretical implications of the sacrifice of national territory for the sake of socialism. Stolberg's claim that "a purely orthodox or puristic position does not answer the problem" suggested that Trotsky should abandon the rarefied atmosphere of theoretical heights, for the more pressing challenges of the real world. Trotsky, however, refused to give up his ideological strictures for the sake of the hardpressed Spanish Left.[33]

Beals's questions during the next two sessions were routine; but in the eleventh session, he pricked an extremely sensitive nerve: the Communists' promotion of worldwide revolution and its possible effects in Mexico around 1920. Trotsky testified that the promotion of revolution outside Russia was not considered by Soviet leadership until 1924. Beals disagreed. He claimed that Michael Borodin, the Russian agent who was stationed in Mexico in the early 1920s, told him of a "controversy" in 1920 in Russia concerning the promotion of revolution in places like Mexico. There followed a heated confrontation:

*Trotsky:* May I ask the source of this sensational communication. Is it published—no?
*Beals:* It is not published.
*Trotsky:* I can only give the advice to the commissioner to say to his informant that he is a liar.
*Beals:* Thank you, Mr. Trotsky. Mr. Borodin is the liar.
*Trotsky:* Yes, it is very possible.[34]

Dewey, with the support of the other commissioners, deemed Beals's question on Borodin and communism in Mexico "inappropriate" and quickly adjourned the eleventh session. Before the next session convened the following morning, Beals resigned.

### Resignation and Reaction

Dewey, Stolberg, La Follette, and Ruehle felt that the Borodin matter jeopardized Trotsky's haven in Mexico. The possibility of Trotsky's role in a plot to stimulate Communist revolution in Mexico would connect him—however indirectly—with the efforts to overthrow the political ancestor of the Cárdenas government. The twelfth session opened with Goldman reading Trotsky's denial of any involvement with Borodin and his accusations against Beals:

I immediately ask the commission to throw light on the source of Commissioner Beals's information. If he has received this information directly from Borodin, then where and when? If he received the information through a third person, through whom and when? I expect that through an investigation into these questions, which involve Mr. Beals's personal honor, a new amalgam will be discovered—a new amalgam will be created with the purpose of preventing me from unmasking the judicial crimes of Mexico.
If Mr. Beals is not consciously and directly involved in this new intrigue, and I will hope that he is not, he must hasten to present all the necessary explanations in order to permit the Commission to unmask the true source of the intrigue.[35]

Suddenly Beals, not Trotsky, was the subject of investigations. Beals had no lawyer to help in his defense nor any friends on the commission to stand with him. Perhaps in anticipation of this situation, Beals submitted his letter of resignation to the commission before Goldman read Trotsky's statement. Omitting any mention of the Borodin issue, he gave his reaction to the larger work of the commission:

Dear Dr. Dewey:
Kindly accept my irrevocable resignation from the commission. This step is for the best interests of Mr. Trotsky, the commission and myself.
The important purpose, among others, for which I became a member of the commission, namely: to give Mr. Trotsky the opportunity which every accused person should have, to present his full case to the world, has been fulfilled to the extent possible with the present arrangements. Unfortunately, I do not consider the proceedings of the commission a truly serious investigation of the charges. For this and other reasons, my further participation in the work of the commission, now that the sessions have been completed, would not prove fruitful.

Sincerely yours,
Carleton Beals.[36]

From a narrow perspective, the dispute hinged on two factors: Beals's memory of his conversation with Borodin seventeen years earlier and the threat of Trotsky's extradition. The first factor can be documented, in part, through an article Beals wrote for the April 1926 issue of *Southwest Review*. The Russian agent Gruzenberg (a name used by Borodin) went to Mexico, in what Beals described as a mission "to stir up anti-American feeling and so provoke internal disturbances, with the hope of precipitating [United States] intervention." The question, therefore, that he posed to Trotsky about Borodin was not simply an imaginative concoction of 1937. It was a perception, although perhaps subjective and overblown, that Beals wrote into a 1926 article, only six years after the alleged mission took place and eleven years before the Trotsky hearings.[37] If Beals was wrong, it was apparently an honest misunderstanding.

On the question of Trotsky's extradition from Mexico to Russia, Beals was technically correct; but in a practical sense, Goldman's fears of expulsion were far from groundless.[38] Trotsky's wayward existence from 1929 to 1937 offered proof that for him, the world was an unfriendly place. From Trotsky's point of view, Beals's mention of his potentially incriminating role in this episode in Mexican history was a real threat to his continued residence in Mexico.

Nonetheless, to claim that Beals's question was prompted by Stalinist plotters, as Trotsky did, was a gross exaggeration. Beals's approaches on Brest-Litovsk and the Spanish Civil War were similar to his questions on the Borodin matter. In all three cases, he posed an example for Trotsky to evaluate. Trotsky's responses were couched in theoretical terms and resembled a philosopher's attempts to explain some distant historical event in terms of an overarching conceptual framework. In response to Trotsky's discussion of the Spanish civil war, Stolberg joined Beals in asking for a more specific answer. This support and the apparent harmony of the previous six sessions created a calm that Beals tested with his questions on Borodin. Trotsky's abrupt and angry reply was unlike his earlier rejoinders and probably surprised Beals, who did not think that extradition was a genuine threat. Although Beals's pursuit of a "tough" line of questioning did not begin with the Borodin case, Trotsky's emotional response to this question spurred the other commissioners to take action against Beals. The charge of Beals's participation in an anti-Trotsky plot, while credible to the Trotskyites, failed to take into account the internal consistency in Beals's pattern of interrogation and his typical bullheadedness in holding firm to his own opinions.

Trotsky and the four remaining commissioners rebuked the departed Beals for his questions and his resignation. Trotsky believed that the questions on Borodin were irrelevant to the hearings and issued a statement to the press claiming that Beals was involved in a Stalinist conspiracy.[39] Although the final report of the commission also mentioned such a plot, it emphasized the strained personal relations between Beals and the other commissioners. The report described Beals as "almost completely aloof" and claimed that he "evaded our request for his new address" in Mexico City.[40]

The records of the hearing seem to contradict the following statement by the commission:

At no time before his resignation did Mr. Beals intimate to the others [sic] members of the subcommission that he was dissatisfied with the attitude of any one of us or with the conduct of the hearings. As a member of the subcommission he was under obligation to express frankly and honestly in private conference any dissatisfaction he may have felt, instead of springing it in public without warning. In this obligation he failed.[41]

Beals's sharp interrogation of Trotsky about his archives, the Brest-Litovsk Treaty, and on the Spanish civil war as well as his exchanges with Goldman on extradition must have alerted his fellow commissioners to his fundamental disagreements with their "attitude" and with their "conduct" of the inquiry.

The commission's report and Beals's article "Fewer Outsiders" suggested another cause for the enmity between Beals and the Trotsky sympathizers: personal misunderstanding. Although both sides wrote in anger, both accounts coincided on this point. Beals's dash from Berkeley to Mexico City was a considerable sacrifice; yet, after his arrival on April 8, the other commissioners left him out of the preliminary work and did not brief him on their preparations. To them, Beals seemed "aloof" and unconcerned about Trotsky's desire to explain his case against Moscow's version of justice. No one on the commission, not even Stolberg, Beals's friend, made an effort before the hearing to apprise him of its real purpose. This serious error explains, to some extent, Beals's separate course, which eventually led to the Borodin confrontation.[42]

Commentators in the U.S. news media found more fault with the commission than with Beals. *The New York Times* correspondent in Mexico City Frank Kluckhon gave much space in two dispatches to the Beals-Trotsky dispute. Although he refrained from an open statement of opinion, his choice of quotations favored Beals.[43] *The Nation* was more direct in its judgment that Beals "was generally considered to be free of bias" and that his resignation implied the other commissioners favored Trotsky.[44] *Time*'s evaluation of the commission was that it "had proved nothing at all."[45]

U.S. Ambassador Josephus Daniels followed the Trotsky hearing and wrote of Beals's resignation in fairly objective terms to Secretary of State Cordell Hull. By contrast, the State Department file on Trotsky included a clipping from a leftist periodical *The Chronicle of World Affairs* that speculated on Beals's connection with Stalin's forces.

What the Stalinites are using in their energetic attempt to discredit the "trial" is the fact that toward its close, Carleton Beals withdrew from the committee, crying to the world that he could not consider the proceedings a serious investigation.[46]

Beals's unfriendly questions and sudden resignation threw him into the intense controversy that raged around Trotsky, the Communist party and the non-Communist Left in the United States. Beals had not been involved in this dispute before the hearing and came to regret his involvement in subsequent months. The U.S. Communist party rejected the commission's final report, but many Communists and Socialists outside the party were satisfied with its findings.[47] The hapless Beals, caught in a factional squabble with no friends in any of the major camps, caught nearly all the blows of battle himself. His papers include no praise filled correspondence from Stalinists or other leftists, but his critics were far from reticent.[48]

Beals and his wife returned to Connecticut to find that the Trotsky affair still hovered over them. The irate Ernest Sutherland Bates—an educator, author of religious books, and a Trotsky sympathizer—wrote a vehement denunciation of Beals for Victor Calverton's *Modern Monthly*.[49] Calverton had misgivings about publishing Bates's letter and instructed him to send a copy to Beals, along with an invitation to reply. Beals was in no mood to extend the quarrel; in his published response, he simply dismissed Bates's charges as unfounded. In a much longer personal letter to Calverton, however, Beals attempted to knock down seven "straw men" that he felt Bates had erected in order to distort what had taken place in Coyoacán. Among the positions Beals defended were the relevance of his questions on Borodin, and his presumption of Trotsky's guilt on the one question of his archives. He expressed dismay that Bates even mentioned the rumor that he had been corrupted by " 'Moscow gold'." Moreover, Beals critizised Bates's reliance on a statement that had been translated several times from English into Spanish, and back again. Based on this much translated statement, Bates claimed that Beals complained he did not know the composition of the commission until his arrival in Mexico City. Beals denied that he ever made such a statement and referred to the likelihood of error made during each translation.[50]

Bates also attacked Beals's statements that seemed to reflect "on the personal integrity of John Dewey," especially the charge that the conduct of the hearings were an example of "childishness." In his unpublished letter to Calverton, Beals expressed respect for the Columbia University philosopher and admitted that Dewey probably thought he was "doing a noble work" in the hearings. Beals, nonetheless, reasserted his denial of the accusation, read by Dewey for the commission, that he (Beals) had associated with Stalinists in Mexico City in the days immediately preceeding the opening session. He explained that the term "childishness" referred to the other commissioners' chagrin with Beals's assumption of "an independent attitude based upon my convictions."[51]

Three days later, Beals poured his feelings into a letter to Calverton. It revealed an immense frustration and a profound disappointment. Beals insisted that the letter remain confidential, a proviso that Calverton honored.

I went on the commission at the cost of time, money and reputation. My question had utterly no intention of embarrassing his [Trotsky's] situation but was pulled out of all context and given unfortunate dramatic prominence because Dewey lifted [adjourned] the session on me. The question was merely the basis for a series of questions on which I had hoped to clarify an entirely different matter. Trotsky's quarrel on this question should be with Dr. Dewey not with me. . . .

Also, I have never at any time or in any way, publicly attacked the personal honesty of Dr. Dewey nor privately, though in the questions at issue I might be tempted to do so. That I did not agree with him on the conduct of the commission goes without saying, and I think his judgement was flagrantly bad. But Bates in his letter has attempted to put me in the position of attacking the good faith of Dewey [and] Trotsky, [and] having sold out to the Stalinists, and he has done this by not examining the published material on the case, by jumping at unwarranted conclusions on insufficient or partial evidence and by ignoring explanations I had made, though he snatches a damning phrase or two out of the very explanations. All of Bates's arguments were just straw men, arbitrarily set up, and based on the assumption that I am a son of a bitch and everybody else is a gentleman and a scholar.[52]

The last sentence expressed Beals's sense of isolation that first appeared in milder form in the early sessions. The letter was tinged with pleas for calm and hints of regret. Beals explained, "I'm not looking for a squabble on this thing and tried to resign as quietly as possible."[53] In the next few months, he found that he could not escape the controversy and that he could find little quiet.

Sidney Hook, a leftist philosopher and an associate of John

Dewey, continued the attack on Beals in a letter to the editor of the *Southern Review*. In his reply, Beals defended his actions and reiterated that he was not an agent of Stalinism. Admitting that he received $250.00 from the Commission, he claimed that this sum represented only a part of his costs. In the conclusion of his letter, Beals was blunt:

"The only question at issue is whether the Trotsky hearings in Mexico represented a sincere effort to get at the truth. In my opinion they did not; they were a farce, and I resigned."[54]

Calverton was caught in a very uncomfortable position between his old friend Beals, now shunned by nearly everyone on the Communist-Socialist Left, and the ardent admirers of Leon Trotsky. At considerable risk to his magazine and himself, Calverton struck a friendly tone with Beals and encouraged the downcast writer to visit him in New York.[55] Perhaps he hoped to reconcile the differences between Beals and the other leftists—typical of his attempts to promote unity among U.S. radicals in the late 1930s. He failed in the Beals case, however, as he did with most of his conciliatory work within the divided left during these years.[56]

Calverton's support did not prevent another attack by the Trotskyites—this one led by Trotsky himself. In October 1937, Calverton suggested to Trotsky that he write something for the *Modern Monthly*. Trotsky replied that "before entering directly into your amiable proposition," Calverton must remove Beals's name from the list of contributing editors to the magazine. Trotsky charged that Beals's explanation of the hearings in Mexico City "was nothing but a series of lies and falsifications dictated by the interests of the GPU [the Soviet political police force]." Trotsky insisted that a contributor to a magazine like the *Modern Monthly* "is bound by a reciprocal bond to all the others [contributors]." Trotsky felt that

"Stalinism is the syphilis of the workers' movement . . . [and that] anybody who chances to be a direct or indirect carrier of such contamination should be submitted to a pitiless quarantine. The hour has struck for the unsparing demarcation of honest people from all the agents, friends, lawyers, publicists and poets of the G.P.U."[57]

Evidently, Trotsky believed that the fatally infected Beals should be removed from the list of contributing editors in order to stop the spread of the virulent Stanlinist plague.

Copies of this letter went to the leading lights of the Trotskyite Left: Diego Rivera, Max Eastman, Sidney Hook, and Ben Stolberg. Calverton, the man in the middle, was under heavy pressure. Max Eastman led the assault by demanding Beals's immediate removal.[58]

Six weeks after Eastman's ultimatum, Calverton gave in to the Trotskyite pressure and dropped Beals from the *Modern Monthly's* editorial board. The removal was not a total victory for Trotsky and his supporters, however, because Calverton rejected their charge that Beals was acting as an agent of the Russian secret police. In a letter to Trotsky, Calverton argued that the published sources and private letters that he had seen "contain[ed] no shred of evidence that Beals acted under instructions from the G.P.U."[59]

One final explosion of emotion occurred, when Diego Rivera, who was angered because Beals was only "removed" and not "ejected," accused Beals of using "lies, slander and low intrigue . . . to hinder the investigations of the crimes of the Stalinist clique."[60] Beals's "ejection" was necessary for the seemingly everpresent Trotskyite concern about "the elementary demands of political hygiene." Therefore, to protect himself from infection, Rivera resigned from the *Modern Monthly.*[61]

Beals wrote his last lines on the Trotsky affair to Calverton in a letter dated April 11, 1938:

Permit me to thank you for stating my case so honestly to the wounded lion in Coyoacán [Rivera].

I am . . . amused by the fact that apparently a wild and hysterical battle has been going on with me at the center of it, without my even having known of its existence and without my having the slightest interest in its outcome. Everybody seems to have stuck up a dummy called Carleton Beals into which they have been plunging their verbal bayonets. I wish them all success in such brave storming of the revolutionary battlements.

It's all cockeyed to me, all these strange revolutionary egos running around loose. In neither Stalinites or [sic] Trotskyites have I found

decency or honor. Stalin for me is a menace to the world. Poor Trotsky reveals all the symptoms of a disordered temperament. I repeat: "a plague on both their houses."
Please accept my warm personal regards. Best to Nina from us both.[62]


## Isolation

It is often difficult to document a period of withdrawal in a person's life simply because inactivity seldom brings contact, through letters or conversations, with other people. In a negative way, Beals's binders of personal correspondence, that he arranged in his study in the early 1960s, testify to his lack of personal involvement. The binders for 1936 and 1938 bulged to overflowing with correspondence; those for 1937 were slim by comparison. Apparently, Carleton and Blanca stayed at home during most of the time from April 1937 to the end of the year, preferring the calm of the Connecticut coast to the storms that raged in New York and Mexico City.

On the surface, the Trotsky episode appeared to be an aberration in Beals's life, a curious contradiction—the staunch prorevolutionary, anti-imperialist journalist attacking a great leader of the non-Stalinist Left. In an ideological and personal sense, however, the episode did coincide with patterns that appeared earlier in Beals's career. He disliked intellectual dogma whether it came from the Right or Left; capitalism and imperialism, Catholicism and communism (either of the Stalinist or Trotskyist variety) all offended him because of the conceptual straightjackets they imposed on their disciples.

He also tended to distrust and oppose established authority. In 1918, he challenged the U.S. military draft. In 1919, he lost his position at the American School in Mexico City because he disagreed with its directors. In 1926, he denounced U.S. policy in Mexico to a hostile audience in Washington, D.C. In 1933, he openly challenged the Hoover administration's policy toward the Machado dictatorship in Cuba. In all these cases, he had the temerity to confront people and organizations with considerable power. In Coyoacán in 1937, he saw the leftist establishment that flocked around Trotsky as an organized power structure; and he rebelled against it by following his own line of inquiry. The main novelty in this instance was that both the intellectual doctrine and the established authority against which he railed were to the extreme Left of the political spectrum, where many of the people he knew and admired placed themselves. The costs of this rebellion were great in terms of Beals's acceptance among leftists and in terms of some of his old friendships. A pro-Trotsky observer of the hearings James T. Farrell was correct when he called Beals's behavior "ill-advised,"[63] an expression that had validity for the public image of the Trotsky commission as well as Beals's personal and professional relationships.

Beals's rebellious radicalism alienated many important figures on the Left, particularly New York-based leftists including Ben Stolberg, Max Eastman and Sydney Hook. This pro-Trotsky group seemed unaware of the populistic nature of the Mexican revolution, which at least in Beals's view, furnished a counterexample to the European-style, elitist revolution that Trotsky often defended. Beals believed in the authenticity of a spontaneous, peasant-worker revolution, which might reject any connection with the Comintern and any theoretical formula derived from a largely European setting. Although this conflict between Third World populistic revolution and European, party-led revolution was never explicitly stated in the course of the hearings in Mexico City, the Trotsky-Beals confrontation seemed, in part, a result of this implicit ideological dichotomy.

Ironically, in 1937 and 1938, Beals reached the high point of his career as a journalist. His connections with Lippincott and with *The Nation,* the *New Republic* and *Current History* remained firm. He completed two volumes of reminiscences: *Glass Houses* (1938) and *Great Circle* (1940). *Glass Houses* was an informative repository of anecdotes and observations, drawn from the lively expatriate community of Mexico City in the 1920s. The scope of the book ranged from the early period (1918–1921), when a variety of strong personalities vied with each other for control of the extreme left in Mexico, to the later 1920s, when a larger, and essentially different, group formed around Edward Weston, Tina Modotti and Diego Rivera. Although the peripatetic Beals had nourished himself upon the variety of their ideologies and the idiosyncracies of their personalities during this period; by 1938, he had cooled in his attitude toward those Bohemian days. He wrote that

The American Bohemians were not, like Poe or Villon or Baudelaire, driven to vices by inner desperation and terror or even cynicism, so much as childish bravura against the smugness of comfortable society. Their bravura smacked slightly of the reformist seriousness of the very Puritans they so despised.[64]

This change of perspective, no doubt the result of experience and not creeping conservatism, enabled him to write some of his most trenchant analyses of people and their circumstances.[65]

In spite of their strengths, neither volume was a model of autobiographical objectivity. Beals showed little inclination toward introspection and a tendency to exaggerate his successes and minimize his failures. He claimed quick acceptance and recognition as a writer in these early years.[67] His struggle to survive as a writer from 1918 to 1923 found no place in the texts, except for a brief mention of a nervous breakdown in Italy; nor did he mention his two unsuccessful marriages.[66] In general, he seemed to vest himself with an implacability in the face of adversity that covered the self-doubt and anguish that surfaced, at times, in his private letters. Probably the trauma of the Trotsky affair intensified his aversion to writing about his personal life. The public image that he cultivated in his reminiscences was not the same Beals who suffered through the loneliness of middle-aged exile from the people and life-styles of his misremembered youth.

# • 11 •

# The War Years

Events in September 1938 presaged Carleton Beals's short-lived triumphs and long-term frustrations during World War II. He and Blanca enjoyed their final leisurely swim of the season early in the month.[1] Within three weeks, however, a massive storm, the infamous hurricane of 1938, destroyed their cottage, along with most of the structures on or near the Connecticut coast.[2] The Bealses soon relocated at Brockett's Point just outside Branford, Connecticut, where they remained for the next two years. Beals continued to write as usual and enjoyed considerable popular, and even financial, success. Like the Bealses's frolics in the September surf, however, this success was ephemeral and marked only a brief time of quiet before a disastrous storm. The temporary acceptance of his work disguised fundamental crises that began to emerge in the war years and, eventually, forced his career into a severe decline.

In the fall of 1938, there was little evidence to suggest Beals's problems in the near future. Like other journalists, Beals focused his attention on heightening international tensions that edged the European and Asian nations into war and threatened to involve the United States and Latin America as well. U.S. reporters found that the public wanted to know more about the expansion of totalitarian power in Germany, Italy and Japan. Adolf Hitler occupied center stage in September 1938 with his seizure of the Sudetenland in Czechoslovakia, to which the British and the French offered only token resistance. Many U.S. politicians advocated an isolationist policy toward this kind of aggression, which reflected public opinion in the early and mid-1930s. As newspapers and magazines warned of "war clouds" over Europe and national radio networks brought live news coverage from European capitals into the living rooms of millions of Americans, however, popular sentiment for U.S. involvement began to rise. Public opinion polls revealed a decided shift toward increased support for Britan and France against Germany and Italy. On October 30, Orson Welles's broadcast of "War of the Worlds," a dramatization of H. G. Wells's tale of an invasion from Mars, caused a huge overreaction across the nation, and furnished a unique example of the instability of the public mind in these months.[3]

As tension mounted in Europe and then burst into open war in September 1939, the U.S. public looked to Latin America in music, films and popular writing, possibly as diversionary relief. Dance bands and radios across the county blared conga music, to whose strains long lines of energetic dancers pranced away the evening hours. This vogue of Latin music owed much to Fred Astaire and Ginger Rogers, who had cavorted to tropical American rythms so pleasingly in *Flying Down to Rio* in 1933. Hollywood producers, always eager to find a successful formula, followed with many other films set in Latin American locales well into the 1940s. Beals and others who wrote on Latin America benefited considerably from the "Latin craze" so prominent in the mass media in the late 1930s and early 1940s.[4]

### The Hemisphere in Doubt

Many journalists had begun to point to the growth of German, Italian and Japanese influence in Latin America. The image that often appeared in the popular media was a sinister Axis agent, seeking not only business and political connections, but also espionage or military adventurism. One popular radio program *Jack Armstrong* featured an episode that involved a secret German airbase hidden away in the Andes

Mountains. More serious coverage in periodicals such as *Current History* gave information on the growth of Axis trade in Latin America and the enduring loyalty of German, Italian and Japanese immigrants in the region to their homelands. *Current History* reproduced an editorial cartoon from a Mexican leftist newspaper *El Machete*, in which a huge caricature of Hitler held a bloody sword aloft as a pitifully small, cowering Getulio Vargas (dictator of Brazil) clutched at his Fascist master's feet. The mass media were responding to a widely held popular concern. Public opinion polls indicated that in the late 1930s almost four-fifths of the people in the United States believed that Germany would make an attempt to gain a foothold in the Western Hemisphere.[5]

As a leading authority on Latin America in the U.S., Beals was in a good position to express his opinions on the extent of Axis influence in the area. His book on the subject *The Coming Struggle for Latin America* appeared in September 1938, at the time that the U.S. public was increasingly aware of Axis expansion in the Americas. Beals wrote to catch the attention of those who had this fear; and at times, he strayed close to sensationalism. On balance, however, his book tended to defuse the fear more than exacerbate it.

Beals saw the Japanese as a definite economic rival of the U.S. but found little evidence of espionage or military activities. He insisted that "to see a Japanese spy under every bush is a bit absurd," although he was concerned about the strategic implications of the Japanese navy's familiarity with the Pacific coastline from Magdalena Bay to Tierra del Fuego.[6] Beals was most impressed by the activities of energetic Japanese businessmen, who hawked their textiles, electronics, cameras and "Datshun (sic) cars" in ever-increasing quantities.[7] Japanese commercial agents and diplomats cultivated cultural relations with Latin Americans on languages, literature and art; and "the gravely formal, courteous, leisurely and punctilious manners of the Japanese" pleased most Latin Americans involved in international business. Beals concluded that Japanese economic and cultural influence was likely to continue to expand.[9]

Germany was the most ominous threat to the hemisphere in Beals's estimation. Over one million German immigrants lived in the area, most of them in Brazil. They constituted a much more serious factor in the internal affairs of the Latin American nations than did the 350,000 Japanese immigrants (with the exception of Peru, where the Japanese had some political impact). Germans were owners of coffee plantations in Brazil and Guatemala and of sugar plantations in Peru; they were distributors of heavy equipment and farm machinery in Mexico and Peru; and they ran banks and breweries in most Latin American countries. Such diversified economic interests gave them a firm foothold, which was reinforced by Hitler's determined trade policy.[10] German trade increased by 500 percent in Central America from 1933 to 1936 and registered less dramatic, but significant, growth in Chile, Brazil, Mexico and Peru. By 1937, Germany was the top trading partner in Brazil. It was second in Chile, Mexico, Nicaragua and El Salvador and held a highly competitive third place in Argentina. Beals felt that Germany's aggressive trade policy and the presence of a large number of successful German emmigrant businessmen gave Hitler a prominent position in Latin America.[11]

Hitler's reich maintained close relations with many German immigrants through the VDA (Volksbund fur das Deutschtum im Ausland), an organization founded in 1882, but revamped by the Nazis to comply with their standards. The VDA strove to build a sense of "blood unity" with Germans around the world by the promotion of feelings of devotion to the fatherland. Beals mentioned an apparently VDA-connected bund in Cali, Colombia, that held its own military maneuvers near the Panamanian border. He also noted the presence of similar youth bunds in Brazil and Argentina.[12] It was in Argentina, however, that Beals found one of the VDA's few open challenges. In Buenos Aires, the German language daily *Argentinische Tageblatt* was published by German Jewish immigrants and was vehemently anti-Nazi; but it had scant influence in the non-Jewish German population of Argentina.[13]

Beals rated the espionage of the notorious Gestapo a much

more serious threat than its Japanese counterpart. The Gestapo organizer for the western coast of South America was Walter Scharpp, a former German consul in Colon, who had contacts from Panama to Chile. Mexico's leftist labor union CTM (Confederación de Trabajadores de México) claimed that the Gestapo had an extensive spy network in that country. The Gestapo recruited its agents from business and professional groups as well as from workers' organizations. It instructed them to encourage loyalty to the reich among the German immigrants residing in Latin America.[14]

One of Germany's great strengths in Latin America, according to Beals, was in the related fields of communications and propaganda. The German news agency Transocean pioneered in the use of a radio teletype system fed by broadcasts from Germany to Latin America, which reduced costs far below AP, UP and other wire services. Supported by a government subsidy, Transocean made large gains in the Latin American press. It opened the way for Nazi propaganda, which, for example, often juxtaposed stories of unemployment and labor unrest in the United States with accounts of busy factories and full employment in Germany. The propaganda directed toward Latin America also called into question the intentions of U.S.-inspired Pan-Americanism and frequently debunked the New Deal as a confused "democracy of noise." The Germans termed U.S. news releases in the Brazilian press the work of "Jewish Yankee telegraph agencies and unscrupulous merchants eager to increase dollar earnings." Beals was convinced that most right-wing conservatives in Latin America welcomed German propaganda. Its anti-U.S., prodictatorial content was an impressive trumpeting of their own views.[15]

What was Germany's purpose in Latin America? Beals had no access to German leaders, so he could only hazard a guess. He saw German economic, espionage and propaganda efforts as parts of a larger campaign "to preserve or create pro-Nazi regimes in Latin America." At most, Beals saw the possibility of open German alliances with rightist dictators, like Getulio Vargas of Brazil. At least, he felt that German agents and sympathizers could stimulate social upheavals and, thereby, reduce the economic contribution several Latin American nations might make to the enemies of the Third Reich.[16]

Beals discounted Italian influence as limited to spontaneous support from her "sons in exile," especially in Argentina and Brazil.[17] He saw a great potential for international fascism, however, in the attraction that Francisco Franco gained from his victories over the Republicans in the Spanish civil war. Beals saw Franco's appeal to conservative elements as more of a threat to the interests of the U.S. than the combined ministrations of Germany, Japan and Italy:

> The fact is that most of Latin America is openly semi-fascist— naturally a fascism of its own brand—and ruled by governments that practice the worst features of Hitlerism. Naturally, they have been pro-Franco.[18]

Franco's victory, aided by German and Italian forces, was a clear-cut triumph for fascism that, in Beals's opinion, was a source of inspiration for the dictatorial Right in most Latin American nations. This conservative political drift drew strength from the common Hispanic heritage that was important in Portuguese-speaking Brazil as well as in Spanish America. Beals, however, was most distressed by the impetus that a solidly emplaced Fascist government in Spain would give to similar regimes already in power in Latin America. He included Vargas of Brazil, Trujillo of the Dominican Republic and Batista of Cuba as the most likely to benefit from a new wave of rightist totalitarianism; and he suggested that would-be dictators out of power in other countries would be encouraged to use violence to reach their political ends.[19]

The possible emergence of rightist governments sympathetic to Franco and his Fascist colleagues posed serious problems for the Roosevelt administration's hemispheric policy. Although such prominent dictators as Vargas, Trujillo and Batista were the assiduously courted friends of the U.S., according to Beals, they were the leaders most likely to turn away from in the U.S. during a crisis or war. He characterized the State Department's relationship with these governments as "false friendships" because it did not consider the domestic policies of the dictators, who often resorted to political persecution, extra-legal repression and other police-state tactics to keep themselves in power. The continuation of this policy would isolate the U.S. from liberal, democratic movements that sought to unseat the pro-Fascist dictators.[20]

Beals was troubled by the growth of fascism in Latin America. His greatest concern, however, was not the externally imposed strategic contest for the region, but the internally generated fight to improve the well-being of the common people.

The struggle of the people of the southern countries against militarism, against feudal enslavement, against mass serfdom, against foreign domination, against ecclesiastical exploitation—that is the only *real* struggle that exists in Latin American, that is the only struggle of importance.[21]

This message may have been lost on most of his readers in 1938 and 1939, who were far more concerned about Axis subversion in the Americas than the absence of social justice. Beals had included the latter theme in most of his earlier books— none of which enjoyed the sales of *Coming Struggle*. (It went through six printings and was revised once.)[22]

While *Coming Struggle* contained elements of the anti-Fascist sentiments typical of the Left in the United States during the Popular Front era of the late 1930s, Beals was not a part of this struggle to unify leftist liberals, Socialists and Communists into one happy family. His traumatic experience in the Trotsky hearings gave him an aversion to Trotsky, Stalin and communism in general. His instinctive skepticism about U.S. policy in Latin America made it difficult for him to accept the Roosevelt administration, in spite of the reformist aspirations of the New Deal. Most importantly, Beals's preoccupation with the issues of land reform, labor organization, economic nationalism and the broadly based social and economic uplift of the masses in Latin America placed him at odds with the Popular Front's sanctification of left-wing unity. The anti-Fascists of the Popular Front placed a higher value on unity through loyalty than on intellectual dissent, which was an attitude that Beals could not accept.[23] From his point of view, liberal democracy in its fight with fascism would have to include, in its battle plans, campaigns against the entrenched power of the landed and industrial upper class, the exploition of peasants and workers, the excesses of dictatorial *caudillos* and the resilient phenomena of imperialism. The Popular Front's fixation with international relations in Europe and Asia made this Latin American agenda largely irrelevant. In the 1940s, Beals was to discover the extent to which reform in Latin America was of little relevance not only to the liberals and radicals, but also to the government and to the publishing industry of the United States.

### All Quiet on the Home Front

The magnitude and rapidity of events in Europe and the Pacific from September 1939 to December 1941 overwhelmed the U.S. public and seemed to heighten interest in Beals's *Coming Struggle*. In January 1942, however, he began to realize that his own immediate future was highly uncertain given the sudden changes that swept across the home front. William Barrett, a Denver-based writer and frequent correspondent with Beals in the early 1940's, shared his doubts about the role of their profession in the war years—both in terms of the availability of government work and in terms of personal survival.[24]

In 1942, Beals submitted a manuscript to Houghton Mifflin, which the company eventually published the next year under the title *Rio Grande to Cape Horn*. Nonetheless, many of Beals's opinions as expressed in the original manuscript were too provocative for Houghton Mifflin's editors. The original version included harsh criticisms of several dictatorial regimes in Latin America and two chapters that roundly condemned United States policy in Panama. This type of commentary was typical of Beals's writing, even in the late 1930s, but such remarks were not well received in the publishing industry during World War II.

Beals's literary agent Maxim Lieber sensed the potential for a negative response to the manuscript because of the atmosphere that existed in the American publishing industry. Lieber wrote to Beals: "One factor that may disturb Houghton Mifflin and, I suspect, almost any other publisher, is the fact that you don't hesitate to speak your mind about vicious dictators in some Latin American countries." Lieber did not question the truth of Beals's statements. He did, however, question the propriety of these statements in view of the State Department's concern for hemispheric support in the war. He suggested that Beals's descriptions might act "like a bombshell whose explosion tends to shatter the United Nations's efforts."[25]

Lieber anticipated Houghton Mifflin's response correctly. Robert Linscott did most of the editorial work on Beals's manuscript and recommended extensive revisions. He felt that several pages should be changed, or perhaps removed entirely, because they "might perhaps be offensive to the State Department."[26] On December 23, Linscott completed a typed four-page memorandum, in which he called for the deletion of large amounts of material, including the two chapters on U.S.-Panamanian relations. He also proposed the elimination of several references to "unsavory military dictatorships," the Puerto Rican nationalist movement and American policy in Argentina and Bolivia, on the grounds that Beals's analysis of these matters might be harmful to U.S. diplomacy in Latin America.[27]

Linscott's justifications for the omission of controversial material was quite explicit. Chapter XXI of the manuscript, entitled "Treason in Puerto Rico," was unacceptable, not because of error in fact or in interpretation, but because "the temper of the article is unfortunate in these times when we are playing for Latin American solidarity with so much at stake." Linscott questioned the historical discussion of Panama because "it seems unnecessary to exacerbate Latin American feeling by digging up injustices of the past which no longer exist." He doubted the wisdom of retaining Beals's six-page delineation of Bolivian grievances against the U.S.—"again for the reason that it hardly seems good policy at this time to put so strong an accent on the subject."[28]

Beals was surprised and disappointed by Linscott's suggestions but found that he had little choice in the matter. Two weeks before Linscott's memorandum, Lieber had urged Beals to accept Houghton Mifflin's editorial suggestions and had accused him of being overly sensitive and stubborn.[29] Under pressure from both the publisher and his agent, Beals faced the possibility of complete rejection of the manuscript by Houghton Mifflin. Lieber saw only slight opportunity for publication elsewhere. Beals concluded that the only way to salvage his work was by extensive revision following Linscott's critique. He rewrote much of the manuscript by substituting geographic description and sociocultural material for his customary acerbic political analysis.[30] He confined his coverage of twentieth century Panama to five short paragraphs in his chapter on Colombia.[31] The publication of *Rio Grande to Cape Horn* in the edited version represented a defeat for Beals and his style of provocative, issue-oriented journalism.

Houghton Mifflin acted on the assumptions, prevalent throughout the publishing industry, that a company should support the war effort and avoid any controversy that might complicate U.S. relations with allies. Beals's views on dictators, such as Trujillo and Batista, and U.S. policy in countries like Panama probably would have caused some embarrassment in the State Department and might have triggered a small "bombshell" in hemispheric relations. His resentment of this indirect, veiled censorship, however, was not lessened by Lieber's explanation of the larger forces at work in wartime publishing.[32]

Houghton Mifflin's advertisement for *Rio Grande to Cape Horn* revealed a kind of duplicity that must have added salt to Beals's wounds. Sandwiched between promotional descriptions of Ester Forbes's patriotic *Johnny Tremain* and Lloyd C. Douglas's pious *The Robe* was an advertisement for *Rio Grande to Cape Horn*, which claimed that the author: "has distilled a lifetime of study of Latin America to give us this picturesque, provocative and *utterly honest* book" (italics added.)[33]

### Flawed Success

The disturbing curtain of silence that descended over inter-American issues in World War II brought Beals personal disappointment. Ironically, however, in the war years, he enjoyed his greatest financial success. In 1940, he completed *Pan America*, a lengthy discourse on the dangers of the growing U.S. dependency on foreign sources of critical raw materials, especially petroleum, in the context of international conflict. While *Pan America* was a fairly impressive catalog of strategic raw materials and their relationship to the complexities of modern industry, Beals offered no real solutions to the conflict between the needs of the U.S. economy and the expectations of the nations, many of them Latin American, that held the raw materials.[34]

The main vehicle for Beals's momentary affluence was *Dawn Over the Amazon*, a futuristic, potboiler novel, with few redeeming literary virtues. The main reason for its financial success was its selection by the Literary Guild in March 1943 as one of the books for sale to members at reduced cost, which meant an immediate order of 125,000 copies from Duel, Sloan and Smith, his publisher.[35] Although the exact amount of money that *Dawn* earned for Beals is not available, there is no doubt that he and Blanca enjoyed a more-than-comfortable lifestyle through the next few years.

The content and style of *Dawn* ranked much lower than Beals's earlier fiction. In *Destroying Victor* (New York, 1929), he attempted to portray the psychological disintegration of a college professor. In *Black River* (Philadelphia, 1934), he pricked the reader's social conscience with his account (partly from personal observation) of the unscrupulous and rapacious struggle for wealth in the Mexican oil fields. And in the *Stones Awake* (Philadelphia, 1936), he described the trials of a Mexican woman as she survived the vicissitudes of the Mexican revolution. All of these novels had some valid psychological, sociological or ethical theme; but not one of them was a financial or critical success.

*Dawn* was a story of wartime adventure set in 1950 as the Germans and Japanese invaded South America, the U.S. Achilles's heal. Beals combined military conflict, with political and business intrigue, ideological polemics and lightly romanticized sex. The central character Grant Hammond was an idealistic engineer from the United States, who had plans to develop the Amazon Basin with help from the enigmatic Peruvian radical Victor de la Hoz, probably modeled on Víctor Raúl Haya de la Torre, the real-life head of APRA. Hammond was a clean-cut, sincere, sympathetic Yankee with the best interest of the common people foremost in mind. His only weakness was for the raven-haired, voluptuous Latin beauties, who continually tempted him with their physical charms in hotels, night clubs, and even jungles, while he tried to remain faithful to Bluebelle, his nagging, bitchy wife from Mobile. Grant ultimately failed in his quest to maintain marital fidelity, but that was his only failure. He and his assorted cohorts beat back Germans, Japanese, tropical vegetation, mountains, rivers, epidemic diseases, racism, reactionary conservatism and other threats of evil manifested in nature and in man, so that, in the end, the way is open for progress and prosperity in the tropics.

In 1943, at the peak of his financial, but certainly not journalistic, achievement, Beals broke off his relationship with Maxim Lieber. Their disagreement seemed to begin with a rather petty matter relating to Houghton Mifflin's rejection of Beals's manuscript "From Hell to Broken Bow," which was an attempt at a popular history of the Populist movement in the United States. Beals was angered by the comments of Houghton Mifflin's editors and, in a brusque letter, he complained of "the uninformed, conflicting, contradictory and irresponsible editorial suggestions that have been flung out over a period of more than two years."[36] In some way not clearly expressed in their correspondence, Beals associated Lieber with Houghton Mifflin's positions on a number of minor matters, including the latter's assumption that he had agreed to a contract for another book. Beals claimed Lieber's attitude was "highhanded (and) unilateral."[37]

Lieber was "amazed and shocked" by Beals's accusations. His response was an honest, but hurtful, appraisal of a critical period in Beals's writing career:

> Years ago you were a pioneer, striking out along new paths and embodying progressive interpretations of political action. Dur-

ing the past few years, others have caught up with and passed you. Recently your interests have turned inward to such an extent that your books have become chores for you rather than exciting creative challenges.

Lieber then explained the details for the termination of their professional relationship.[38]

Another painful experience for Beals in these years was the death of his father. The last time he saw his father was in the winter of 1940-1941, when he and Blanca visited his parents in California.[39] In early September 1941, Leon Eli Beals died peacefully of complications from influenza. He had worked in trying circumstances in California for many years; he seemed always to take a humble background position in the family in comparison with the strong influence of his wife. Beals was deeply moved and expressed sincere filial admiration in the telegram he sent to his grieving mother: " . . . he was a grand and noble man . . . a civilized man who lived his life staunchly and bent the knee to none, yet who did no man evil. (He was) the most honest man I ever knew."[40]

The impact of his father's death, the abrupt termination of his relationship with Lieber and his frustrations in journalism suggest that Beals was undergoing a serious emotional crisis in the early 1940s. An April, 1944 letter, from an old friend of his mother, who had known her years earlier in Berkeley, contained similar implications. Mrs. Maurice Katz wrote to Beals pleading with him to write his mother because she had not heard from him for a disturbingly long period of time. The urgency of Mrs. Katz's plea to a fifty-one year old, well-known and prosperous author to write a simple letter to his nearly frantic mother suggests that his behavior was far from normal.[41]

The basic cause of Beals's distress was not discussed openly in any of his letters. One can only speculate about the pressures that drove him to the self-imposed withdrawal that so concerned Lieber and his mother. His own serious writing was more frequently rejected in the early 1940s than in the two previous decades. In addition, he must have been dismayed

by the shift in public attention away from Latin America, the
only continent other than Antarctica left out of the fighting in
World War II. His marriage to Blanca, while seemingly happy
in its first years, may have become less supportive and more
stiffling in these difficult times. Beals's desire for travel, satisfied by jaunts to California and Florida in the late 1930s, was
completely blocked during the war by the rationing of gasoline.
The death of his father in 1941 must have reminded Beals of his
own mortality and may have led him to question his own accomplishments. (This was the kind of introspection that Lieber
felt hurt his work and threatened to throw his career into decline.) Moreover, letters such as the one he received from
Howard Phillips in the summer of 1943 could easily have jog-
ged his memory of his youthful days in Mexico; of friendships
with Diego Rivera, who was by then an enemy; with Ernest
Gruening and Frank Tannenbaum, who were by then very distant; with Julio Mella, Tina Modotti and Edward Weston, who
by then were dead; and of former passions, both ideological
and romantic.[42] Buffeted by the memories of his past, the
frustrations of the present and an awareness of his limited
longevity, Beals must have sensed that he had reached the end
of a period in his life. He must have looked with great uncertainty to the future.

# • 12 •

# Comeback

In early February 1946, Carleton and Blanca Beals embarked upon an extensive eight-month tour of a dozen Latin American countries in hopes of stimulating his journalistic productivity. Frederick Lewis Allen of *Harper's* and Morris Rubin of *The Progressive* expressed interest in articles that Beals planned to write during and after the trip.[1] What Beals observed on his return to familiar places was unsettling. The rapid growth of large cities and their stark contrasts between wealth and poverty escaped the attention of most of the news media in the United States in the 1940s. Mexico City, Beals's home for most of the 1920s, was dissected by new avenues, which were choked with automobiles and flanked by new highrise buildings. The old residential neighborhoods and market places had been obliterated to make way for these monuments to progress. In the South American cities of Buenos Aires and Rio de Janeiro, he found more indications of industrial and urban expansion. They returned to Sachem's Head in late September to find a check from Morris Rubin for some of the articles Beals had written for *The Progressive*.[2] In spite of the sense of accomplishment he derived from the trip, Beals was to discover over the next decade that the interests of the reading public in the United States did not include economic expansion, social change or any other aspect of the Latin American scene.

While on his Latin American trip, Beals began to express grave doubts about the editorial priorities of the postwar publishing industry. Institutional and economic factors were important, but Beals saw an ideological dimension. In an article for *The Progressive* datelined from Santiago, Chile, Beals described the Good Neighbor Policy as mostly "pap and piffle." He believed it was an extended propaganda effort that convinced many people in the Americas that utopia existed on both continents. Neighborly propaganda threatened to continue as the postwar tourist trade blossomed in Mexico, the Caribbean and South America. Beals complained that most publishers avoided any material that might negate the image of the Latin American nations as "perfect little paradises with eternal sun and beauty and the most modern comforts." At the same time, dictators were in charge in Nicaragua and Honduras. In effect, a slumbering press corps, lulled into somnambulism by the necessity of winning the approval of the United States diplomatic representative, who wanted only "sweetness and light" in print, shielded them from exposure. Beals saw very little chance for serious, probing journalism under those circumstances.[3] That *The Progressive*, with its small readership, was the only periodical to accept his articles on a regular basis offered additional evidence that Beals's style of slashing, controversial reportage was expendable in the oppressive climate of the late 1940s and early 1950s.

Central America was the scene of an important example of the Left versus Right dichotomy in the region. Beals found the reformist government of Guatemalan President Juan José Arévalo a source of encouragement that for a few years served as a counterpoint to the repressive Somoza regime in Nicaragua. Nonetheless, Beals was unable to find a major journal that would publish his analyses of Central America in the late 1940s or early 1950s. The policy of the United States reinforced Beals's cynicism. Eisenhower and Dulles, staunch supporters of the Somoza dictatorship, undermined and eventually overthrew Arévalo's leftist successor in Guatemala in 1954. Beals reported in the *Christian Century* that the United States played a leading role in the overthrow by supplying arms and paramilitary personnel. He surmised that "in the rest of Latin America, old fears of 'dollar diplomacy' have been aroused and the general opinion is that the bonafide Good Neighbor Policy has come to an end." Beals also attacked the State Department's "white paper" on Communist infiltration in Guatemala. He claimed that it failed to prove that Communists controlled the government. Although the right-wing revolt had removed Communists and suspected Communists from the government, Beals acknowledged that the social and economic environment conducive to radical agitation remained among the impoverished Guatemalan lower classes.

At this critical time, the editors of two stalwart liberal periodicals *The Nation* and *The Progressive* decided not to publish Beals's articles on Guatemala. Carey McWilliams expressed an interest in one of Beals's manuscripts, but it never found its way into print. *The Nation*, however, did publish two articles that pointed to possible U.S. involvement in the overthrow of Arbenz. The editors of *The Progressive* decided not to publish one of Beals's articles at the last moment because sudden changes in Guatemala might make the article seem "a bit dated."[4]

### Hard Times

The rejection of Beals's leftist commentary was only one example of a much broader trend in the decade after World War II: the Second Red Scare. More deeply rooted than the First Red Scare of 1919-1920, it produced an intensely conservative mood that pervaded nearly every aspect of the nation's political and cultural life. In the late 1940s, the House Un-American Activities Committee (HUAC) conducted public hearings in which many writers, government officials and politicians found themselves trapped into making admissions about earlier left-wing connections or about currently held leftist beliefs. Many of these hapless radicals, who had found the 1930s congenial to their ideologies, were suddenly the victims of demagogic browbeating, public alienation and professional ostracism. Senator Joseph McCarthy emerged in 1950 as the cham-

pion of right-wing excess. He raised public fears of communism to a new high and exploited this atmosphere in a ruthless
quest for publicity. Like most leftist writers who remained
faithful to their convictions, Beals felt the full impact of this
overwhelming assault on two bastions of leftist expression: periodical and book publishers that, in the previous decade, had
trumpeted a variety of radical ideas and commentary.[5]

Evidence of the onset of hard times appeared even before
Beals's Latin American trip. Varian Frye, an editor for the leftist
periodical *Common Sense*, wrote Beals in December 1945 to explain the return of a manuscript. *Common Sense* was no longer
able to meet its expenses; therefore, the publisher decided to
cease publication. Postwar adjustments in the United States
were sudden and often painful. The publishing industry was
as adversely affected as any field. In addition to rising labor
costs, many leftist periodicals faced declines in readership as
the national mood slid from wartime patriotism to postwar
conservatism. The stalwart *Progressive*, shocked by Joseph Mc-
Carthy's defeat of incumbent Wisconsin Senator Robert La Follette (president of the magazine's parent company) in 1946,
barely survived a major financial crisis in 1947.[6]

Beals's friend Cap Pearce of Duel, Sloan and Pearce expressed the general state of confusion in the industry in a letter
that accompanied a returned manuscript:

It dismays me to have to tell you that we think it would be un-
wise to publish your forthcoming book. The reasons for coming to
this decision have nothing to do with the book itself in an editorial
way, but are hard-headed and businesslike. Lately we have had
increasingly unhappy and discouraging experiences with topical
books of every kind. The world seems to move too fast, and these
days the radio and the magazines seem to cover much more important themes and a much wider territory than they did some years
ago.
With the production slowdown we have been confronted with of
late, books dealing with current events are faced with a pretty in-
different public by the time they are published, even if only the
surface of the material is dated. We have a particularly bad taste of
this in publishing Sydney Morrell's book *Spheres of Influence*, though

everyone who can claim any knowledge of the stuff it deals with considers it the most intelligent and informative work that has appeared in its field. In short, reviews were wonderful and the sales haven't paid one half of the printer's cost. We may be wrong, but we have convinced ourselves that we might have a similar experience with your book and, since printers get paid more every day, it's an experience we simply can't afford.[7]

The demand for writing on Latin America remained weak, while at the same time, journalists and an ever-increasing number of academics submitted manuscripts for publication. In the 1920s, Beals was one of only a few journalists from the United States fluent in Spanish, knowledgeable of Latin America and well-travelled in the region. By the late 1940s, international studies programs had become institutional fixtures at many universities. Experts on Latin America emerged from the portals of academe to do field work among the Maya ruins of Yucatan, in the National Archives in Mexico City or in the high mountain villages of the Andes. As a result, the field became crowded. Beals's suggested piece on Argentina for *Harper's* met a reluctant "no" from Frederick Lewis Allen, because Hubert Herring, now a professor at Claremont College, had written a similar article for an earlier issue.[8]

By January 1947, Beals was nearing desperation. In a letter to Mavis McIntosh, Beals's new literary agent, he confessed that he needed an immediate publication to bring in some money. "The trip south cost me nearly five thousand dollars, and I have not been able to capitalize on it as on previous occasions, so it has been all outgo and nothing coming in."[9]

In the 1920s and 1930s, Beals had been an outgoing, ebullient person; but by the late 1940s and early 1950s, his tendency to withdraw from social contacts, first noted by Maxim Lieber in 1944, became more pronounced. Old friends complained that they saw him infrequently; they also began to realize the extent of his professional and financial distress. In 1949, Frances Toor sent him money "as a grateful friend," who expected no repayment. Two years later, she invited the Bealses to move in with her in Mexico City and implored: "Dear Carl, please never again talk to me of indebtedness, for it makes me feel small when I think of what you have done for me."[10]

During these years of struggle, Beals's mother frequently expressed concern for his career and his welfare. In the summer of 1950, she tried to console him by expressing her inability to understand "why you are so unsuccessful in getting your work placed."[11] Her support and sympathy had been with him since his early childhood and was especially important in his early years as a writer in Mexico City and Rome. On February 3, 1954, death took her at a time already frought with great stress for Carleton Beals. Ralph Beals, by this point firmly established in the UCLA Department of Anthropology, handled the funeral arrangements and sent Carleton his share of her small estate.[12]

At the point when Beals's fortunes seemed lowest, there was one more heavy blow to absorb. A February 1953 letter from Howard Phillips in Mexico City presaged this new cause for anguish—marital dissolution. Phillips described in restrained, but poignant, prose the deterioration of his relationship with Lolita, his wife of many years.[13] Phillips was one of Beals's closest friends who was in a similar situation—a disintegrating marriage. Within two months, Carleton left Blanca to begin a separation that eventually resulted in divorce. It was a rancorous breakup. Blanca was quite bitter. It was no doubt unpleasant for Carleton, who had subdued his penchant for meandering for nearly two decades, but who could no longer tolerate the restrictions of the marriage.[14]

Near the bottom of his professional and personal crises, Beals's luck began to change. In 1952, after four years of vacillation among three literary agents, Beals signed with Bertha Klausner.[15] She helped him through the continued bad times of the 1950s, after which their collaboration found some success and endured until his death in 1979. Beals, like many other experienced writers, turned to textbooks as a convenient way to earn financial rewards for the use of his skills. He authored a series of three books on New England history for high schools.

His research on one of these volumes *The Making of Bristol* attracted the attention of the FBI.[16] A clarion call of warning under the letterhead of the Connecticut Daughters of the American Revolution went directly to the office of FBI Director J. Edgar Hoover. The author of the letter (whose anonymity is preserved by the FBI) proclaimed herself "panic-stricken" because Beals's name appeared in an article by William Fulton in the *American Magazine* on radical influences in U.S. scholarly foundations. Apparently, the Guggenheim Fellowship that Beals held in the early 1930s carried an improbable legacy. The anonymous Bristolean not only overstated the case, but also ignored the rules of parallel sentence structure as she reported to Hoover: "This man has been here for months, has had access to our records, been (sic) through our factories, and everywhere else (sic). What is he up to? I am simply worried to death and I dare not tell a soul except you."[17]

The danger of a left-wing history of Bristol was too great a risk for Hoover to take. He ordered the New Haven office of the FBI to begin a full investigation of Beals. Hoover reassured his frantic correspondent in Bristol that the FBI would soon have the full story on Beals. The first "break" in the case came in January 1953, when an alert FBI agent uncovered the name of the financial supporter of the Bristol history. It was the Barnes Foundation, a charitable organization formed by Fuller Forbes Barnes, a Bristol businessman.[18] Barnes, perhaps acting on information from the FBI, summoned Beals to his office to request his resignation as historian of Bristol. Beals refused to be removed; instead, he wrote a sweeping denial of any Communist connections. He pointed out in detail his unfriendly relationships with many Communists since the Trotsky affair.[19]

Meanwhile, New Haven agents made a "neighborhood investigation" that uncovered little of value. One informant said that Beals lived "'a quiet and uneventful life keeping very much to himself.'" Other neighbors gave much the same report and were unable to cite any indications that Beals was a subversive. The New Haven agents summarized their observations with only one comment of a derogatory nature: he "drinks excessively."[20]

FBI agents around the nation made studies of his passport applications, family background and military record—none of which turned up any incriminating evidence.[21] An agent in New York City talked with some FBI sources "who have some knowledge of Communists and Communist activities in the New York area" and concluded that there were no leads to follow, which matched the report from Mexico City.[22] Perhaps the most telling evidence came from a bureau review of Clifford Odets' testimony before HUAC on May 19, 1952. The playwright admitted that he was a member of the Communist party at the time that he and Beals collaborated on *Rifle Rule in Cuba* (1937), but he did not name Beals as a party member.[23]

After twenty-one months of investigation, Hoover, having obtained only lists of a few articles in left-wing journals and membership in some short-lived front groups, decided to drop the case. He concluded that:

A Review (sic) of the bureau file on the subject, a writer, reflects that he was affiliated with various Communist party front groups during the 1930s and up until the early 1940s. He has never been reported as a Communist party member and has not taken part in subversive activities in recent years.

In view of the above, it does not appear that an interview of the subject would serve a useful purpose and your request to interview him is denied.

You are instructed to close this case.[24]

It remained for Vice-President Richard Nixon, in a classic example of bad timing, to request that the FBI start another investigation of Beals. Unaware that Hoover had made the first inquiry, the vigilant Nixon read an article by Beals that described the U.S.-backed Castillo Armas government in Guatemala as "a military dictatorship."[25] Nixon felt that this article "espouses the Communist line" and told an FBI agent that the Senate Internal Security Subcommittee might begin its own investigation of Beals.[26] The FBI did not make a new investigation; however, it merely reviewed its earlier findings on Beals. Apparently, Nixon's fears were allayed by this report.[27]

Beals completed his history of Bristol on schedule. He was unaware that even in the hysteria of the early 1950s, the intrepid, bulldog guardian against communism, J. Edgar Hoover had found his record clear of any hint of a subversive nature. Beals would have been furious had he known of the investigation, and he probably would have been a bit insulted by its conclusion. The absurdity of the investigation was that his innocuous history of Bristol, not his numerous defenses of revolution and attacks on imperialism, was its inspiration.

## Storm Clouds over Cuba

Beals began a more settled life in the summer of 1957. He married Carolyn Kennedy, a graduate of Skidmore, who after many years of employment with Consolidated Edison of New York, capitulated to her preference for country life. Her secure financial situation, owing largely to her inheritance from her father's estate built up during his years as a banker, made it possible for the two of them to purchase a thirty-acre farm a few miles north of Killingworth, Connecticut. Their the home, a two-story colonial structure, was in good condition and had ample living space for the two of them. There she indulged her love of cats, goats and horses, and he converted a large one-room schoolhouse (moved from the original site in the town) into a study lined with shelves heavily loaded with books, magazines and manuscripts.

Beals was very pleased with this new environment and even more so with his new wife. She gave him freedom to travel and to write, while she was busy with the many chores associated with the caring the animals and the grounds. With no offense to Beals and often to his amusement, she gave little attention to the tasks of housewifery. About a year after their marriage, Carleton expressed his happiness in a letter to his brother Ralph: "Carolyn has been most lovely about every-thing, (is) an excellent cook, rotten housekeeper, mostly interested in two horses, three goats and this part of a horse, yours truly."[28]

As Beals knew only too well, U.S. public interest in Latin America had nearly disappeared in the middle 1950s. Russia, the Cold War and the Suez Crisis dominated the headlines while the 1954 CIA-instigated coup in Guatemala gained only

fleeting interest in the press. The one exception to public disin-
terest in Latin America was the Cuban Fidel Castro. Through
the stories of *The New York Times* correspondent Herbert L.
Matthews, he became a well-known figure in the United
States—even before the overthrow of Batista in January 1959.
An abortive revolt on July 26, 1953 nearly cost the flamboyant
Castro his life. Three years later, Castro and eighty-one fol-
lowers returned to Cuba from exile aboard a leaky yacht the
*Granma*. They set out upon what many contemporary observers
objectively considered a quixotic quest: the overthrow of the
Batista dictatorship. Matthews responded to a call from *The
New York Times* Havana-based reporter Ruby Hart Phillips and
went to Cuba to interview Castro. With the help of a Castro
agent as a guide, he located the bearded rebel at his camp in the
Sierra Maestra Mountains of eastern Cuba. Matthews described Castro as a revolutionary for "liberty, democracy [and]
social justice" and against the evil and oppressive Batista regime.[29] Largely as a result of the Matthews's articles, Castro
burst into the U.S. media as a khaki-clad rebel, engaged in an
idealistic struggle for reform.

Three months before Matthews's article appeared in *The
New York Times* and nearly two weeks before the *Granma* landed
on the south coast of Oriente Province, Beals wrote an analysis
of Batista's violent reaction to the growing unrest in Cuba for
the *Christian Century*. Borrowing his title "Rifle Rule in Cuba"
from a pamphlet he helped to edit in the 1930s, Beals drew
parallels between the endemic violence that preceded the overthrow of Gerardo Machado in 1933 and the deterioration of the
social order in Cuba in the 1950s. As in the 1930s under Machado, the Batista government attempted to crush student agitation at the University of Havana. Beals predicted that Batista
could not quell unrest by intimidation and police-state tactics.
He also noted that "trouble in Cuba means trouble for all of us,
since most of the island's cultivated land and its industries
belong to absentee United States corporation, which means
that our policies are shaped accordingly."[30]

Carey McWilliams, editor of *The Nation*, called on Beals for
some background information about Cuba in December 1956.

Beals's response, written in January 1957, placed Castro in a fairly prominent position, more than seven weeks before Matthews's famous interview. Beals listed four opposition movements, including the Cuban Communist party and a group he identified as the *Novembristas* headed by Fidel Castro. Unaware of Castro's December landing in Oriente, Beals believed that the opposition clique was in Mexico.[31] Matthews's February article from the Sierra Maestra, however, made it clear that eastern Cuba was the center of action.

In June 1957, Beals departed for Cuba, armed with letters of introduction from McWilliams to verify his status as a reporter for *The Nation*.[32] Beals's first impression of Castro and his supporters was not favorable. While he did not weaken his previous condemnation of the Batista government, Beals could find nothing in Castro's rebellion in the Sierra Maestra or among his young supporters in Havana that promised to redeem the awful costs in human life and suffering. After talking with "more than a dozen student leaders, several closely linked with the terrorists' movement," Beals concluded that their only source of unity was their "passion" to overthrow Batista. Beals did not talk to Castro or any of his followers in Havana, but his investigations gave him an impression that the rebel leader was a "quick-tempered, impatient, imperious, violence-prone adventurer, whose father built a landed empire on theft and corruption and left his son the legacy of a youth shattered by his father's flaunted infidelity." Castro's unstable personality troubled Beals less than the apparent absence of a clearly articulated set of revolutionary goals, a litmus tests for revolutions that Beals had used for years.[33]

Such a blanket condemnation of the nascent rebel movement by a venerable defender of leftist causes surprised and disappointed at least one of Castro's intellectual supporters— Mario Llerena, who was in Mexico City in the summer of 1957. Llerena had the task of writing a statement of revolutionary aims, which he did under the title *Nuestra Razón (Our Cause)*, a thirty-three page pamphlet, that appeared first in June or July 1957. Soon after, Llerena read Beals's "Rebels Without a Cause" and sent the North American writer a copy of *Nuestra Razón* to show that Castroism did have an intellectual foundation. The program contained in Llerana's manifesto drew heavily from liberal democratic thought—"the traditional philosophy of freedom and human dignity that any schoolboy could find in the works and lives of Thomas Jefferson and José Marti." Some twenty years later, Llerena recalled that he was influenced by such democratic leftists as Romulo Betancourt of Venezuela, José Figueres of Costa Rica, Victor Raúl Haya de la Torre of Peru and North American writers John Dos Passos, Waldo Frank and Carleton Beals.[34]

While Llerena's manifesto was only one of several such expressions from the Castro movement in these early years, Beals felt that it was important enough to publicize. He summarized the document in a letter to *The Nation* in September 1957. In his study of Llerena's calls for land reform, labor unionization and economic nationalism, Beals located some evidence of ideological maturity in the movement.[35]

Llerena and Beals had much in common in their assessment of Castro's personality. In his memoir of the period, Llerena recalled that Beals's

article went into much scandalous detail on Castro's upbringing and family, particularly his father, who was described as, among other things, a former cattle thief and now a shady country squire who kept a harem somewhere in the Oriente jungle. In time, I learned that, although some of the details were not strictly accurate, there was a considerable amount of truth in the charges.[36]

Later in his book, Llerena observed that Castro's father was a distant, authoritarian figure, "who could hardly communicate with or show affection for his family." Castro emerged from this setting as "a hyperactive individual with an uncontrollable urge toward the adverturous and the catastrophic."[37]

In December 1958, Beals saw that Batista's collapse was imminent. In an unpublished letter to Carey McWilliams, he insisted the mounting terrorism in the cities and the growing disarray of the Cuban army meant a major political change in the immediate future. Beals predicted that, baring direct interference of the army, Castro would displace Batista.[38]

## Cuban Hurricane

On January 1, 1959, Fulgencio Batista fled Havana for exile in Florida. Suddenly the game of guessing Castro's intentions once in power preoccupied not only a few journalists and academics, but also a substantial part of the foreign policy establishment in Washington, the business community in New York and a number of well-known and highly respected intellectuals. Historian Robert Freeman Smith observed that the serious study of Cuba in the United States was the domain of a dedicated few before 1959. Their considered conclusions, according to Smith, were obscured and distorted in the public mind by the naive assumption that a benevolent Uncle Sam had bestowed political freedom and economic prosperity on Cuba since 1898. U.S. domination of the island was a "normal condition requiring little thought, effort or understanding."[39] In 1959 and 1960, Castro destroyed this belief and disturbed its believers by starting one of the world's few social revolutions only ninety miles from U.S. shores. The formerly benevolent Uncle Sam had by then become Cuba's enemy because of its alliance with Russian communism.

Carey McWilliams again relied on Beals to provide much of *The Nations* coverage of Cuba. Beals wrote a quick assessment of the revolution, in which he warned that the U.S. was likely to pay dearly for past aid and accolades to Batista. Castro's movement was the most recent manifestation of the anti-imperialist tendency which was evident in Mexico in the 1910s and Nicaragua in the 1920s and which continued to surface not only in Latin America, but also in Africa and Asia. The conciliatory statements of Milton Eisenhower, the President's brother and chief spokesperson on Latin America, came too late and offered too little. Beals detected one flaw in Castro's power base—the absence of support from organized labor—but expressed confidence in his ability to take charge of Cuba. Beals felt that "a revolution has been set in motion and there is little likelihood that it can be stopped short of its objectives either by outside interference or by incompetent or recalcitrant leadership."[40]

McWilliams expressed admiration for the article and for Beals:

When you pass away—which I hope will never, never happen—
your epitaph will be: "Here was the last of the really great freelance foreign correspondents."
That piece was excellent, and I don't know how you knocked it out
so quickly, and the filler that you sent by cable was just exactly
what we wanted.[41]

McWilliams's letter reached Beals by American Express in
Havana. After remaining in Cuba for three weeks in order to
make sense of the confusion that seemed to reign there, Beals
departed suddenly because he was ill with a virus.[42] His reputation as an advocate of left-wing causes was indicated by the
words of the *Diario Nacional,* a Cuban newspaper that described
him as a "very intelligent U.S. journalist and sociologist" and a
"biographer of the crimes of Machado."[43] Undoubtedly, his
failure to obtain an interview with Castro, was a great disappointment for Beals. The exact reasons for Beals's failure to
reach the "First Chief" remain unclear. An internationally
known Cuban historian and commentator on current events
Herminio Portel Vilá, however, saw Beals's departure as a
missed opportunity of some importance. Portel Vilá argued
that Castro needed to reach the important segment of the U.S.
public that read *The Nation* and similar periodicals. He pointed
out that Obregón and Calles had benefited from the work of
Beals and his colleagues Frank Tannenbaum and Ernest Gruening in the 1920s.[44] Two years later, Portel Vilá wrote that Beals
left Cuba "very resentful" because he had been unable to interview Castro; but this experience did little to dampen his enthusiasm for the revolution.[45]

One of Castro's earliest and most vocal critics was Senator
Wayne Morse, chairman of Senate Foreign Relations Committee, who accused the Cuban government of complete disregard
of proper judicial process and large-scale miscarriage of justice
in its dealings with ex-Batista officials. Beals's memories of
Batista's terror campaign, especially the memory of his friend
Octavio Seigle's death in the 1930s, were vivid. In his view,
Castro's methods were not nearly so excessive. Some of his old
anger welled up—this time against Morse and his congressional colleagues:

American liberals' onslaughts on and uninformed criticisms of the new regime come with bad grace. Where were some of the gentlemen during the long years when the human spirit was defiled in Cuba as terribly as it ever was on the face of the earth?

Where were our good liberals when our government was shipping arms to Batista and our army officers were training his men and pinning medals on his worst assassins?[46]

Beals argued strenuously against any U.S. intervention to force a North American version of justice on the Cuban courts. Senator Morse urged such action on the assumption that convictions and executions under Castro were far more numerous than they should have been. Beals disagreed. In the trials that he studied, the treatment of the accused persons was both fair and humane, a rather remarkable circumstance because of the tension and the strong feelings against the former Batista officials that existed in Cuba.[47] While this evaluation contains some of Beals's propensity to minimize revolutionary excess and to maximize dictatorial brutality, historian Hugh Thomas has pointed out that "the extent and horror of the Batista era became apparent only after it had ended. Bodies and skeletons, torture chambers and tortures were discovered and photographed by the press." The trials conducted by the Castro government in early 1959 were, according to Thomas, "unfair" in that higher officials of the Batista regime escaped the island, leaving the lower ranks to the revolutionary courts. His overall conclusion, however, was that "the trials were fair, in the sense that a genuine effort was made to establish the guilt or innocence of the accused."[48]

Beals found U.S. press coverage of the Castro government in early 1959 unjustifiably hostile. He singled out *Time* as leading the field in "McCarthy-type smear reporting," that exaggerated the influence of Communists in the new government. He admitted that some Communists held some important positions in labor unions, but they had done so since the 1930s. Beals reported that Castro was aware of his negative image in the United States and was attempting to improve it. For political and ideological reasons, Beals rated as very small the chances of success for Castro's media campaign. He implied that the journalistic establishment opposed Castro largely because of his intentions to restructure Cuban society in a radical revolution that had little sympathy in the United States. It did not matter whether the revolution carried the Communist label.[49]

Most of his 1959 articles were heavily pro-Castro, but Beals did express some doubts about the future in Cuba. His unequivocal defense of Cuban justice in January and February weakened in May. By then, he observed that: "A new edict, making all counter-revolutionary activity against Castro's provisional government punishable by death, has an ominous ring."[50]

This concern about justice was well placed. The arrest, trial and conviction in late 1959 of Huber Matos, a Fidelista from the early days in the Sierra Maestra, opened a new epoch for the Cuban courts, in which enemies and alleged enemies of the revolution were the subject of arbitrary treatment. The death penalty was used with some frequency, and the number of political prisoners on the island grew substantially in the next few years. (They numbered as many as 40,000 by 1965.[51])

Castro's prominence in the U.S. media brought a large surge of interest in Cuba and in Latin America in general. It also brought a substantial improvement in Beals's ability to find publishers for his articles. Relying on *The Nation* and *Christian Century*, Beals placed nine articles in 1959. His friend Fernando Ortiz wrote to congratulate him on his coverage of the revolution.[52] Harvey O'Connor, an expert on Cuban economic affairs, gave him a much larger compliment: "Everywhere in Latin America the name of Carleton Beals elicits respect, admiration and cariño—Latins are really wonderful in the way they appreciate their friends."[53]

Beals also found publishers more receptive to his other projects. He commented to Albert K. Dawson that half a dozen of his old manuscripts, that had "gone the rounds for from ten to twenty years" now suddenly had better prospects.[54]

With his career apparently on the rise again, the sixty-six year old journalist chose not to pursue the main attraction of the times. In the last half of 1959, he refused twice to go to Cuba for McWilliams.[55] A younger Beals probably would have accepted the opportunity with little hesitation; but in his schoolhouse-office in Connecticut, he was busy on several projects that held the prospect of some immediate financial, if not critical, reward. One was the writing of a lengthy report for the New Haven Housing Authority.[56] The others included the revision of manuscripts.[57]

Why Beals did not write a book about Cuba in the early 1960s remains one of the larger anomalies of his career. His decision to turn away from Cuba for several months in 1959 was perhaps understandable in terms of his age and the strenuous efforts firsthand investigation would have required. He did, however, miss an opportunity to enhance his position as one of the leading commentators on Cuban affairs.

### Fair Play

In 1960, Beals returned to the polemics of the Cuban revolution. His most pernicious act, according to conservatives and moderates, was to join the Fair Play for Cuba Committee (FPCC), a loose coalition of U.S. leftists determined to present events in Cuba from a Castroite perspective. Beals took up this cause with great relish. On his second trip to Cuba since the fall of Batista, Beals was excited by the contagious optimism of a newborn social revolution, in which almost anything seemed possible. His writing in 1960 was full of an ebullience that, at times, boardered on naiveté. He failed to detect, or perhaps refused to allow himself to see, that Castro was headed ever closer to Russia.

The reputation of the Fair Play for Cuba Committee suffered irreparable damage in 1963, when Lee Harvey Oswald, the assassin of President John F. Kennedy, used its name as a front for his dubious activities in New Orleans and Dallas, just prior to the assassination. Long before that sad event, the FBI and the news media subjected the FPCC to fairly close inspection. Peter Khiss of *The New York Times* reported that Beals and Waldo Frank served as "honorary co-chairmen" of the organization at its inception in November 1960. These two veteran leftists were sympathetic to the Cuban revolution, as were such other prominent writers as Columbia University sociologist C. Wright Mills, independent journalist I. F. Stone and long-time anti-imperialist Scott Nearing. But none of these founding members had any interest in assisting international assassination plots. J. Edgar Hoover concluded that the FPCC was merely an arm of Cuban propaganda, a designation that probably would not have surprised its members.[58]

George Sokolsky, a conservative columnist for the *New York Journal-American,* attacked the FPCC by citing a letter set by Beals to Robert Taber, one of the founders of the organization. The means through which Sokolsky obtained the letter remains unclear; but in the letter Beals expressed to Taber serious concerns about the independence of FPCC:

Two things I would have to be reassured about: (1) That no Communist is part of the Committee or is asked to become a sponsor. This would blow the whole thing out of the water. (2) That funds are from voluntary contributions and that no money is derived from the Cuban government or their representatives, either directly or indirectly.[59]

Beals did not want this letter to be made public and most certainly not by a conservative like Sokolsky, who used the quotation to imply that the FPCC was a propaganda tool of the Castro regime and that its members were either Communist sympathizers or Communist dupes. Beals, who had been a member of the FPCC for over a year, felt these assertions were incorrect.[60] Beals retained his sincere, if at times impractical and self-injurious, concern about the integrity of left-wing organizations.

In May and June, Beals made his second trip to revolutionary Cuba, a venture that was immensely stimulating for him. Isolated from the hotbeds of the Latin American Left since the mid-1930s, except for a brief visit to Arevalo's Guatemala in 1946, Beals enjoyed the heady atmosphere that prevailed in Havana in 1960. Undoubtedly, he came under the influence of some of the "techniques of hospitality" described by sociologist

Paul Hollander in *Political Pilgrims*. Using this technique, the revolutionary leaders diverted Beals's attention in directions that they preferred.[61] At the time of Beals's arrival, Castro had the support of labor unions; his land reforms brought him the loyalty of peasants; and his massive push in education gave him a solid phalanx among teachers.[62] Beals met people in these three occupations; and even though the meetings were somewhat structured,[63] it reminded him of youthful days in Mexico of the 1920s.[64] In an interview with Waldo Medina of the legal department of INRA (National Agrarian Reform Institute), he confessed to a surge of long-absent enthusiasm: "I feel much younger. I feel rejuvenated. It seems that everything around me is filled with youthful energy."[65]

Beals's first piece on Cuba after his return to Killingworth in early July contained an overly optimistic assessment of Cuba's economic situation and a long list of Cuban complaints about U.S. foreign policy. His utopian version of land redistribution, accompanied by growth in agricultural productivity, told more of Beals's hopes for Cuba than the reality. Nonetheless, his recounting of the Cuban position vis-à-vis the United States was an accurate reflection of the Castro government's point of view, which Beals insisted did not get a fair hearing in the United States. A central issue of the summer of 1960 was Castro's seizure of refineries owned by private oil companies. It was the government's reaction to companies' refusal to refine shipments of Russian crude oil purchased by the Cuban government. Beals admitted that Cuba was "certainly not blameless, according to business standards," but that the burden of blame for the growing rupture in U.S.-Cuban relations lay in Washington. According to Beals, the State and Defense departments quietly, but effectively, punished the island by blocking the sale of military equipment and farm machinery and by allowing Batista exiles to carry on anti-Castro activities from the United States.[66]

Beals's conviction about the always present threat of U.S. intervention found substantial reinforcement in late 1960. In his article "Cuba's Invasion Jitters" in the November 12 issue of *The Nation*, Beals reported that the Castro government was concerned about the buildup in Guatemala of men and equipment for a possible invasion of Cuba. The Castro government was also concerned about the shipment of military aid to "Papa Doc" Duvalier of nearby Haiti and the staging of an incident at Guantanamo to justify a large-scale U.S. invasion.[67] The last two fears were apparently groundless; but the Guatemalan operation, the product of CIA collaboration with pro-Batista Cuban exiles, resulted in the Bay of Pigs disaster in April 1961. While Beals culled his information from Cuban government sources, Ronald Hilton of Stanford University learned of the CIA base on a trip to Guatemala and published his discovery in the *Hispanic American Report*. Carey McWilliams combined these two stories in the November 19, 1960 issue of *The Nation* and editorialized against this "dangerous and hair-brained project" five months before the invasion took place. He also complained of the curious lack of interest in the U.S. press about CIA activity in Guatemala, even though local newspapers and television had revealed the existence of the base.[68] Ironically, President Kennedy voiced a similar complaint about the decision of *The New York Times* only a few days before the actual event, not to publish news of the Bay of Pigs invasion plan. Kennedy felt that such an exposé might have provoked a cancellation of the ill-fated venture.[69] As McWilliams, Beals and Hilton knew, the plot was already exposed; but obviously, not enough people had taken the warning seriously in November 1960. By April 1961, it was conveniently forgotten.

## The Limits of Independent Journalism

When Beals made his second trip to revolutionary Cuba in January 1961, he was still a whole-hearted supporter of the movement. He went as an official of the FPCC and as a representative of Prensa Latina, a Cuban-based press syndicate, that had ambitions of supplying a leftist alternative to Reuters, UPI and AP throughout Latin America. Beals had found only reluctant acceptance in most of the U.S. journalistic and publishing establishments since the 1940s, therefore, Prensa Latina seemed a particularly good opportunity for him to express his ideas to a receptive audience. He wrote at least five articles for Prensa Latina in 1960 and 1961. Each was critical of various aspects of U.S. foreign policy, and one carried a strong warning against presidential candidate John Kennedy, whom Beals saw as simply another cold warrior who would not recognize the validity of the Cuban revolution.[70]

In late March of 1961, Beals began his biggest undertaking since 1946—a fast-paced, six-nation tour as representative of Prensa Latina. This three-month trip was as much a physical as journalistic challenge for Beals, who because of his age (sixty-seven) and his health (he was a chain smoker for most of his life), had limited stamina and often overestimated his ability to deal with the stress of almost constant activity. In a letter to his wife Carolyn dated March 22, he indicated the hectic pace and his own disorientation in Mexico City, a place he knew intimately in the 1920s.

I hardly recognize the city any more and lose my way constantly. It has grown to an abominable size, nearly four million people, and skyscrapers a dime a dozen, the old landmarks destroyed or submerged.
Have not been able to contact any old friends yet, too busy, dazed or weary or something. Monday a big press conference. Tuesday a smaller one. Met the Cuban ambassador, very nice and amusing person. Visited Chapultepec museum. Took in a cabaret night show till very late hour. Very good and more decorous than those in N.Y. This afternoon leave for Guadalajara to talk at the university, back tomorrow morning. Speak at Chapingo Agricultural School tomorrow. Will also speak at Toluca University, perhaps also in Tampico. Will likely leave Sunday for Panama as scheduled.[71]

The Kennedy State Department was aware of Beals's trip for Prensa Latina. A circular to U.S. Latin American diplomatic posts warned of Beals's plans and characterized him as having "close relations with causes opposing U.S. policy interests." It also suggested discrete use of this information, presumably to discredit his statements.[72]

Beals's letter of May 3 contained a cryptic account of another exhausting experience: a whirlwind tour of the Colquiri

tin mine in the Bolivian Andes, whose entrance was approximately 14,000 feet above sea level. A much younger person in
the prime of health would have been staggered by Beals's itin-
erary:

They wisked me off to look at the Fundición, which sprawls up
and down the mountain for about ten stories, and my tongue was
hanging out (while I was) running up and down iron steps: ore
crushers, conveyor belts, more curhsers (sic), grinders, shakers,
sievers, revolving puddles, stirrers, mixers, drying ovens, and the
big hunks of ore end up in 70 percent concentrate, fine as talc,
being bagged by men of mars with snout-like masks.
From there, no chance to rest, I was rushed off, my tongue really
hanging out, to talk to about 500 miners, mostly Aimara Indians,
but they knew the score about everything from Laos to Algiers, the
Congo and the Cuban revolution. Many questions. Lasted till
about eight. When I emerged it was night and freezing cold,—and
the damn place is "dry," not a nip. I was too cold to eat anything,
and the soup, which was good, was nearly cold, so I let that go
by, and settled for bad coffee and doughy bread and butter.[73]

In Chile, the State Department watched Beals's activities.
Although denied permission to speak at the University of Chile
and limited largely to radio addresses, he did relay his messages in a manner "unnecessarily critical of the United States."
The political officer of the embassy in Santiago noted Beals's
assertions that the "Latin American politician sells himself and
his country to imperialism too cheaply" and that land reform
was a prerequisite for economic development in the region.
The report concluded that these words were "the gratuitously
harmful remarks" of "a professional critic of United States policy."[74]

By the time of his arrival in Asunción, Paraguay, Beals was
exhausted and ill. He wrote Carolyn that he had both bron-
chitis and laryngitis; a week later from Sao Paulo, he wrote an
intemperate letter complaining of high prices, poorly laid side-
walks and a foul stench from an incomplete sewer system. In
spite of these discomforts, Beals was cheered by warm recep-
tions at most of his stops. He was in demand as a speaker, and
his audiences (usually university students, workers and intel-

lectuals) responded positively to his defense of the Cuban revolution and his criticisms of the United States.[75]

His return to Killingworth gave him a much needed rest, but it also brought a sudden decision to leave Prensa Latina. On his trip, Beals had worked as writer for the syndicate and was a willing proponent of the Cuban revolution. He had taken the position with Prensa Latina on the assumption that it would provide an independent leftist perspective on the news for the hemisphere; but by June, he was greatly disappointed. Beals seemed to work harmoniously with Jorge Ricardo Masseti, a transplanted Argentine writer, who was head of Prensa Latina when Beals joined in January 1961. As the Castro government moved to the Left, Prensa Latina came under the domination of Communists, who removed Masseti in May or June.[76] The new head of the agency was Fermin Revueltas, a man Beals saw as a heavy-handed editor, who did not understand the virtues of a free-spirited style.

Beals explained his limited relationship with Prensa Latina by telegram to Revueltas in late June. He added a tersely worded note to the explanation later:

Since you are new in your post, you are apparently unaware that you have no right to instruct any correspondent of yours anywhere to clear what I may say or write with your office before it is released. I am not in the emply (sic) of Prensa Latina. I am not a correspondent of Prensa Latina. I am an independent writer who agreed to send you articles for payment, as I am doing to United States and other publications elsewhere in the world. What I write or say is therefore none of your business, and I shall continue to write and say what I consider to be the truth.

In a letter to Sam Shapiro, a Michigan State history professor with an interest in contemporary Cuba, Beals explained his views on the internal politics in Prensa Latina. Beals charged that it had become "Communist lock stock and barrel and has degenerated into a combination censorship bureau (for Cubans) and a propaganda bureau abroad." Beals had hoped that Pensa Latina might become an independent Latin American news agency, but he concluded that under Revueltas's heavy-handed leadership, such independence was impossible. His concern about Communist control of Prensa Latina paralleled his growing worries about Communist influence in Cuba. To Shapiro, he expressed "hope that the CPs (Communists) will moderate their grab for power in Cuba or the whole revolution is going to be wrecked. They are difficult and intransigent people."[78]

Beals next attacked Pensa Latina in a more public forum, the *Independent*, a leftist journal edited by Lyle Stuart. Beals gave his view of the degeneration of Prensa Latina from a promising news agency under Masseti to a narrow Communist propaganda organ under Revueltas. Beals's decision to work for Masseti grew out of his conviction that "international news is at present largely dished out from the point of view of the United States," which was sadly inadequate in explaining the complexities of events in Third World nations. Beals knew that many well-informed Latin Americans distrusted U.S. news coverage of events in Africa, Asia, and the Western Hemisphere. He felt that readers in the United States would benefit from exposure to news from a Latin American viewpoint and that even Washington might be encouraged "to avoid some of its more egregious blunders in Latin America."[79]

A few weeks later, Beals withdrew from FPCC, thereby completing his disassociation from pro-Castro institutions. Richard Gibson of FPCC asked him to reconsider, because "You are too valuable a person to lose because of the stupidities of one man or even a clíque," Gibson argued.[80] His pleas were to no avail.

### Unrelenting Watchdogs

Beals's articles and speeches on Castro's Cuba and his work for Prensa Latina and the FPCC attracted the attention of the FBI. The bureau's office in New Haven assembled a report on Beals in February 1961, in which the agency's informants denied the existence of any formal ties between the reporter and the Communist party, although party leaders suggested to members that he "was to be used as a speaker . . . whenever possible." Apparently the Communist party attempted to place Beals in speaking engagements. In that sense, it used him for their purposes which, in the early 1960s, included an attempt to discredit U.S. policy toward Cuba.[81] Beals did not know of his exploitation by these methods.[82] His earlier statements, however, indicate that the views he expressed were his own and not those foisted on him by the Communist party. One FBI informant described him as an "extremely self-centered (person who) would not have any 'real loyalty' to any cause, including communism."[83] FBI surveillance yielded insufficient evidence to convince Director Hoover to place Beals's name on the agency's list of pro-Cuban subversives.[84]

In the summer of 1961, a few weeks after Beals broke with Prensa Latina and the FPCC, the United States Information Agency Office of Research and Analysis completed a report on him that resembled, in some ways, the accusatory findings of the War Department and the State Department in the 1920s. The USIA document compiled some of Beals's most inflamatory statements from five of his Prensa Latina articles and placed heavy emphasis on an essay by Herminio Portel Vilá in *Bohemia Libre* of February 5, 1961. The Cuban historian, then in exile, wrote with great dismay about the Communists' recent take-over of Prensa Latina. He complained that Beals, "the great liberal North American writer of former years became a firm collaborator." Portel Vilá understood the full meaning of the ouster of Masseti five months before Beals did; however, as soon as Beals recognized the imprint of dogmatic propaganda, he left Prensa Latina. Although Portel Vilá's judgments had validity in February 1961, when they were written, the USIA report was out of date soon after its completion.[85] Beals removed himself as a "collaborator" later the same month.

The USIA sent Hoover a copy of its report on Beals, but it seemed to have little effect on the FBI's inquiry. In early 1962, the special agent in charge of the New Haven office wrote Hoover of his decision not to interview Beals. The agent justified this course on the grounds that it was unlikely that Beals would cooperate. The agent felt that Beals might use the interview as a pretext to criticize the agency and to make "a self-serving statement—for example, that his association with Prensa Latina was that of an independent, objective reporter who sold articles to Prensa Latina."[86]

In spite of the accumulation of information that indicated Beals was not a serious threat to national security, the FBI continued to watch him and to make additions to his file. The quality of the information deteriorated substantially after 1962. One informant concocted a highly imaginary character assessment tinged with right-wing paranoia. The FBI agent wrote that this informant:

Volunteered further information to the effect that the subject is a pervert. ——— ——— this affliction has become worse in recent years. ——— ——— In the past subject has maintained contacts with other perverts who were "left-wing" writers. ——— ——— of the opinion that many of his "bad" associations resulted from this weakness on his part.[87]

In 1964, the FBI found an informant who gave a more realistic picture of Beals as living a quiet, sedentary life with few personal contacts, even in the local community. According to this source, Beals "remains at home most of the time . . . devoting time to his writing." The New Haven special agent in charge observed that Beals was "an old man now," who had become "somewhat of a recluse in his declining years and devotes most of his time on (sic) his farm in Killingworth to his writings and seldom leaves the area."[88] At seventy and in semiretirement, Beals finally moved beyond the purview of government agents, which ended a mutually acrimonious relations that lasted forty-six years.

In the two decades after World War II, Beals experienced both the depths of professional frustration and the heights of personal adulation. He was unable to find an editor who consistently would accept his left-wing commentary on inter-American relations because of the paranoia produced by congressional witchhunts and McCarthyite extremism during this decade. In the late 1950s, the fall of Batista and the rise of Castro brought Cuba and the rest of Latin America back to the center of journalistic attention. Beals's colleague and friend

Carey McWilliams of *The Nation* called on the veteran Latin Americanist for coverage of the quickly changing Cuban scene. Obviously swayed by his friendly reception in revolutionary Havana, Beals penned a dozen articles on Cuba in the early 1960s. Although he remained a defender of the Cuban revolution, his aversion to hardline Marxism led him to leave the Cuban-controlled Prensa Latina and the ill-fated Fair Play for Cuba Committee. Through his triumphs and tribulations, the FBI maintained a watchful eye on Beals's activities and examined his past. In spite of his leftist beliefs, the bureau concluded that Beals had no significant ties with the Communist party or any other radical organization. Retired in Connecticut, Beals remained isolated from all organizations and institutions, whether Left or Right, much as he had in his youth and middle age.

# An Assessment

Carleton Beals died on June 26, 1979, as the result of complications from an abdominal operation.[1] Most of the last fifteen years of his life were spent in the calm of his study in Killingworth. In the 1960s, through the help of his loyal agent Bertha Klausner, he found publishers for seven books, the majority of which were in the field of popular history.[2] He also worked on a detailed autobiography in which he gave extensive attention to his childhood years in California.[3] After 1970, he was unable to locate a publisher for his writing, in spite of the valiant efforts and frequent encouragement of Klausner.

To characterize these years as a time of withdrawal and depression for Beals would be wrong. He and Carolyn enjoyed life, and each other, on their small farm. She was a vigorous woman, who continued to care for her animals and, when necessary, her husband. Although he gave up horseback riding in these years, he developed affectionate relationships with other members of their menagerie, especially a large, gray, male cat named Smokey.[4] The imperious feline established the study as *his* territory by driving away other pet pretenders and often aided Beals in his writing by leaping on to the author's large desk to assist in the turning of pages, the moving of pencils or perhaps the typing of a manuscript. When Beals took a siesta on a small bed in the study, the helpful Smokey would take a position on the slumberer's stomach or back (depending upon which was most available) and proceed to knead the area enthusiastically until it was properly arranged for a catnap. Beals regarded Smokey as a welcome companion and laughed at these frequent interruptions.

Beals followed news events in the 1960s and 1970s through newspapers, magazines and radio—but not television. Unlike most leftists, he had little confidence in President John F. Kennedy's ability to lead the nation to a better future. The image of youthful idealism did not convince Beals that the Massachusetts-born president could overcome the legacy of family wealth and the elitism to become a proponent of democratic reform at home and abroad of the east-coast establishment. Like most leftists, however, he was highly critical of U.S. involvement in Vietnam and found amusement and satisfaction in Richard Nixon's fatally inept handling of Watergate. Although Beals found few heroes in positions of responsibility and power in the world of the 1960s and 1970s, he saw some sparks of hope in the tumult that surrounded the war protesters and civil rights demonstrators in the U.S. and the peasant and worker movements in Latin America. These groups which touched his populist sentiments, seemed to offer some possibility for the betterment of the human condition.

In 1963, Beals found publishers for a book that, if nothing else, reaffirmed his basic ideological stance. *Latin America: World in Revolution* was one of the earliest condemnations of Kennedy's Alliance for Progress. Beals saw the highly-touted alliance merely as camouflage for the creation of a capitalist Western Hemisphere that would surround and isolate Castro's leftist government in Cuba. Lashing out against the liberal establishment once more, Beals criticized Kennedy and his advisors as "arrant romantics" who hoped to build an international economic system that the Latin American nations could not afford to tolerate.[5]

Such charges against a U.S. president were typical of the remarks Beals made in his half century as a journalist, during which he wrote 34 books and over 200 articles. With publication of *Rome or Death* and *Mexico: An Interpretation* in 1923 Beals won the recognition of other writers, book critics and editors as an important and controversial journalist. His most audacious reporting was the Sandino interview, which solidified his reputation as an advocate of leftist causes. His best-selling effort was *The Coming Struggle for Latin America*, which attracted a broad spectrum of readers because of widespread fears of totalitarian penetration of the Americas on the eve of World War II. Beals's highest achievement in terms of his own preferences in style and content was probably *Mexican Maze* (1931). Indulging his predilection for effusive, colorful prose, Beals conveyed his deep feelings for Mexico, its people and its revolution, which at the time of writing, was floundering. He was in full command of his talents for observation and description. Beals used the book to present his ideal of the revolution as a vehicle for the liberation of the common people and his critique of the Mexican government's failure to pursue this goal.

Beals's decline as a professional journalist in the late 1940s and early 1950s, however, was not the result of his authorial idiosyncracies, but rather grew out of the oppressive intellectual atmosphere of the "Second Red Scare." Carey McWilliams, as editor of *The Nation*, worked closely with Beals in the 1950s and was aware of the effects of these forces on his colleague. McWilliams saw Beals as an intuitive writer, who produced his stories quickly and who, at times, was "a rather slapdash journalist as were many of his generation." Beals's impressionistic style and his "slapdash" methods disconcerted many of his critics, who failed (or refused) to see his strong points. Mc Williams, however, saw through these surface defects and rated Beals highly as a journalist whose "sharp insights" produced conclusions that were "generally right." The editor of *The Nation* "thought of (Beals) as a fine journalist and valued contributor and as a good friend." McWilliams insisted that Beals's articles on Sandino and on the early phases of Castro's revolution were of Pulitzer Prize quality, although they did not gain recognition as such. According to McWilliams, "probably the key factor" in explaining Beals's troubles in the late 1940s and early 1950s was "the repressive atmosphere of those years."[6]

Neither hostile critics nor friendly editors fully appreciated what Beals attempted to do through most of his half-century in journalism. Beals was one of the first U.S. writers to report on a vital area in what is now called the Third World. His commentaries faced two major barriers: public ignorance of and indifference to the region he covered and public hostility towards his ideological perspective. While tumultuous Mexico was in the headlines in the 1920s, Beals's work on Mexico was in demand. As public interest in Nicaragua and Cuba peaked in the late 1920s and early 1930s, Beals found ready acceptance for his manuscripts. While the United States and totalitarian powers vied for influence in Latin America, he had wide recognition as an expert on the foreign rivalry within the region. His fundamental assumptions, however, that revolution by the masses was the best way to social justice in some countries and that the United States was guilty of heartless, self-serving imperialism did not find a popular reception in a reading public that accepted a middle-class value system, including an aversion to news of such unpleasantness from foreign lands.[7] Beals's attempt to bridge the chasm between the relatively affluent United States and what is now called the Third World was a thankless task; yet, his bullheaded determination and left-wing ideals held him to his chosen path, in spite of its obvious pitfalls.

The leftist populism that Beals espoused consistently throughout his life had its origins in the United States. Beals's identification with Eugene V. Debs, the hero of his youth, and with the rural, western socialism of his parents had a lasting impact on his values and ideas. His enjoyment of the Bohemian life in Mexico City in the 1920s, his sensitivity to peasant life, his frequent allusions to peasant art, to the spontaneous, to the rhythmical, and to the mystical marked him as a member of what John P. Diggins has called the Lyrical Left.[8] The confrontations with Borodin, Trotsky and Prensa Latina revealed Beals's profound aversion to the rigidities of dogmatic Marxism. Beals was a radical with the ethos of small-town America (Medicine Lodge, Pasadena and Berkeley) who followed the tradition set by Emerson, Debs and Reed. His use of leftist populism to explain revolution and imperialism in Latin America was probably the first application of this intellectual tradition as an analytical framework in which to study realities and issues of the Third World.

Although a supporter of revolutionary movements in Latin America, Beals was willing to criticize them when he saw an apparent dereliction of purpose. Unlike Paul Hollander's political pilgrims, Beals quickly developed a facility for critical evaluation of the revolution. His criticisms of the Mexican revolution between 1927 and 1934 irritated governmental authorities and, in part, caused his arrest and brief incarceration by the Mexican military. The Cárdenas administration restored his faith in the revolution; but subsequent Mexican leaders' fascination with economic growth at the expense of social reform, again, prompted him to fault government policies. Although Castro's revolution initially swept up Beals along with a phalanx of other leftist intellectuals, he also expressed doubts about Fidel's personal stability. Eventually, Beals quit Prensa Latina because of its excessive devotion to Marxist rigidities. Beals was enraptured by the radical promise of Mexico and Nicaragua in the 1920s, Guatemala in the 1940s and Cuba in the 1960s captivated Beals; but he quickly passed beyond the point of unquestioning devotion—and much earlier than Hollander's implicit model for "political pilgrims."[9]

Beals's issue-oriented style of journalism gave him a perspective on Latin America that resembled the approach followed by many students of Third World nations in the 1960s and 1970s. His study of social change led him to question the effects of "development" or "modernization."[10] His espousal of anti-imperialism placed him close to such leftists as Parker Moon, Scott Nearing and Joseph Freeman, who were the intellectual predecessors of the pro-Cuban and pro-North Vietnamese writers of the 1960s and 1970s. Without too much exaggeration, Beals and his contemporaries would claim to have "discovered the Third World" in the 1920s through their identification of the basic issues that underline the questions of the effect of socio-economic change is this region. These are still the core issues that dominate debates about the consequences of modernization in the developing nations and the relationship between these nations and the more industrialized countries. Of course, Beals and his colleagues did not use the vocabulary of post-World War II social science; their research often lacked scholarly breadth and depth; they were, however, pioneers. The cumulative effect of their writings formed the first stage in the building of the conceptual framework used by later generations of experts in Third World studies.[11]

The impact of Beals's many books and articles is difficult to gauge. The most definite example of his influence is documented in the files of the State Department. In the 1920s Beals's defense of the Mexican revolution and the Sandinista cause in Nicaragua excited cries of consternation, and even alarm, from the Coolidge administration's diplomats. By the end of the decade, U.S. Ambassador Dwight Morrow understood Beals's importance as did Josephus Daniels in the 1930s. In 1931, the State Department warned the Mexican government of the potential harm in Beals's arrest because of his reputation as an expert on Mexican affairs, and because of his profession as a writer for journals of liberal opinion in the United States. During his Latin American trip for Prensa Latina in 1961, the USIA found his articles and speeches too radical for the best interests of the United States. Officials in Washington for nearly five decades regarded him as a leading, although hostile, commentator on Latin America.

Moreover, Beals appealed to another audience: Latin American intellectuals and politicians, who saw him as an insightful and therefore important, political and social critic. It was his literary approach to journalism, however, as well as his ideas that garnered Beals praise in private letters and published reviews from such intellectuals as Mexicans Luis Quintanilla and Isidro Fabela, Costa Ricans Vicente Sáenz and Joaquín García Monje, Peruvians Luis Alberto Sanchez and Ciro Alegría, and Cubans Fernando Ortíz, Jorge Manach and Mario Llerena. Latin American politicians were typically more interested in content than in style. Leftists like Haya de la Torre of Peru and Juan José Arevalo of Guatemala were receptive to Beals's simpatico writing, but high officials in Mexico in the Calles years were disturbed by his criticism of their government. Although many of these people read his work in English, at least eight of Beals's books were translated into Spanish and marketed in Latin America, which broadened the impact of his writing.[12] Whether they were in accord with his basic conclusions or not, these Latin American political and intellectual leaders recognized Beals as an influential commentator on hemispheric affairs.

If Beals had a primary target, it was the reading public of the United States. Intellectuals in his homeland usually saw him as a dedicated leftist defender of revolution and anti-imperialism in Latin America. It seems reasonable to assert that although Beals reached a considerable audience, both friendly and unfriendly, through the publication of his numerous articles in and the review of his book by *The Nation, New Republic, Current History* and similar magazines, his influence on the larger reading public was not as great. His two "best-sellers" *The Coming Struggle for Latin America* and *Dawn Over the Amazon* contained few references to imperialism and revolution, although these were the subjects of paramount interest in most of his work. Probably Beals's typical readers were intellectuals, politicians, government officials, academics and businessmen who had some connection with Latin America. While these people were influential in their own fields, they were not numerous enough to keep Beals's name on the best-seller list for any length of time.

Always the romantic leftist, Beals seemed to carry individualism to the extreme. His inability to tolerate bureaucratic encumbrances ruled out employment in business, academics and publishing. His rejection of any impingement on his ideological commitments earned him enemies, even among liberals and leftists. These spirited assertions left him isolated from old friends and large institutions. In his own intense and well-meaning way, he alienated himself from others for the sake of his perception of ideological purity and personal integrity.

His critical dissent was usually lonely, but it served a purpose well within the democratic traditions of the United States. Beals was a secular prophet who challenged middle-class comfort and conformity with the disturbing reminder that most of the people in the western hemisphere did not fit into the bourgeois mold. His singular advocacy of the legitimacy of revolution and the illegitimacy of imperialism constituted a personal campaign against the expansionist, business-oriented, materialistic, and individualistic society that he rejected. Yet, through his commitment to left-wing populism, Beals exemplified the uncompromising individualism he often decried.

# Abbreviations

| | |
|---|---|
| AGN | Archivo General de la Nación, Mexico City. |
| AREM | Archivo de la Secretaría de Relaciones Exteriores de México, Mexico City. |
| CBC | Carleton Beals Collection in the Special Collections Division of the Mugar Memorial Library, Boston University, Boston, Massachusetts. (All citations are from the personal correspondence section unless otherwise noted.) |
| CB Interview | Author's interviews with Carleton Beals in Killingworth, Connecticut, 1973 |
| DS | Records of the United States Department of State in the National Archives, Washington, D.C. |
| FBI | Records of the Federal Bureau of Investigation, Washington, D.C. |
| WD-MID | Records of the United States War Department, Military Intelligence Division in the National Archives, Washington, D.C. |
| RB Interview | Author's interview with Ralph Beals, Los Angeles, Ca., 1975. |

# Notes

**Chapter 1**

1. Carleton Beals, *Banana Gold* (Philadelphia, 1932), 264–267 and Neill Macauley, *The Sandino Affair* (Chicago, 1967), 106–107.

2. Among the many histories of twentieth century United States-Latin American relations are: Cole Blaiser, *The Hovering Giant* (Pittsburgh, 1976); Gordon Connell-Smith, *The United States and Latin America* (New York, 1974); and Frederico Gil, *Latin American-United States Relations* (New York, 1971).

Interpretive studies in this field include Alonso Aguilar, *Pan-Americanism from Monroe to the Present* (New York, 1968); Samuel Flagg Bemis, *The Latin American Policy of the United States* (New York, 1943); Isidro Fabela, *Buena y mala vecindad* (Mexico, 1958); Pablo González Casanova, *Imperialismo y liberación* (Mexico, 1978); Dexter Perkins, *A History of the Monroe Doctrine* (Boston, 1955); and Gregorio Selser, *Diplomacia, garrote y dolares en America Latina* (Buenos Aires, 1962).

3. Two general surveys of the mass media in the United States are George N. Gordon, *The Communications Revolution* (New York, 1977) and Edwin Emery, *The Press in America* (Englewood Cliffs, 1972). The few studies on the work of the American press in foreign countries include Philip Knightly, *The First Casualty* (New York, 1975); two books by John Hohenberg, *Foreign Correspondence* (New York, 1964) and *Between Two Worlds* (New York, 1967); and Mort Rosenblum, *Coups and Earthquakes: Reporting the World for America* (New York, 1979).

An important synthesis of the role of journalism as a facet of United States relations with the Third World is Emily Rosenberg, *Spreading the American Dream* (New York, 1981). For an excellent study of journalists' (and other writers') views of the Mexican revolution see Eugenia Meyer, *Conciencia historica norteamericana sobre la revolución de 1910* (Mexico, 1970). Three studies that emphasize the narrow, ethnocentric perspective of U.S. media coverage of the Third World are Anthony Smith, *The Geopolitics of Information* (New York, 1980), Camilo Taufic, *Periodismo y lucha de clases* (Buenos Aires, 1974); and Jeremy Tunstall, *The Media Are American: Anglo-American Media and the World* (London, 1977).

4. Smith, *Geopolitics*, 19–28.

5. Paul Hollander, *Political Pilgrims* (New York, 1981).

6. CB Interview, January 1973; Leon Beals obituary, Berkeley *Daily Gazette*, Oct. 6, 1941; Kansas State Historical Society, *History of Kansas Newspapers* (Topeka, 1916), 104; William F. Zornow, *Kansas: A History of the Jayhawk State* (Norman, Okla., 1957), 204; and Raymond C. Miller, "The Populist Party in Kansas" (Ph.D. diss., University of Chicago, 1928), 39–40, 141–142.

7. Leon Beals obituary, and CB Interview, January, 1973.

8. CB Interview, January, 1973.

9. *Ibid.*

10. RB Interview, July, 1975. On the Socialist Party in California, see Royce Delmatier, Clarence McIntosh and Earl G. Waters eds., *The Rumble of California Politics* (New York, 1970), 178–181.

11. CB Interview, January, 1973.

12. *Ibid.*

13. *Ibid.* and Carl Blick Beals, Application for Admission to the University of California, June 9, 1911, Office of Admissions and Records, Berkeley.

14. CB Interview, January, 1973.

15. Verne E. Stadtman, *The University of California, 1868–1968* (New York, 1970), 186–193.

16. CB Interview, January, 1973.

17. Carleton Beals, University of California transcript, Office of Admissions and Records.

18. CB Interview, January, 1973 and "James Bryce Historical Essay Prize," a list of prize winners in the university archives, Bancroft Library, Berkeley; and James Sutton to C. Beals, May 17,

1916, CBC. Unfortunately, a copy of Beals's prize-winning essay did not survive.

19. *Blue and Gold* (University of California Annual), (1917): 81.

20. CB Interview, January, 1973, and Robert Sproul (University assistant comptroller) to Whom it may concern, August 31, 1916, CBC.

21. CB Interview, January, 1973.

22. Carleton Beals, "The Old Alma Mater," *Student Opinion*, (March 6, 1915): 2, 8.

23. Carleton Beals, "The American Intellectual Declaration of Independence," *Student Opinion*, (August 31, 1915): 5, 7.

24. CB Interview, January, 1973, and RB Interview, July 6, 1975. See also Carl B. Beals, "The Self-Sufficient City State" (Master's thesis, Columbia University, 1917), 2–3.

25. Donald Johnson, *The Challenge to American Freedoms* (Lexington, 1963), 30–34. See also Paul L. Murphy, *World War I and the Origin of Civil Liberties in the United States* (New York, 1979).

26. M. Hon. M. Johnson to C. Beals, June 15, 1917, CBC.

27. "The Account of the Case of Mr. Carl Beals," December 29, 1917, CBC.

28. *Berkeley Daily Gazette*, August 11, 1917, 1.

29. "The Account . . .," " CBC.

29. New York City Local Exemption Board No. 135, to Carleton Beals, Telegram, December 13, 1917, CBC.

30. "The Account . . .," " CBC.

31. Local Board No. 135 to Beals, Telegram, December 22, 1917, CBC.

32. Roger Baldwin to Elvina Beals, Telegrams December 27, 1917, and December 29, 1917, both in CBC.

33. Johnson, *Challenge to American Freedoms*, 30–34.

34. "The Account . . .," " CBC. Positivism, as Beals understood it, called for a dedication to the rational study of humanity as the means to study civilization's problems. Obviously, war represented the ultimate degradation of human life and posed the most serious problem for the Positivists.

35. CB Interview, January, 1973.

36. Report on Carleton Beals, September 1, 1953, FBI.

37. Johnson, *Challenge*, 34–54.

38. Nick Salvatore, *Eugene V. Debs, Citizen and Socialist* (Urbana, 1982), 342–343. See also 220–242.

39. CB Interview, January, 1973.

40. Salvatore, *Debs*, 292–302, 317–328.

## Chapter 2

1. For general discussions of the revolution's early years, see Ramón Eduardo Ruiz, *The Great Rebellion: Mexico, 1905–1924* (New York, 1980); Alvaro Matute, *La carrera del caudillo* (Mexico, 1980); Linda Hall, *Alvaro Obregón* (College Station, Texas, 1981); and William Weber Johnson, *Heroic Mexico* (Garden City, N. Y., 1968).

2. CB Interview, June-July, 1973. RB Interview, July 6, 1975, and Carleton Beals, *Brimstone and Chili* (New York, 1927).

3. Beals, *Brimstone*, 287–297 and CB Interview, June-July, 1973.

4. *Brimstone*, 292–297, 302–304.

5. Ibid., 319. For a slightly different version of the "English Institute" see Carleton Beals, *Glass Houses* (Philadelphia, 1938), 16.

6. *Brimstone*, 324 and Carleton Beals, *Mexico: An Interpretation* (New York, 1923), 228–229.

7. CB Interview and *Brimstone*, 325–326.

8. Quote from *Brimstone*, 326. See also *Glass Houses*, 22–23.

9. *Glass Houses*, 31–35.

10. *Brimstone*, 328–329.

11. Ibid., 289–291.

12. Ibid., 313–315.

13. Ibid., 323–329.

14. Ferris to Secretary of State, September 15, 1920. WD-MID, 1917–1941, 10058–0–20 and Report on C. Beals, September 1, 1953, FBI. They may have been engaged before Carleton went to Mexico. Beals to Mother, May 1924, CBC.

15. Undated memorandum, WD-MID, 10516–533–30.

16. Beals, *Glass Houses*, 71.

17. Ferris to Secretary of State, September 15, 1920, WD-MID, 10058–0–20. For an investigation of Haberman made by U.S. Department of Labor, see Robe Carl White to Frank B. Kellogg, August 27, 1926, DS 812.20211/38. For another view of this group, see Pablo González Casanova, *La clase obrera en la historia de México en el primer govierno constitucional (1917–1920)*, (Mexico, 1981), 139–205.

18. Ferris to Secretary of State, September 15, 1920, WD-MID, 1917–1941, 10038–0–20. (Newspaper clipping and abridged translation of article attached.)

19. CB Interview, June-July, 1973.

20. *Glass Houses*, 49–53.

21. *Ibid.*, 43–44.

22. Typed copy of an article from *Gales' Magazine* attached to Ferris to Secretary of State, September 15, 1920, WD-MID, 1917–1941, 10058–0–20.

23. *Glass Houses*, 50. For an account of the Communist party in Mexico, see Karl Schmitt, *Communism in Mexico* (Austin, 1965), 4–7.

24. Beals, *Glass Houses*, 35–37.

25. Report from Barcelona to MID, December 28, 1920, WD-MID, 1917–1941, 10058–928.

26. W. L. Hurley to General Douglas-Nolan, September 30, 1920, and John M. Dunn to W. L. Hurley, October 5, 1920, both in WD-MID, 1917–1941, 10058–0–02; and Beals, *Glass Houses*, 75–76.

27. *Brimstone and Chili.*

28. Weeks to Beals, April 3, 1920, CBC.

29. *Current History*, 12 (May 1920): 355–356. The other two articles were "Mexico Changes Its President," *North American Review*, 212 (August 1920): 168–180 and "Mexico Is Also Going Dry—But Slowly," *World Outlook* (September 1920): 4–5. Relevant correspondence includes: Marjorie Barstow Greenkie to Beals, April 10, 1920, and Adelaide Lyons to Beals, July 12, 1920, both in CBC.

30. CB Interview, June-July, 1973. For rejection notice, see Ernest Gruening to Beals, May 29, 1920, CBC.

31. "Mexico Is Also Going Dry . . . " and "The Status of Prohibition in Mexico," *Current History*, 12 (May, 1923), 355–35.

32. "The Mexican as He Is," *North American Review*, 214 (October 1920), 338–546.

33. Eugenia Meyer, *Conciencia Historica norteamericana sobre la revolución de 1910* (Mexico, 1970), 46–47 and John Reed, *Insurgent Mexico* (Introduction by James Wilkie.) (1914; reprint New York, 1969).

34. Harry H. Stern, "Lincoln Steffens in Mexico," *American Journal of Economics and Sociology* 34 (April 1975): 197–212 Justin Kaplan, *Lincoln Steffens* (New York, 1974), 196–213 and Lincoln Steffens, *Autobiography of Lincoln Steffens* (New York, 1931), 724–731.

35. On Reed in Russia, see Theodore Draper, *The Roots of American Communism* (New York, 1957), 282–293; Robert A. Rosenstone, *Romantic Revolutionary* (New York, 1975), 357–382 and John P. Dig-

gins, *The American Left in the Twentieth Century* (New York, 1973), 96–100.

36. John Kenneth Turner, *Barbarous Mexico* (Introduction by Sinclair Snow) (1911; reprint, Austin, 1969); Meyer, *Conciencia*, 30–32, 49, 54–55, 67–74 and Diana Christopulous, "American Radicals and the Mexican Revolution, 1900–1925" (Ph.D. diss., State University of New York at Binghamton, 1980), 71–132, 219–222, 254–277, 327–329 and 402–406; and Ethel Duffy Turner, *Revolution in Baja California* (Detroit, 1981). See also Beals, *Interpretation*, 45.

37. "Mexico Changes Its President" *North American Review* 212, (August 1920) 168–180 and *Glass Houses*, 58–64.

38. Ferris to Secretary of State, September 15, 1920, WD-MID, 10058-0-20.

39. Christopher Lasch, *The New Radicalism in America, 1889–1963* (New York, 1965), 256.

40. *Glass Houses*, 94. For the European background in the 1920s, see George Lichtheim, *Europe in the Twentieth Century* (New York, 1972), 118–164. On Mussolini's Italy, see Dennis Mack Smith, *Mussolini* (New York, 1982).

41. Beals to Mother, August 1921, CBC. The end of the marriage is discussed in Chapter 3.

42. *Glass Houses*, 109.

43. *Ibid.*, 172.

44. Beals to Mother, August 1921, CBC.

45. John P. Diggins, *Mussolini and Fascism: The View from America* (Princeton, 1972), 42–57.

46. Beals, *Rome or Death*, 310–314, 337–341.

47. *Rome or Death*, 254–255 and Diggins, *Mussolini and Fascism*, 53. Over a decade later, George Seldes condemned Mussolini in greater detail in *Sawdust Caesar* (New York, 1935). Beals expanded his criticisms of Mussolini in 1938 in *Glass Houses*, 159–160. For Steffens's view of Mussolini, see Steffens, *Autobiography*, 808–837.


## Chapter 3

1. On the Wilsonian view of revolution, see Robert Freeman Smith, *The United States and Revolutionary Nationalism in Mexico, 1916–1932* (Chicago, 1972) and N. Gordon Levin, *Woodrow Wilson and World Politics: America's Response to War and Revolution* (New York, 1968).

2. *American Left*, 88–106.

3. Documents on the divorce are Beals to Mother, May 1924, CBC and Report on Carleton Beals, September 1, 1953, FBI.

Porter's story "That Tree" appeared first in *Virginia Quarterly Review* 10 (July, 1934): 351–361 and was reprinted in revised form in *The Collected Stories of Katherine Anne Porter* (New York, 1965), 66–79. Porter made the revisions of the original in 1935 for publication in *Flowering Judas* (New York, 1935), a collection of short stories.

4. Lupe? to Beals, Dec. 16, 1924; Mercedes Modotti to Beals, Jan. 6, Dec. 23, 1926, and two undated letters, Angie? to Carleton, Sept. 16 and Oct. 28, 1926 all in CBC. See also *Glass Houses*, 243, and Photographs in CBC.

5. *Glass Houses*, 179, 184–185.

6. For a moderate statement on the revolutionary nature of the revolution, see Michael Meyer and William Sherman, *The Course of Mexican History* (New York, 1983). José Manuel Puig Casauranc, *El Sentido social del proceso historico de México* (México, 1936) gives a progovernment perspective from one of the leading political figures of the 1920s. Also relevant are Victor Alba, *Las ideas sociales contemporaneas en México* (Mexico, 1960) and Pablo González Casanova, *La clase obrera en la historia de México en el primer gobierno constitucional: (1917–1920):* (Mexico, 1980).

On the growing doubts about the meaning of the revolution, see Arnaldo Córdova, *La ideología de la Revolutión Mexicana* (Mexico, 1967); Ramon Eduardo Ruiz, *The Great Rebellion: Mexico, 1905–1924* (New York, 1980); Mary Kay Vaughan, *The State, Education and Social Class in Mexico, 1880–1928* (DeKalb, 1982); and Richard Tardanico, "State, Dependency and Nationalism: Revolutionary Mexico, 1924–1928," *Comparative Studies in Society and History*, 24 (July 1982): 400–423.

Three valuable studies of U.S. intellectuals' perceptions on the revolution are Eugenia Meyer, *Conciencia histórica norteamericana sobre la Revolución de 1910* (Mexico, 1970); Donald Zelman, "American Intellectual Attitudes Toward Mexico" (Ph.D. diss., Ohio State University, 1969); and Diana Christopulus, "American Radicals and the Mexican Revolution, 1900–1925" (Ph.D. diss., State University of New York at Binghamton, 1980). Meyer identified a "new current" in U.S. intellectuals' growing sympathy toward the Mexican revolution as eaily as 1918 (see *Conciencia*, 67–124). Beals, Gruening and Tannenbaum continued the tendency to reject presumptions about the futility of the revolution commonly held by U.S. observers and began to point out many positive reforms that Mexico's leaders had implemented in the 1920s.

7. Bertram Wolfe, *A Life in Two Centuries* (New York, 1981), 276–359; Ella Wolfe Phonotapes, Bertram Wolfe Collection, Hoover Institution, Stanford University; Ella Wolfe interview with author, July 24, 1984; Beals to Ella Wolfe, July 10, 1925 and Ella Wolfe to Beals, July 20, 1925, both in CBC.

8. *Glass Houses*, 257.

9. For example, see Herbert Croly, "The Way Out of the Mexican Muddle," *New Republic* 49 (Jan. 19, 1927): 234–235; "The Imperialist as Snob," *New Republic* 49 (Feb. 9, 1927): 314–316; and "Mexico and the United States," *New Republic,* 50 (March 30, 1927): 159–164.

10. Ernest Gruening, *Mexico and Its Heritage* (New York, 1928), ix and CB Interview, June-July, 1973.

11. CB Interview, June-July, 1973.

12. *Glass Houses*, 245. For examples of Gold's writing, see the *New Masses* in 1926.

13. George D. Beelen, "Harding and Mexico: Diplomacy by Diplomatic Persuasion," (Ph.D. diss., Kent State University, 1971), 51–55 and Beals to Tannenbaum, Dec. 9, 1923, Frank Tannenbaum Papers, Columbia University, New York.

14. Frank Tannenbaum, *The Balance of Power in Society,* Introduction by John Herman Randall (London, 1969), x–xi and Idem., *Wall Shadows: A Study of American Prisons* (New York, 1922).

15. Beals to Mother, October 5, 1921, CBC.

16. Huebsch to Beals, December 18, 1922, CBC.

17. *Interpretation,* 151–161.

18. *Ibid.,* 69–144.

19. James G. McDonald Book Review, *New Republic* 40 (Oct. 29, 1922): 231.

20. Ernest Gruening Book Review, *The Nation* 112 (December 5, 1923): 660. See also Frank Tannenbaum Book Review *Survey* 52 (May 15, 1924): 251.

21. The author purchased Murray's annotated copy of *Mexico: An Interpretation* in the Strand Book Store in New York City in the summer of 1973. The book contains Murray's signature on the title page and many hand written comments, probably dating from 1925, by Murray. 61 and 111.

22. *Glass Houses*, 190 and CB Interview, June-July, 1973.

23. CB Interview, June-July, 1973, and *Glass Houses,* 172.

24. Quote from Beals, "The Obregón Regime," *Survey* 52 (May 1, 1924): 135–137, 188–189. See also Beals, "Mexico's New Era of Peace," *Current History,* 20 (August 1924): 720–725.

25. *Glass Houses,* 57 and CB Interview, June-July, 1973.

26. CB Interview, June-July, 1973.

27. On Morones in the 1920s, see Enrique Krauze, Jean Meyer and Cayetano Reyes, *La reconstructión económica* (Mexico, 1977), 183–199 and Barry Carr, *El movimiento obrero y la política en México, 1910–1929* (Mexico, 1976): 29–63.

28. *Glass Houses,* 195–196. Beals did not name Morones as the labor leader in *Glass Houses* but confirmed his identity in CB Interview, June-July, 1973. For a different version of the same event, see José Vasconcelos, *El Desastre* (Mexico City, 1968), 180–181.

29. For example, on Gruening, see Soledad González to Arturo M. Elías, Feb. 24, 1925, and Manuel Tellez to Soledad González, Dec. 1, 1926, both in AGN, Ramo Obregón-Calles, 104–A–36. On the work of the Mexican Press Agency, see Francisco Benavides to Calles, Oct. 28, 1927, AGN, Ramo Obregón-Calles, 721–I–6.

There are numerous examples of the Mexican Ministry of Foreign Relations interest in the U.S. press (mainly newspapers) in AREM 628 (010/l L–E–554–1 and AREM 628 (010/1 L–E–552–2).

For a perceptive assessment of the Calles government's policies towards the United States and its concern with U.S. press opinion, see Christopher Jay McMullen, "Calles and the Diplomacy of Revolution: Mexican-American Diplomatic Relations, 1924–1928" (Ph.D. diss., Georgetown University, 1980).

30. *Mexican Maze* especially 107–128. Quotation from 122–123.

31. *Interpretation,* 113–114.

32. Beals, "Tasks Awaiting President Calles," *Current History,* 21 (Feb. 1925): 681–682.

33. Beals, "Has Mexico Betrayed Her Revolution?" *New Republic* 67 (July 22, 1931): 249–258. Beals did not discuss land reform in *Mexican Maze,* an indication of his aversion to what he considered the central issue of the revolution in the 1920s. For a comparable assessment of land reform under Calles, see Enrique Krauze, Jean Meyer and Cayetano Reyes, *La reconstrucción economica* (Mexico, 1977), 107–182 and Hans-Werner Tobler, "Las paradojas del ejército revolucionario: su papel social en la reforma agraria mexicana, 1920–1935" *Historia Mexicana* 21 (Julio-Septiembre 1971): 38–79.

34. Croly to Beals, January 20, 1927, CBC; and Beals, "Whose Property is Kellogg Protecting," *New Republic* 50 (February 23, 1927): 8–11.

35. Croly to Beals, February 3, 1927, CBC.

36. On the history of church-state relations in Mexico, see J. Lloyd Mecham, *Church and State in Latin America* (Chapel Hill, 1966), Chap. 15–16; Robert Quirk, *The Mexican Revolution and the Catholic Church* (Bloomington, 1973) and Alicia Olivera Sedano, *Aspectos del conflicto religioso de 1926 a 1929* (Mexico, 1966).

37. Beals, "The Mexican Church on Trial," *Survey* 57 (Oct. 1, 1926): 12–15, 47–49.

38. Croly to Beals, March 18 and idem., March 30, 1927, CBC.

39. Beals to Croly, June 23, 1927, CBC.

40. Beals, "Civil War in Mexico," *New Republic* 51 (July 6, 1927): 166–169.

41. Beals, "Whither Mexico," *New Republic* 53 (December, 1927): 133–135.

42. Boletín 163 de la Agencia Mexicana de Prensa, AGN, Ramo Obregón-Calles, 721–I–6.

43. CB Interview June-July, 1973 and Oficina del Presidente en el Palacio Nacional to Beals, June 18, 1924, AGN, Ramo Obregón-Calles, 728–M–28.

44. On the split between Calles and Obregón, see Rafael Loyola Díaz, *La crisis Obregón-Calles y el estado mexicano* (Mexico, 1980).

45. Beals to Croly, Sept. 27, 1927; Croly to Beals, Nov. 7 and Idem., Dec. 12, 1927; and Rublee to Beals, Nov. 2, 1927, all in CBC. Quotation from Beals, *Glass Houses*, 266–267. Among many accounts of the *modus vivendi*, see Quirk, *Mexican Revolution and the Catholic Church*, 215–247.

46. Meyer, *La cristiada.*

47. Gruening to Beals, Nov. 16, 1923, Dec. ?, 1923 and Jan. 24, 1924, all in CBC. Review in *The National* 117 (Dec. 5, 1923): 660; and Gruening, *Mexico and Its Heritage* (New York, 1928).

48. Beals to Tannenbaum, n.d.; Idem., June 25, 1928; and Tannenbaum to Beals, July 25, 1928, all in Frank Tannenbaum Papers, Columbia University.

49. Beals, *Interpretaton,* 75–114. See also *Mexican Maze,* 70–93, 121–138, 151–163 and 190–204. From 1925 to 1930, Beals wrote some of his least opinioned pieces for the North American News-

paper Alliance on a variety of subjects including land reform, labor organization and church-state conflict. Since these NANA dispatches appeared irregularly in member newspapers, the best sources for these articles are the original typescripts of the Beals Dispatches in the CBC.

50. This comparison of the Tannenbaum and Gruening analyses of the revolution is based on Tannenbaum, *The Mexican Revolution* (Washington, 1929), 393–426; Idem., *Peace by Revolution* (New York, 1933), 187–224; and Gruening, "The New Era in Mexico," *Century* 109 (March, 1925), 649–658 and *Mexico and Its Heritage*, 91–108, 393–493 and 657–664.

51. Thomas to Beals, May 28, 1928 and Idem., July 3, 1928, CBC and Beals to Calles (with translation of Thomas statement) July 13, 1928, AGN, Ramo Obregón-Calles, 217–E–40. On Thomas, see W. A. Swanberg, *Norman Thomas, The Last Idealist* (New York, 1978), 108–112 and Bernard Johnpoll,*Pacifist's Progress* (Chicago, 1970), 50–67.

## Chapter 4

1. Samuel P. Huntington, *Political Order in Changing Societies* (New Haven, 1969) and Theda Skocpol, *States and Social Revolutions* (New York, 1979).

2. On U.S.-Mexican relations in the 1920s, see Robert Freeman Smith, *The United States and Revolutionary Nationalism in Mexico, 1916–1932* (Chicago, 1972); two books by Lorenzo Meyer, *México y Estados Unidos en el conflicto petrolero, 1917–1942* (Mexico, 1962) and *Los Grupos de presión extranjeros en el México revolucionario* (Mexico, 1973); Karl M. Schmitt, *Mexico and the United States, 1921–1973* (New York, 1974); Luis Zorilla, *Historia de las relaciones entre México y los Estados Unidos de América 1808–1950* 2 (Mexico, 1966); Joseph Tulchin, *The Aftermath of War* (New York, 1971); and McMullen, "Calles and the Diplomacy of Revolution" (Ph.D. diss.).

3. Catt to Beals, November 1, 1926, CBC and "Tentative Program of the Second Conference on the Cause and Cure of War," (typescript), Carrie Chapman Catt Papers, Library of Congress, Washington, D.C., and Catt to Beals, November 12, 1926 and Idem., November 16, 1926, both in CBC.

4. *New York Times*, December 10, 1926, 14. See also *Glass Houses*, 250–251 and *Washington Post*, December 10, 1926.

5. Catt to Beals, December 17, 1926, CBC.

6. Wilson to Scott, December 20, 1926; Scott to Butler, December 22, 1926; Butler to Catt, n.d.; and Catt to Beals, January 4, 1927, all in CBC.

7. Beals to Catt, January 18, 1927 and Beals to Wilson, January 12, 1927, CBC.

8. Catt to Wilson, January 27, 1927, CBC.

9. Wilson to Beals, December 29, 1926 and Wilson to Catt, January 14, 1927, both in CBC. For Murray's articles on "Huerta and the Two Wilsons," see *Harper's Weekly* 62 (March 25-April 29, 1916): 301–303, 341–342, 364–365, 402–404, 434–436, 466–469.

10. For Murray's articles, see *El Universal*, April 25, 26, 28, 1926, all on page 2. For Wilson's published account, see Henry Lane Wilson, *Diplomatic Episodes in Mexico, Belgium and Chile* (Garden City, N.Y., 1927), 252–335. For historical appraisals, see Berta Ulloa, *La revolución intervendia: Relaciones diplomáticas entre los México y Estados Unidos* (Mexico, 1971); John P. Harrison, "Henry Lane Wilson, El trágico de la decena," *Historia Mexicana* 6 (Jan.-March, 1957): 374–405; and Martín Luis Guzmán, "Henry Lane Wilson: Un embasador malvádo," *Cuadernos Americanos* 129 (1963): 203–208.

11. "Ten Questions to the Secretary of State," *The Nation*, 114 (May 24, 1922): 614–615.

12. As quoted in Beelen, "Harding and Mexico," 72.

13. Ibid., 72–73.

14. Ignasias, "Reluctant Recognition," 118–122.

15. Horn, "Diplomacy by Ultimatum," 25–33; and Idem., "U.S. Diplomacy and the 'Specter of Bolshevism' in Mexico (1924–1927)," is a revised version of Chapter 6 of the dissertation.

16. Sheffield to Kellogg, July 1, 1926, Sheffield Papers, Yale University, New Haven, Conn.

17. Sheffield, "Mexico" (Unpublished memoir of his ambassadorship), Sheffield Papers.

18. Memorandum, Division of Mexican Affairs, February 15, 1926, DS 711.12/695.

19. Sheffield to Secretary of State, December 11, 1926, DS 812.20211/45; Idem., December 31, 1926, DS 812.20211/47; and Memorandum by Weddell, December 30, 1926, DS 812.20211/51.

20. Grew to Weddell, Oct. 9, 1925, DS 812.20211/39; *Glass Houses*, 338–356; and Beals to author, April 17, 1974. Beals knew

Gruzenberg and Roy. The remainder of Grew's assertions were never proven by the State Department and, according to Beals, had no basis in fact.

21. Horn, "Diplomacy by Ultimatum," 128–157.

22. Beals to author, April 17, 1974; Gruening, interview with author, March 20, 1974, and Tannenbaum to Secretary of State, February 18, 1926, DS 711.12/732.

23. McMullen, "Calles," 135–138 and L. Ethan Ellis, *Frank B. Kellogg and American Foreign Relations, 1925–1929* (New Brunswick, N.J., 1961), 25–43.

24. Horn, "Diplomacy by Ultimatum," 73–95.

25. "No, Mr. Coolidge—No!" and Beals, "Mexico's Bloodless Victory," both in *The Nation*, 124 (January 26, 1927): 80, 85–86.

26. "Whose Property Is Kellogg Protecting," *New Republic*, 50 (February 23, 1927): 8–11.

27. Smith, *The U.S. and . . . Mexico*, 239–240 and Horn, "Diplomacy by Ultimatum," 164–167.

28. Horn, "Diplomacy by Ultimatum," 178–186.

29. Gruening to Morrow, Oct. 8, 1928; Morrow to Gruening, March 27, 1929; Gruening to Morrow, March 28, 1929; Morrow to Gruening, April 5, 1929; and Tannenbaum to Morrow, September 3, 1927, all in the Dwight Morrow Papers, Amherst College, Mass.

30. Morrow to George Rublee, February 2, 1928, Morrow Papers.

31. W. A. Swanberg, *Citizen Hearst* (New York: Bantam Books, 1961): 467–471.

32. Croly to Beals, April 7, 1927, CBC.

33. Beals to Croly, December 23, 1927 and Beals to Oswald Villard, December 23, 1927, CBC.

34. Beals to Croly, January 31, 1927 (sic, 1928), CBC; "The Meaning of the Hearst Documents," *New Republic*, 53 (January 18, 1928): 243–244; U.S. Congress, Senate, Hearing *Before a Special Committee to Investigate Propaganda or Money Alleged to Have Been Used by Foreign Governments to Influence United States Senators* (Washington, D.C., 1927–1928); and Weddell Memorandum, December, 1926, DS 812.20211/51.

35. For an assessment of the importance of the awakening of interest among U.S. intellectuals in Mexican culture in the 1920s, see Helen Delpar, "'The Present Vogue of Things Mexican: U.S. Travelers to Mexico, 1920–1932.'" Paper delivered to the Con-

ference of the Latin American Studies Association, Mexico City, September 1983.

36. Mildred Constantine, *Tina Modotti: A Fragile Life* (New York, 1975), 72.

37. For an early assessment of the American and English expatriates in Mexico City in the 1920s, see Drewey Wayne Gunn, *American and British Writers in Mexico, 1556–1973* (Austin, 1973), 76–101; *Glass Houses*, 176–177, 240–248, 313–323; and CB Interview, June-July, 1973.

38. Ella Wolfe to Beals, June 10, 1925, CBC. For Bertram Wolfe's recollection of these years, see his *A Life in Two Centuries* (New York, 1981), 276–314, 338–372.

39. *Glass Houses*, 338–343.

40. *Mexican Maze*, 279–283.

41. Anita Brenner, *Idols Behind Altars* (1929; Reprint Boston, 1970).

42. Jean Charlot, *Mexico's Mural Renaissance* (New Haven, Conn., 1967), 280–285.

43. Porter, "Where Presidents Have No Friends," *Century* 104 (July, 1922): 373–384. This article and several others on Mexico in the 1920s are reprinted in Porter, *The Collected Essays and Occassional Writings of Katherine Anne Porter* (New York, 1970). See also Porter, *Outline of Mexican Popular Arts* (Los Angeles, 1922).

44. CB Interview, June-July, 1973.

45. Frances Toor, *A Treasury of Mexican Folkways* (New York, 1947).

46. Edward Weston, *The Daybooks of Edward Weston*, edited by Nancy Newhall (vol. 1) (Millerton, N.Y., 1973), 58.

47. *Ibid.*, 137.

48. *Ibid.*, 139 and Constantine, *Modotti*, 71.

49. Beals, "Tina Modotti," *Creative Art*, (February 1929) No. 11: xliv–li.

50. Diggins, *American Left*, 88–106; Morton White, *Social Thought in America* (Boston, 1957), 180–202; and Robert M. Crunden, *From Self to Society* (Englewood Cliffs, N.J., 1972), 76–131.

51. Gunn, *American and British Writers*, 76–101 and Zelman, "American Intellectual Attitudes."

52. Richard Tardanico, "State, Dependency and Nationalism: Revolutionary Mexico" *Comparative Studies in Society and History*, 24 (July 1982), 400–423.

53. Gunn, *American and British Writers*, 76–101 and Zelman, "American Intellectual Attitudes," 71–119, 172–218.

54. *Interpretation* 89–114, 151–161, 217–247.

55. Ibid., *Mexico*, 3–17, 75–85, 200–214; Beals, "The Mexican As He Is," *North American Review* 214 (October 1921): 538–546; and "The Obregón Regime," *Survey* 52 (May 1, 1924): 135–137, 188–189.

56. In the 1930s Beals was more explicit in his critique of the government's plans for rural Mexico. See Chapter 10.

57. John A. Britton, "In Defense of Revolution: American Journalists in Mexico, 1920–1929," *Journalism History* 5 (Winter, 1978–1979): 124–130, 136 and "United States Anti-Imperialism and the Mexican Revolution, 1913–1928," unpublished ms.

58. Roger Owen and Bob Sutcliffe eds., *Studies in the Theory of Imperialism* (London, 1972); Robin Winks, "On Decolonization and Informal Empire," *American Historical Review* 81 (June 1976): 540–556; and Tony Smith, *The Pattern of Imperialism* (Cambridge, 1981).

For example, see Scott Nearing and Joseph Freeman, *Dollar Diplomacy* (New York, 1925) and Parker Moon, *Imperialism and World Politics* (New York, 1926). These authors stressed the formal aspects of imperialism. They gave little attention to purely economic domination and virtually no recognition to informal political factors. They saw economic motives behind imperial ventures, but the idea of control by means of financial and other economic devices, without military intervention or formal annexation, was not a major consideration in their analyses. In brief, these students of imperialism subscribed to the rather mechanistic view that economic penetration was followed almost inevitably by political interference, military intervention, and finally formal annexation. This approach led them to under-estimate the impact of economic dominance per se.

For a succinct statement of this position, see Nearing and Freeman, *Dollar Diplomacy*, 17–18.

In the case of Cuba, however, these three authorities pointed out the overwhelming economic preponderance of the United States without formal annexation. While Nearing and Freeman emphasized the political control exercised by the U.S. under the Platt Amendment, Moon made a case for "a more subtle" form of imperialism on the basis of financial and economic domination. See Moon, *Imperialism*, 415–422.

59. Diggins, *American Left*, 73–106.

60. Probably anthropology was the only academic discipline to study Third World peoples in depth in the 1920s, but the anthropological perspective usually focused on small communities some distance from the centers of socioeconomic change. For an overview, see Crunden, *Self to Society*, 10–13 and various works by Franz Boas, Margaret Mead, Ruth Benedict, and Roger Redfield.

## Chapter 5

1. Diggins, *American Left*, 88–106; Nearing and Freeman, *Dollar Diplomacy*; and Moon, *Imperialism*.

2. Joseph A. Baylen, "Sandino—Bandit or Patriot," *Hispanic American Historical Review* 31 (August 1951): 394–419 and Neill Macauley, *The Sandino Affair* (Chicago, 1967): 83–84.

3. "Baron Banana in Puerto Barrios," *The Nation* 123 (September 15, 1926): 241–243. Also in *Banana Gold*, 139–147; and "The Nicaraguan Farce," *The Nation* 123 (December 15, 1926: 631–632.

4. "Mexico is Seeking Central American Leadership," *Current History* 34 (September, 1926): 839–844.

5. "Nicaraguan Farce," 632.

6. Quintanilla to Beals, December 8, 1926, CBC. For Quintanilla's assessment of Beals's visit to Guatemala, see Luis Quintanilla to the Mexican Ministry of Foreign Relations, June 24, 1926, Mexican Foreign Relations Archive, III /510(728.1–0) "926"/1,39–8–79.

7. William Kamman, *A Search for Stability: U.S. Diplomacy Toward Nicaragua, 1925–1933* (Notre Dame, 1968), 12–16. For a good, brief account of U.S.-Central American relations, see R. Lee Woodward, *Central America: A Nation Divided* (New York, 1976), 194–202.

8. Joseph Tulchin, *The Aftermath of War* (New York, 1971), 185–190.

9. Kamman, *Search for Stability*, 30–35, 41–43, 66–68, 83.

10. *Ibid.*, 69–81.

11. Henry Stimson, *American Policy in Nicaragua* (New York, 1927), 85.

12. *Ibid.*, 44–45.

13. Villard to Beals, January 5, 1928, CBC; also in *Glass Houses*, 290–291.

14. Beals to Villard, January 5, 1928; also in *Glass Houses*, 291 and Beals to Kirchwey, January 6, 1928, CBC.

15. Beals to Kirchwey, January 10, 1928, CBC; also in *Glass Houses*, 292.

16. *Banana Gold*, 178–184.

17. *Ibid.*, 189–194.

18. *Ibid.*, 184–190; and *Glass Houses*, 293.

19. Beals to Kirchwey, January 14, 1928, CBC. Also in *Glass Houses*, 292.

20. *Banana Gold*, 192–196.

21. *Ibid.*, 219–223.

22. Macauley, *The Sandino Affair*, 99–105.

23. *Banana Gold*, 49.

24. *Ibid.*, 250–263.

25. *Banana Gold*, 264–265.

26. Beals, "Sandino Himself," *The Nation* 126 (March 14, 1928): 289. Much of the substance of the six articles published on Sandino in *The Nation* also appeared in *Banana Gold*. (Some details omitted from the book, however, are cited in this paper from the articles. In cases of duplication, only the book is cited.)

27. Beals, "Sandino—Bandit or Patriot?" *The Nation* 126 (March 28, 1928): 340.

28. *Banana Gold*, 269–270.

29. Beals, "Send the Bill to Mr. Coolidge," *The Nation* 126 (March 21, 1928): 314.

30. "Sandino," *The Nation*: 340 and *Banana Gold*, 266.

31. *Ibid.*, "Sandino," 341.

32. *Banana Gold*, 272–278. Beals narrowly escaped an exchange of fire at San Rafael del Norte between Marine airplanes and Sandinistas later the same morning, only because both sides were under orders not to fire at the time. Macauley, *Sandino Affair*, 106–107.

33. *Ibid.*, 277; Beals to Gruening, May 2, 1932, Gruening Papers, University of Alaska, Fairbanks, Alaska; and CB Interview, August 1974.

34. *Banana Gold*, 284.

35. Beals to *The Nation*, Telegrams, February 10, 18, and 27, 1928, CBC.

36. Beals to Kirchwey, February 11, 1928; Elvina S. Beals to edi-

tor of *The Nation*, March 12 and items 16, 1928; and Beals to Kirchwey, n.d., all in CBC.

37. Kamman, 108–113.

38. Salomon de la Selva, "Sandino," *The Nation* 126 (January 18, 1928): 63.

39. Moncada to Beals, February 12, 1928, CBC.

40. *La Noticia*, February 15, 1928, Printed Matter, CBC. For a brief discussion of the Managua press, see Ramón de Belauste-guigoitia, *Con Sandino en Nicaragua* (Madrid, 1934), 211–214.

41. *La Prensa*, February 12, 1928, Printed Matter, CBC.

42. Idem., February 14, 1928, Printed Matter, CBC.

43. *La Noticia*, February 16, 1928, Printed Matter, CBC.

44. Davis to Secretary of State, March 9, 1928, DS 811.91217/20.

45. *La Nueva Prensa*, March 6, 1928, Printed Matter, CBC.

46. Davis to Secretary of State, March 9, 1928, DS 811.91217/20.

47. Beals to Chief of Police in Tegucigalpa, Telegram, CBC; *La Nueva Prensa*, March 6, 1928, Printed Matter, CBC; and *Banana Gold*, 341–342.

48. Davis to Secretary of State, March 9, 1928, DS 811.91217/20 and *Banana Gold*, 343.

49. Beals, "Mexico Seeking Central American Leadership," *Current History* 34 (Sept. 1962): 839–844.

50. Geissler to Secretary of State, March 14, 1928, DS 811.91217/21.

51. Beals to the editor of *Diario de Guatemala*, March 22, 1928, CBC.

52. Geissler to Secretary of State, March 29, 1928, DS 811.21217/25.

53. *Ibid.*; Geissler to Secretary of State, March 22, 1928, DS 811.91217/22 and /23; Beals to Kirchwey, n.d.; and Idem, April 8, 1928, CBC.

54. *Banana Gold*, 352.

55. Caffery to Secretary of State, January 30, 1928, DS 811.91217/13.

56. Eberhardt to Secretary of State, February 2, 1928, DS 811.91217/9 (message repeated in Caffery to Secretary of State, February 4, 1928, DS 811.91217/18). Beals stated that he did not know any of the Nicaraguan contacts or Ernesto Vacasey, the reputed author of the letters of introduction, nor was he aware of the two bank drafts mentioned in the State Department letters. Beals to author, August 23, 1974.

57. Summerlin to Secretary of State, February 4, 1928, DS 811.91217/10.

58. Caffery to Secretary of State, February 4, 1928, DS 811.91217/19.

59. Beals to Kirchwey, February 8, 1928, CBC and *Banana Gold*, 285–290.

60. Beals to Kirchwey, February 11, 1928, CBC.

61. *Banana Gold*, 291–292.

62. *Ibid.*, 293.

63. Beals to Kirchwey, February 8, 1928, CBC; *Banana Gold*, 296–298; *Glass Houses*, 295; and *The Nation* 126 (March 21, 1928): 315–317.

64. Unsigned and undated memorandum to Oswald Garrison Villard (perhaps from Kirchwey), CBC.

65. Beals, *The Nation* 126 (March 21, 1926): 315–317.

66. Macauley, *Sandino Affair*, 109–110.

67. Eberhardt to Secretary of State, March 3, 1928, DS 817.00/5439.

68. Beals to Kirchwey, May 1, 1928, CBC.

69. Hammond to Secretary of State, May 9, 1928, DS 811.91217/26; Idem; May 10, 13, 17, and 20, 1928, DS 811.91217/27; and Idem, May 27 and June 4, 1928, DS 811.91217/28.

70. Caffery to Secretary of State, March 14, 1928, DS 817.00/5524.

71. Weddell to Secretary of State, June 6, 1928, DS 810.43 Anti-Imperialist League.

72. *Ibid.*

73. Weddell to Secretary of State, July 4, 1928, DS 810.43 Anti-Imperialist League.

74. Beals to Kirchwey, n.d., CBC.

75. Gannett to Beals, July 10, 1928, CBC.

76. *Banana Gold*, 284.

77. Kirchwey to Beals, March 30, 1928, CBC.

78. Beals to Kirchwey, April 12, 1928; Idem; May 19, 1928; and Kirchwey to Beals, May 16, 1928, all in CBC.

79. Gannett to Beals, July 10, 1928, CBC.

80. Beals to Gruening, May 21, 1928, Gruening Papers.

81. Anastasio Somoza, *El verdadero Sandino* (Managua, 1936), 82.

82. Gustavo Alemán Bolaños, *Sandino* (Mexico, 1932), 67–69; and Ramón de Belausteguigoitia, *Con Sandino en Nicaragua*, 128.

83. Baylen, "Sandino—Bandit or Patriot?" *Hispanic American Historical Review 31,* 408.

84. Charles E. Frazier, "The Dawn of Nationalism and its Consequences in Nicaragua" (Ph.D. diss., University of Texas, 1958), 436.

85. Kamman, *A Search for Stability,* 136–142.

86. Macauley, *Sandino Affair,* 105–107, 112, 127.

87. *Banana Gold,* 299–300.

88. *Ibid.,* 294–295.

89. Davis to Secretary of State, March 9, 1928, DS 811.91217/20.

90. *The Nation* 126 (April 11, 1928): 406 and Beals to Kirchwey, April 18, 1928, CBC.

91. Beals to Father, April 1928, CBC.

92. Bryce Wood, *The Making of the Good Neighbor Policy* (New York, 1961), 13–47.

93. For a convenient collection of contemporary articles, see Lamar Beman, *Intervention in Latin America* (New York, 1928).

## Chapter 6

1. CB Interview and *Universal,* January 11, 1929, 1, 9.

2. *Universal* and *Excelsior,* January 12, 13, 14, and 15, 1929 and Constantine, *Modotti,* 129–150.

3. *Universal,* January 20, 1929, 1, 8.

4. *Universal,* January 14, 1929, 11. Constantine refers to him as Pepe Magriña.

5. *Universal,* January 13, 1929, 1, 7.

6. *Universal,* January 15, 1929, 1, 8 and Constantine, *Modotti,* 136.

7. Beals, *Great Circle* (Philadelphia, 1940), 215–217 and Constantine, *Modotti,* 148–149.

8. Constantine, *Modotti,* 149–150.

9. Weston, *Daybooks,* Vol. 2, 110.

10. L. F. Bustamante, "El enigma de Tina Modotti," *Jueves de Excelsior* (January 15, 1942).

11. Beals, *Great Circle,* 215–217. Later events seemed to confirm Beals assertion, although no one was convicted of the murder. See Constantine, *Modotti,* 149.

12. See Chapter 8.

13. *Mexican Maze,* 278.

14. Jean Meyer, *La cristiada*, 3 Vols. (Mexico: Siglo Vientiuno Editores, 1973–1974) and David Bailey *Viva Cristo Rey!* (Austin: University of Texas Press, 1974).

15. Beals, *Great Circle*, 202–205 and *Mexican Maze*, 324–327.

16. Beals, *Great Circle*, 199–213 and *Mexican Maze*, 327–332.

17. Idem, "The New Democracy in Mexico," *New Republic* 56 (Oct. 3, 1928): 169–171.

18. Idem, "Plutarco Elías Calles: A Record of Statesmanship," *Current History* 29 (January 1929): 554–559.

19. *Ibid.*, 558–559 and Beals, "Mexico Rises Out of Chaos," *The Nation* 128 (April 13, 1929): 392–393.

20. Beals, "Mexico's New Leader," *New Republic* 61 (December 11, 1929): 62–64.

21. *Ibid.*, Beals's prediction that Rodríguez Triana would outpoll Vasconcelos was wrong. Vasconcelos received over 110,000 votes to Rodríguez Triana's 23,279 and Ortiz Rubio's nearly 2 million. See Dulles, *Yesterday in Mexico*, 476.

22. Bliven to Beals, February 5, 1930, CBC.

23. Beals to Bliven, February 10, 1930, CBC.

24. José Vasconcelos, "Nuestros Amigos," *Repertorio Americano* (June 28, 1930): 373–374.

25. "Una Repuesta a José Vasconcelos." (Unpublished type-script) dated 1931, CBC.

26. Beals to U.S. Department of State, February 18, 1930, DS 312.1121-Beals, Carleton/8.

27. Ibid.

28. Ibid.

29. Colonel Gordon Johnston to Assistant Chief of Staff, G-2, February 18, 1930, WD-MID, 1917–1941, 100–58–30, and Herschel Johnson to Secretary of State, February 16, 1930, DS 312.1121 Beals, Carleton/4.

30. Johnston to War Department, February 18, 1930, WD-MID, 1917–1941, 100–58–0–30.

31. Johnson to Secretary of State, February 16, 1930, DS 312.1121 Beals, Carleton/4.

32. Signature illegible to Secretaría de Relaciones Exteriores (hereafter SRE), Feb. 17, 1930, AREM, Expediente III, 534 (73–0) (04), Mexico City.

33. Beals, memorandum of conversation of Colonel Johnston and Carleton Beals with Señor Chazaro, private secretary to Presi-

dent Ortiz Rubio. Enclosed with letter from Herschel Johnson to Secretary of State, February 18, 1930, DS 312.1121 Beals, Carleton/7.

34. *Great Circle*, 246–247 and Johnston to War Department, February 18, 1930 DS 312.1121 Beals, Carleton/7 mentioned the Chazaro phone call but implied that it took place after the meeting.

35. Beals to Bliven, January 10, 1930. (Copy in CBC.)

36. Memorandum of Conversation . . . Johnson to Secretary of State, February 18, 1930 DS 312.1121 Beals, Carleton/7 and Johnston to War Department, February 18, 1930, WD-MID, 1917–1941, 100–58–0–30.

37. Beals, "Mexico and the Communists," *New Republic* 62 (February 17, 1930): 10–12.

38. Signature illegible to S.R.E., February 17, 1930, AREM, Expediente III, 534 (73–0) (04).

39. Beals to Bliven, February 18, 1930, CBC.

40. Idem., February 29, 1930, CBC.

41. Elías to Beals, February 19, 1930, CBC.

42. Beals to Elías, April 26, 1930, CBC.

43. Elías to Beals, April 28, 1930, CBC.

44. Beals to Elías, April 29, 1930, CBC.

45. For an old, but useful, discussion, see Alexander De Conde, *Herbert Hoover's Latin American Policy* (Stanford, 1951).

46. Beals, "The Mexican Fascisti," *Current History* 19 (November, 1923): 257–261; Idem, "Mexico's Labor Crisis," *The Nation* 128 (March 13, 1929): 327–329; and Idem, "Mexico's New Leader," *New Republic* 61 (December 11, 1929): 62–64.

47. Beals, "Mexico Turns to Fascist Tactics," *The Nation* 132 (January 28, 1931): 110–112.

48. Beals, "Has Mexico Betrayed Her Revolution?" *New Republic* 67: 249–250.

49. Quintanilla to Beals, no day or month, 1931, CBC.

50. Dawson to Beals, Nov. 18, 1931, CBC.

51. Father to Beals, Dec. 19, 1931; William Spratling to Beals, March 30, 1932; Mother to Beals, Dec. 11, 1932 and "Carleton Beals," *Current Biography*, New York, 1941, 49–51.

52. For reviews of *Mexican Maze*, see *Books* (May 31, 1931): 1; *The Nation* 133 (Sept. 16, 1931): 287; and *Saturday Review of Literature* 7 (June 7, 1931): 907.

For reviews of *Banana Gold*, see *Bookman* 75 (May 1932): 185; *The Nation* 134 (June 15, 1932): 684; and *Saturday Review of Literature* 8 (July 9, 1932): 827.

53. Beals, *House in Mexico* (New York, 1958).

54. For reviews of *Porfirio Díaz, Dictator of Mexico*, see *New York Times*, Nov. 27, 1932; *Bookman* 75 (Dec. 1932): 863; *Saturday Review of Literature*, 9 (Jan. 14, 1933): 375; and *Commonweal* 17 (Jan. 25, 1933): 385.

*Porfirio Díaz* caused an extended controversy in the Mexico City press. For example, see Salvador Quevedo y Zubieta, "Los Generales Presidentes Porfirio Díaz y Manuel González, el Sr. Carleton Beals y Yo," *Excelsior*, Nov. 9, 1934, 5, 8 and Beals, "Los Generales Presidentes Porfirio Díaz y Manuel González, el Señor Salvador Quevedo y Zubieta y Yo," *Excelsior*, Nov. 12, 1934, 5 and Ibid., Nov. 13, 1934, 5, 7. See also Quevedo y Zubieta to Beals, Sept. 6, 1931, CBC and Quevedo y Zubieta, *El General González y su gobierno* (Reprinted in 1885 and 1928, Mexico, 1884.)

For another Mexican review, see Jesús Guiza y Azevedo, "Porfirio Díaz, por Carleton Beals," *Excelsior*, (five-part review) Feb. 8–12, 1933.

## Chapter 7

1. Carleton Beals, *The Crime of Cuba* (Philadelphia, 1933), 38–39.

2. Hugh Thomas, *Cuba, the Pursuit of Freedom* (New York, 1971), 569–602; Luis E. Aguilar, *Cuba 1933 and Politics in Cuba, 1913–1921*, (Pittsburgh, 1978).

3. Aguilar, *Cuba*, 77–78, 104–106, 117–118.

4. Ibid., 121–124.

5. Robert Freeman Smith, *United States and Cuba, Business and Diplomacy, 1917–1920* (New York, 1960), 114–133 and Benjamin, *The United States and Cuba* (Pittsburgh, 1974), 28–68.

6. Beals, Interview in *La Prensa*, typed translation, Oct. 19, 1932, CBC.

7. Octavio Seigle to Beals, Nov. 12, 1932, CBC and Thomas, *Cuba*, 594.

8. Francis V. Jackman, "America's Cuba Policy during the Period of the Machado Regime" (Ph.D. diss., Catholic University, 1964), 190–191.

9. Seigle to Beals, November 12, 1932, CBC.

10. Ibid., See Chapter 6.

11. Beals, "The Crime of Cuba," *Common Sense* 1 (December 29, 1932): 10–11, 29–32. Beals continued his attack on Machado and

Guggenheim in *Common Sense* 1 (January 19, 1933): 20–24, and (February 1, 1933): 22–26.

12. *New York Times,* December 23, 1932, 13. Cuban authorities soon released the owner of the news service.

13. Alfred M. Bingham to Secretary of State, Dec. 25, 1932; H.T.M. to Baker, Dec. 29, 1932 and H.T.M. to E. C. Wilson, Dec. 29, 1932, all in DS 837.918/45–/46; and Percy A. Brient to Department of State, Jan. 26, 1933 and Franklin White to Percy A. Brient, Feb. 8, 1933, both in DS 837.000/3441.

14. Duggan to Beals, Oct. 11, 1932, CBC.

15. Ortiz to Beals, Nov. 11, 1932, CBC.

16. Benjamin, *U.S. and Cuba,* 59 and Thomas, *Cuba,* 519, 524, 532 and 602.

17. "Cuban American Friendship Council." Statement of "Basic Principles," January 22, 1933, CBC.

18. Ortiz to Beals, February 9, 1933, CBC.

19. Ortiz to Beals, February 9, 1933; Idem., February 29 (?), 1933; Idem., March 18, 1933; Idem., March 22, 1933; and Idem., April 6, 1933, all in CBC.

20. Idem., April 15, 1933, CBC.

21. *Great Circle.*

22. *The Nation* 126 (May 12, 1929): 209 and Idem., (Oct. 2, 1929: 339.

23. Gruening, "Cuba Under the Machado Regime," *Current History* 34 (May 1931): 214–219.

24. For a general discussion of the U.S. press and Machado, see Jackman, "America's Cuban Policy" (Ph.D. diss.) 181–244.

25. Guggenheim to Billikopf, Nov. 18, 1932, copy in CBC. (Gruening probably gave the copy to Beals.

26. Billikopf to Gruening, Nov. 28, 1932. Copy, CBC.

27. Beals to Billikopf, December 8, 1932. Copy, CBC.

28. Billikopf to Beals, December 16, 1932, CBC.

29. See Herring "Attempts to Discredit American Policy in Cuba." Copy, CBC. See also Beals to editor of the *New Republic,* March 16, 1933 and Bruce Bliven to Beals, March 30, 1933, both in CBC.

30. Beals to Herring, March 24, 1933. Copy, CBC.

31. Harry F. Guggenheim, *The United States and Cuba* (1934; Report New York, 1970), 184–191.

32. Smith, *Business and Diplomacy,* 130–133 and Benjamin, *U.S. and Cuba,* 68–71.

33. Beals, *Crime,* 32.

34. Jones to Beals, April 21, 1933, CBC.

35. Beals, *Crime,* 342.

36. Evans to Beals, June 25, 1933, CBC. Six years later, Evans achieved recognition in *Let Us Now Praise Famous Men* (Boston, 1939), a collaborative effort with James Agee.

37. The photographs appeared on the last thirty-one pages of *Crime.*

38. *Crime,* 40–44.

39. Ibid., 85–89.

40. Ibid., 323.

41. Ibid., 195, 296–300.

42. Ibid., 160.

43. Ibid., 182–183.

44. Ibid., 383–398.

45. Ibid., 355–368.

46. Jones to Beals, Sept. 14, 1933, CBC.

47. Thomas, *Cuba,* 586, 686 and Smith, *Business and Diplomacy,* 142–143.

48. Beals, *Crime,* 398–399.

49. Ibid., 241–242.

50. Ibid., 250–251.

51. Ibid., 308–312.

52. Ibid., 330–333, 343–352.

53. Jackman, "America's Cuban Policy," (Ph.D. diss.), 244.

54. *Books,* review, (Aug. 30), 1933:3.

55. *Yale Review,* review, (Winter, 1933):405.

56. *The Nation,* review, (Sept. 6, 1933):275.

57. Grau San Martín to Beals, Sept. 28, 1933, CBC.

58. Mañach to Beals, Dec. 26, 1933, CBC.

59. "A Cuban" to Beals, Dec. 16, 1933, CBC.

60. Gruening to Beals, Sept. 6, 1933, CBC.

61. Beals, "American Diplomacy in Cuba," *The Nation* 138 (Jan. 17, 1934): 68–70.

62. Phillips to Beals, Feb. 7, 1934, CBC.

63. Beals, "Saving Cuba," *The Nation* 140 (Feb. 13, 1935): 196–199.

64. *New York Times,* March 28, 1935, 22.

65. Mcrritt Bond to Beals, April 8, 1935, CBC.

66. Beals to Bond, April 11, 1935. Copy, CBC.

67. Phillips to Beals, May 2, 1935, CBC.

68. Beals, "Censorship in Cuba," *The Nation* 140 (May 22, 1935): 601.

69. International Committee for Political Prisoners, Press release June 20, 1935, CBC. The committee also sent letters of protest to President Mendieta and Secretary of State Cordell Hull.

70. Beals, "New Crime of Cuba," *New Republic* 83 (July 3, 1935): 216–219 and "The New Machado," *The Nation* 141 (August 7, 1935): 152–154.

71. Ibid.

72. Beals and Odets, "Rifle Rule in Cuba" (New York, 1935).

73. Phillips to Beals, July 11, 1935, CBC.

74. Komorowski to Beals, August 9, 1935; Idem., September 21, 1935; and Idem., October 18, 1935, all in CBC. Beals's contribution was originally intended for a newspaper, but "Rifle Rule" appeared before the newspaper was able to use it. Beals thereby lost the revenue it might have produced, if it had been published by the newspaper.

75. Aguilar, *Cuba*, 211–215 and 223–226, and Gellman, *Roosevelt and Batista*, 14–33, 55–83, 97–99, 154–156. Aguilar seems closer then Gellman to Beals's thesis that U.S. diplomats subverted the course of political change in Cuba, although Beals was somewhat more skeptical than Aguilar of the potential of the short-lived Grau San Martín government.

## Chapter 8

1. Thomas to Beals, no month or day, 1934, CBC.

2. Williams to Beals, Oct. 11, 1934, CBC.

3. *Time* 31 (April 25, 1938): 70.

4. For an analysis of the U.S. intellectual Left in the 1930s, see Richard Pells, *Radical Visions and American Dreams* (New York, 1973).

5. Toor to Beals, May 19, 1934, CBC.

6. James to Beals, Sept. 10, 1934 and Diffie to Beals, Oct. 27, 1934, both in CBC.

7. Beals chose not to discuss his marital history in interviews with the author.

8. Mother to Beals, May 28, 1934, CBC.

9. Daniels to Beals, Aug. 28, 1934, CBC.

10. Leona A. Pazzi to Beals, Aug. 24, 1934, CBC.

11. Bliven to Beals, Aug. 23, 1934 and Leiber to Beals, Sept. 13, 1934, both in CBC.

12. Steve Stein, *Populism in Peru* (Madison, 1980), 83–202.

13. Frederick Pike, *The Modern History of Peru* (London, 1967), 268–271.

14. Stein, *Populism*, 49–82.

15. Frederick Pike, *The United States and Andean America* (Cambridge, Mass., 1977), 226–233. For the historical debate surrounding Haya's position on the role of the Indian in Peruvian life, see Stein, *Populism;* Thomas Davies, *Indian Integration in Peru* (Lincoln, Neb., 1974); and Peter Klarén, *Modernization, Dislocation and Aprismo* (Austin, 1973).

16. Markel to Lieber, December 1933, CBC.

17. Ossa to Beals, December 1933, CBC.

18. *Acción Aprista,* April 21, 1934, Printed Matter, CBC and *America South*, 403–404.

19. *America South*, 407–409 and *Fire* 415–416.

20. *Fire*, 434–436.

21. Ibid., 317–447.

22. Ibid., 414.

23. Ibid., 422–423 and *America South*, 397–399. For a discussion of Haya in Mexico, see Richard V. Salisbury, "The Middle American Exile of Víctor Raúl Haya de la Torre," *The Americas* 40 (July 1983): 3–7.

24. *America South*, 398–401 and *Fire*, 423–425.

25. *Fire*, 423–426.

26. Ibid., 426.

27. Sánchez to Beals, July 9, 1935, CBC.

28. Alegría to Beals, Nov. 8, 1936, which included Ciro Alegría, "Datos sobre la vida y obra de Ciro Alegría" and "Informes sobre política Peruana," all in CBC.

29. Alegría to Beals, Jan. 24, 1936; Idem., May 1, 1936; Idem., June 27, 1936; Idem., July 4, 1936; Idem., Sept. 3, 1936; Idem., Nov. 8, 1936; Idem., Oct. 22, 1937; and Idem., Feb. 27, 1940, all in CBC.

30. For an evaluation of Alegría's work, see Kessel Schwartz, *Spanish American Fiction* (Coral Gables, Fla., 1971), vol. 1; 55–61.

31. *Fire*, 448. For a brilliant interpretation of the mystical nature of Haya's thought, see Frederick Pike, "Vision's of Rebirth: The Spiritualist Facet of Peru's Haya de la torre," *Hispanic American Historical Review* 63 (August, 1983): 479–516.

32. *Saturday Review of Literature* 11 (Dec. 15, 1934): 369.

33. Beals to the editor of the *Saturday Review of Literature*, Feb. 7, 1935, CBC.

34. Toor to Beals, CBC May 19, 1934, CBC.

35. Daniels to Beals, Jan. 5, 1935 and Idem., Jan. 29, 1935, both in CBC.

36. E. David Cronon, *Josephus Daniels in Mexico* (Madison, 1960).

37. Ibid., 82–111; Meyer, *La cristiada*, and John A. Britton, *Educación y radicalismo en México* (Mexico, 1976), vol. 1; 23–47, 97–159.

38. Cronon, *Daniels*, 82–111.

39. Beals's account of his speeches in Beals to Daniels, Feb. 17, 1935; Daniels to Beals, Feb. 27, 1935; Herter to Beals, Feb. 21, 1935, all in CBC.

40. Beals, "Socialism on a Platter," *The Nation* 140 (April 10, 1935): 414–416.

41. *America South* 359–381, (quote from 380–381). Beals found the general reform program more acceptable than socialist education, which was only a part of the whole. His views on collectivism in Mexico seemed to change from 1935 to 1937.

## Chapter 9

1. Beals, *America South* (New York, 1937).

2. Ibid., 224–240.

3. Ibid., 246.

4. Ibid., 269–283, (long quote from 301).

5. Ibid., 359–381, 397–409.

6. Ibid., 343–348.

7. Ibid., 351–354. The economic aspect of Beals's analysis is treated in more depth later in this chapter.

8. S. N. Eisenstadt, *Modernization: Protest and Change* (Englewood Cliffs, N.J., 1966).

9. For an overview, see Eisenstadt, "Studies of Modernization and Sociological Theory," *History and Theory*, 13:3 (1974): 225–252. For more specialized studies, see Oscar Lewis, *Life in a Mexican Village* (Urbana, 1951); Michael Belshaw, *A Village Economy* (New York, 1967); F. LaMond Tullis, *Landlord and Peasant in Peru* (Cambridge, 1970); and Klarén, *Modernization, Dislocation and Aprismo*.

10. Arnaldo Córdova, *La ideología de la Revolución Mexicana* (México, 1973), 262–351 and John Y. F. Dulles, *Yesterday in Mexico* (Austin, 1961).

11. *Interpretation* 84–114 and *Mexican Maze* 70–93.

12. *Interpretation*, 85, 106–109.

13. Ibid., 114.

14. *Mexican Maze*, 176–204.

15. Ibid., 135–138 and *Interpretation*, 84, 89–92.

16. *Mexican Maze*, 49–54.

17. Ibid., 137.

18. Beals, "The Revolution in Mexico," *New Republic* 52: 255–256.

19. *Mexican Maze*, 67–68 and Beals, "Church on Trial," *Survey* 57; 12–15, 47–49.

20. For discussions of the Cristero movement, see Meyer, *La cristiada* and David Bailey, *Viva Cristo Rey!* (Austin, 1974).

21. *Mexican Maze*, 301–302 and "Mexican Church Goes on Strike," *The Nation* 123 (August 18, 1926): 145–147.

22. Beals "Frontier Teachers," *Bulletin of the Pan American Union* 59 (May, 1925): 443–452.

23. *Mexican Maze*, 186–188.

24. Beals to Croly, June 23, 1927, CBC.

25. *Mexican Maze*, 188.

26. Ibid., 50–54, 162, 329.

27. Pike, *Modern Peru* (London, 1967), 269–270 and Klarén, *Modernization*, 119–141.

28. *Fire* 325–348.

29. Ibid., 310.

30. Ibid., 311–313.

31. Davies, *Indian Integration* 110–112 and Klarén sees him as an astute observer sincerly concerned about rural problems. For a sampling of Haya's public statements on the Indian problem, see his *Construyendo el Aprismo* (Buenos Aires, 1933), 104–116, and *Politica Aprista* (Lima, 1933), 23.

32. *Fire*, 342. Beals made frequent use of Sáenz's *Sobre el indio Peruano y su incorporación al medio nacional* (México, 1933).

33. *Fire*, 348.

34. Ibid., 401, 426.

35. Ibid., 427–429.

36. Ibid., 431.

37. Pells, *Radical visions*, 96–150.

38. *Mexican Maze*, 107–151, 176–204 and *Fire*, 325–348.

39. Stuart Chase and Marian Tyler, *Mexico: A Study of Two Americas* (New York, 1931); Robert Redfield, *Tepoztlán, Peace by Revolution*. For general studies of the response of U.S. intellectuals, see

Zelman, "American Intellectual Attitudes;" E. Meyer, *Conciencia histórica Norteamericana sobre la Revolución de 1910.*

40. Joseph S. Tulchin, *Aftermath of War,* chap. 6. On the U.S. government and private efforts in this cultural offensive, see Robert N. Seidel, *Progressive Pan-Americanism: Development and United States Policy Towards South America* (Ithaca, 1973); Frank A. Ninkovitch, *The Diplomacy of Ideas: United States Foreign Policy and Cultural Relations, 1938–1950* (Cambridge, 1981); and Emily S. Rosenberg, *Spreading the American Dream: American Economic and Cultural Expansion* (New York, 1981), chap. 9–10.

41. Beals, *The Coming Struggle for Latin America* (New York, 1938), 178–186.

42. Quoted in *Coming Struggle,* 189. See also 185–193.

43. Ibid., 198–199.

44. Ibid., 212–216.

45. Ibid., 200–201.

46. Ibid., 202–205.

47. Ibid., 206–207.

48. Ibid., 208, 220.

49. For historical studies of the Good Neighbor Policy, see Bryce Wood, *The Making of the Good Neighbor Policy* (New York, 1961) and Gellman, *Good Neighbor Diplomacy: United States Policies in Latin America, 1933–1945* (Baltimore, 1979). For critical views of FDR's Latin American policy, see Lloyd Gardner, *Economic Aspects of New Deal Diplomacy* (Madison, 1964) and Clayton R. Koppes, "The Good Neighbor Policy and the Nationalization of Mexican Oil: A Reinterpretation," *Journal of American History* 69 (June, 1982): 62–97.

50. *Coming Struggle,* 219–222.

51. Ibid., 253–254. See also Cordell Hull, *The Memoirs of Cordell Hull* (New York, 1949), Vol. 1 335–336.

52. *Coming Struggle,* 256.

53. Ibid., 271. The highly complicated issues involving anti-imperialism, economic nationalism and dependency theory are discussed by Anthony Smith, *The Pattern of Imperialism* (Cambridge, 1981) and Roger Owen and Bob Sutcliffe eds., *Studies in the Theory of Imperialism* (London, 1972). Some recent work on the application of dependency theory in Latin America include C. Richard Bath and Dilmus James, "Dependency Analysis of Latin America," *Latin American Research Review* II (1976): 3–54; D. C. M. Platt, " Dependency in Nineteenth Century Latin America: An Historican Objects," and Stanley J. and Barbara H. Stein, "D. C. M. Platt, The

Anatomy of 'Autonomy,' " both articles are in *Latin American Research Review* 15 (1980): 113–149.

54. *America South*, 410–411.

55. Ibid., 410–427.

56. Tannenbaum, *Whither Latin America* (New York, 1934), chap. 2.

57. *America South*, 424.

58. *Coming Struggle*, 354–374.

59. *America South*, 424–426.

60. Ibid., 426–427.

61. *Fire*, 401–404.

62. Beals, "The Mexican Challenge," *Current History* 48 (April, 1938): 28.

63. Ibid., 28–30 and *The True Facts about the Expropriation of the Oil Companies Properties in Mexico* (Mexico, 1940), 81–85.

64. "Mexican Challenge," Current History 48: 30.

65. Beals's argument in favor of government-controlled industrial development resembled the action of the Mexican government as described by Koppes, "The Good Neighbor Policy and the Nationalization of Mexican Oil," *Journal of American History* 69: 62–97. Koppes distinguishes clearly between expropriation, i.e., the government's explusion of foreign oil companies, and nationalization or the creation of a government agency to develop petroleum. U.S. business and diplomatic interests accepted the former reluctantly but were irreversibly opposed to the latter. Beals was a consistent advocate of economic development through nationalized industries.

66. For example, see Archibald MacLeish, "South America III: Chile," *Fortune* 17 (May, 1938): 156–172; Herring, *Good Neighbors*; and John T. Whitaker, *Americas to the South.* (New York, 1940).

67. Louis G. Dreyfus (counselor of Peruvian embassy) to Secretary of State, January 22, 1934, DS 811.91223/33; Robert Frazer (of the Salvadorean legation) to Secretary of State, November 30, 1938, D.S. 616.6217/4; and Lt. Colonel J. B. Pete (Military Attaché, Costa Rican legation) to Military Attaché Office, War Department, November 14, 1938, WD-MID 2315-P-19.

68. On populism in Latin America see Michael L. Conniff, ed., *Latin American Populism in Comparative Perspective* (Albuquerque, 1982).

69. For examples of Beals's appreciation of the mystical in Mexico and Peru, see Beals, *Mexican Maze*, 9–17, 23–30, 34–35, 49–138, 284–306 and *Fire*, 9–24, 139–168, 212–284, 430–448.

**Chapter 10**

1. Frances Grossel to Beals, Feb. 27, 1937, CBC.
2. Beals to Calverton, March 15, 1937, Calverton Papers, New York Public Library.
3. Stolberg to Beals, March 12, 1937, CBC.
4. Novak to Beals, March 19, 1937, CBC.
5. Stolberg to Beals, Telegram, March 25, 1937, CBC.
6. Alan Wald, "Memories of the John Dewey Commission: Forty Years Later," *Antioch Review* 135 (Fall, 1977): 447.
7. Beals to Calverton, April 8, 1937, Calverton Papers.
8. Calverton to Beals, April 14, 1937. Copy, Calverton Papers.
9. Jan van Heijenoort, *With Trotsky in Exile* (Cambridge, 1978).
10. Issac Deutscher, *The Prophet Outcast* (New York, 1963), 358–366.
11. Wald, "Memories," *Antioch Review* 135: 446–447; Deutscher, *Prophet Outcast*, 37 and Constance Ashton Myers, *The Prophet's Army* (Westport, Conn., 1977): 134–135.
12. Dewey to Beals, July 22, 1926, CBC.
13. See above, chap. 7.
14. Myers, *Prophet's Army*, 133–137.
15. Beals, "The Fewer Outsiders the Better," *Saturday Evening Post* 209 (June 12, 1937): 23, 75.
16. Deutscher, *Prophet Outcast*, 374–376 and *New York Times*, April 18, 1937. See also James T. Farrell, "Dewey in Mexico," in *John Dewey: Philosopher of Science and Freedom* Sidney Hood ed. (Westport, Conn., 1976), 363 for a more moderate appraisal.
17. Novak to Beals, March 19, 1937, CBC.
18. *The Case of Leon Trotsky* (London, 1937), xxiii.
19. *Case*, 52.
20. Ibid.
21. Ibid.
22. Ibid.
23. Ibid., pp. 53–54.
24. "The Fewer Outsiders," *Saturday Evening Post* 209: 74–76.
25. *Case*, 66–70.
26. Ibid., 70.
27. "The Fewer Outsiders," *Saturday Evening Post* 209: 77.
28. *Case*, 110.
29. Ibid., 110–11.
30. Ibid., 296.

31. Ibid.
32. Ibid., 298–299.
33. Ibid.
34. Ibid., 412–413.
35. Ibid., 415–416.
36. Ibid., 416–417.

37. Beals, "How Mexico Nearly Lost Its Mayan States," *Southwest Review* April, 1926: 232–245. The War Department was aware of Borodin's activities in Latin America in 1920 and listed him and Beals (incorrectly) among other "leaders of (a) Communist movement." WD-MID, 1917–1940, 10058–928.

See also *Glass Houses,* 45–51.

Mexican historian and sociologist Pablo González Casanova describes Borodin's work in Mexico in his *La Clase obrera en la historia de México (1917–1920)* 154–170.

Dan Jacobs in his *Borodin: Stalin's Man in China* (Cambridge, Mass., 1981) documents Borodin's presence in Mexico as an agent of the Comintern with the general purpose of spreading revolution (59–74).

Beals objected to Deutscher's characterization of the Trotsky confrontation in *The Prophet Outcast* when it appeared in the fall of 1963. His objections led Oxford University Press to revise that section of the book (374–376) soon after publication.

Beals to Oxford University Press, September 15, 1963; Benjamin H. Stern and Raymond Reubens to Beals, Oct. 21, 1963; and Fon W. Boardman to Beals, Nov. 18, 1963, all in CBC.

38. Richard Swift, *International Law* (New York, 1969), 388–389.
39. *New York Times,* April 18, 1937 and *Excelsior,* April 18, 1937.
40. *Case,* xxvi.
41. Ibid.
42. "Fewer Outsiders," *Saturady Evening Post;* 209 75–78; *New Hvaen Register,* April, 1937 (article for North American Newspaper Alliance); and *Case,* xxiii–xvii.
43. *New York Times,* April 18 and 19, 1937.
44. *The Nation* 144 (May 1, 1937); 496–497.
45. *Time* 29 (May 17, 1937): 20.
46. Daniels to Secretary of State, April 30, 1937 and undated clipping both in D S 861.00 Trotsky, Leo/84–85.
47. Myers, *Prophet's Army,* 133–142.
48. An FBI investigation of Beals in the 1950s reached the conclusion that he had no affiliation with a Stalinist or any other sig-

nificant left-wing organization. See chapters 12 and 13 for a discussion of the FBI investigations of Beals.

49. Bates to Beals, May 14, 1937, Calverton Papers, and *Modern Monthly* (May, 1937): 9–10.

50. Beals to Calverton, May 19, 1937, Calverton Papers. Beals also wrote that soon after his resignation he telegraphed President Cárdenas to request that Trotsky receive asylum in Mexico. The impact of Beals telegram is uncertain, but the Mexican government allowed Trotsky to stay in Mexico where he remained until his assassination on August 20, 1940 by Jaime Ramón Mercader, a Spanish-born Communist sent by Stalin. See Issac Don Levine, *The Mind of an Assassin* (New York, 1959).

51. Beals to Calverton, May 19, 1937, Calverton Papers.

52. Idem, May 22, 1937, Calverton Papers. There is no evidence that Beals received the $500 offered him in the Stolberg telegram on March 25.

53. Ibid.

54. Sidney Hook to the editor and Beals to the editor, *Southern Review* 3 (1937–1938): 406–411. (Complete copy of Beals's letter in CBC.)

55. Calverton to Beals, May 31, 1937. Copy, Calverton Papers.

56. Daniel Aaron, *Writers on the Left* (New York, 1977), 322–333.

57. Trotsky to Calverton, October 15, 1937, Calverton Papers. (Copy in CBC.)

58. Eastman to Calverton, October 23, 1937, Calverton Papers.

59. Calverton to Trotsky, December 6, 1937. Copy, Calverton Papers.

60. Rivera to Calverton, November 3, 1937, Calverton Papers.

61. Rivera to the editor of *Modern Monthly* (Calverton), January 18, 1938, Calverton Papers.

62. Beals to Calverton, April 11, 1938, CBC.

63. Farrell, "Dewey in Mexico," in Sidney Hook, ed., *John Dewey: Philosopher of Science and Freedom* (Westport, Conn., 1976), 363.

64. *Glass Houses*, 34–35.

65. Ibid, pp. 9–78, 174–265. In the late 1930s, Beals frequently wrote on contemporary events in the United States including a biography, *The Story of Huey P. Long* (Philadelphia, 1935); a commentary on the farm crisis, *American Earth* (New York, 1939); and a series of articles on the Scottsboro Trials for *The Nation*. The Latin

American focus of this study, however, precludes an analysis of his writings on the United States.

66. Ibid., 172–173.

67. Ibid., 73. In *Great Circle* (Philadelphia, 1940), he also avoided mention of personal disappointments.

**Chapter 11**

1. Minna Lieber to Beals, Sept. 2, 1938, CBC.

2. William Manchester, *The Glory* and the Dream (Boston, 1973), vol. 1, 183–188.

3. Cabel Phillips, *From the Crash to the Blitz* (New York, 1969), 548–550 and Manchester, *Glory,* I, 189–196.

4. Geoffrey Parrett, *Days of Sadness, Years of Triumph* (New York, 1973), 162–165.

5. "Jack Armstrong" on *Golden Days of Radio* (a phonograph record released by the Longines Symphonette Society) *Current History* 48 (Jan. 1939): 16. See also, Genaro Arbaiza, "Are the Americas Safe?" *Current History* 47 (Dec., 1937): 29–34 and 48 (April, 1938): 6. On public opinion polls, see Gellman, *Good Neighbor Diplomacy* 111.

6. Beals, *The Coming Struggle for Latin America* (New York, 1938), 13–18.

7. Ibid., 23–35.

8. Ibid., 36.

9. Ibid., 44.

10. Ibid., 50.

11. Ibid., 53–60.

12. Ibid., 66–68.

13. Ibid., 69.

14. Ibid., 68–69.

15. Ibid., 60–62, 72–77.

16. Ibid., pp. 81–85. Most historians do not place Vargas as far to the right as Beals did, but Stanley Hilton in his *Brazil and the Great Powers, 1930–1939* (Austin, 1975) views Brazilian policy in the 1930s as essentially a calculated attempt to take advantage of U.S.-German rivalry. At times, therefore, Vargas was quite friendly with Berlin. For a similar view, see Alton Frye, *Nazi Germany and the American Hemisphere* (New Haven, 1967), 126–130.

On German espionage and intelligence networks in South America, see Stanley Hilton, *Hitler's Secret War in South America, 1939–1945* (Baton Rouge, 1981).

17. Beals, *Coming Struggle*, 86–104.

18. Ibid., 156–167.

19. Ibid., 159–174 and 374–379. Beals distinguished between European and Latin American fascisms. Although there were many similarities, Beals argued that Latin American fascism had its roots in the political chaos of the nineteenth century, whereas the European version was of twentieth century vintage. The various Fascist political parties of the 1930s in Latin America were artificial imports only remotely connected to history. For a more recent discussion of fascism, and more precisely, corporatism, see Fredrick Pike and Thomas Stritch eds., *The New Corporatism* (Notre Dame, 1974).

20. Beals, *Coming Struggle*, 169–174.

21. Ibid., 380.

22. *Crime of Cuba* had four printings in 1933–1934 and was re-printed by Arno Press in 1970. Beals wrote two new chapters for the second edition of *Coming Struggle* that appeared in 1939.

23. Pells, *Radical Visions*, 292–329 and Diggins, *The American Left*, 107–136.

24. Barrett to Beals, Jan. 7, 1942, CBC.

25. Lieber to Beals, Nov. 6, 1942, CBC.

26. Robert Linscott to Paul Brooks, Nov. 24, 1942. copy, CBC.

27. Linscott to Lieber, Dec. 23, 1942, CBC.

28. Ibid.

29. Lieber to Beals, Dec. 8, 1942, CBC.

30. CB, interview, Aug. 14, 1978.

31. Beals, *Rio Grande to Cape Horn* (Boston, 1943), 171–172.

32. For historical studies of government pressure on the publishing industry, see John M. Blum, *V Was For Victory* (New York, 1976) and Perrett, *Days of Sadness*, 248–252.

33. *Harper's* 188 (May, 1944): Book Section.

34. Beals, *Pan America* (Boston, 1940). See Peter Drucker's review in *Saturday Review of Literature* 23 (Dec. 21, 1940): 14.

35. Lieber to Beals, March 15, 1943, CBC. Beals, *Dawn Over the Amazon* (New York, 1943).

36. Beals to Lieber, April 12, 1944, CBC.

37. Beals to Lieber, May 9, 1944; Lieber to Beals, May 15, 1944; and Beals to Lieber, May 16, 1944, all in CBC.

38. Lieber to Beals, May 22, 1944. The final break occurred with the exchange of Lieber to Beals, Aug. 17, 1944 and Beals to Lieber, Oct. 18, 1944, both in CBC.

39. Lieber to Beals, Jan. 15, 1941 and Feb. 17, 1941, both in CBC.

40. Beals to Mother, Telegram, Sept, 1941. Copy, CBC.

41. Katz to Beals, April 3, 1944, CBC.

42. Phillips to Beals, July 18, 1943, CBC.

**Chapter 12**

1. Allen to Beals, Jan. 21, 1946 and Rubin to Beals, Feb. 4, 1946, both in CBC.

2. Rubin to Beals, Oct. 4, 1946, CBC.

3. Beals, "Getting The Truth About Latin America," *The Progressive* (July 15, 1946): 8, 10. See also his "Nicaragua: Land of Despair," the *Progressive* (May 20, 1946): 4, 11 and "Crisis in Chile," *The Progressive* (July 29, 1946): 8.

4. Britton, "Carleton Beals and Central America After Sandino: Struggle to Publish," *Journalism Quarterly* 60 (Summer, 1983): 240–245, 310. On U.S. involvement in the 1954 coup, see Richard Immerman, *The CIA in Guatemala: The Foreign Policy of Intervention* (Austin, 1982).

5. Among many studies on the Second Red Scare, see David Caute, *The Great Fear* (New York, 1978); Walter Goodman, *The Committee* (New York, 1968); Richard Rovere, *Senator Joe McCarthy* (New York, 1968) and Allen Weinstein, *Perjury: The Hiss-Chambers Case* (New York, 1978).

6. Fry to Beals, Dec. 28, 1945 and Rubin to Beals, Nov. 26, 1947, both in CBC. On general conditions in the publishing industry, see George N. Gordon, *The Communications Revolution* (New York, 1977), 247–248 and James Aronson, *The Press and the Cold War* (Boston, 1970), 1–63.

7. Pearce to Beals, Jan. 9, 1947, CBC.

8. Allen to Beals, Nov. 7, 1947, CBC and Robert A. Mc Caughey, "In the Land of the Blind," *The Annals of the American Academy of Political and Social Science* 449 (May, 1980): 1–16.

9. Beals to McIntosh, Jan. 16, 1946 (sic, 1947), CBC.

10. Toor to Beals, April 23, 1949 and Idem., Jan. 10, 1951, both in CBC.

11. Mother to Beals, July 14, 1950, CBC.

12. Ralph Beals to Carleton Beals, Feb. 10 and Idem., Aug. 10, 1954, both in CBC.

13. Phillips to Beals, Feb. 19, 1953, CBC.

14. Carleton to Blanca, April 12, 1953, CBC.

15. Beals to Klausner, Dec. 5, 1949; Klausner to Beals, Dec. 29, 1952; and Klausner to Beals, Sept. 28, 1952, all in CBC.

16. Beals, *Our Yankee Heritage: The Making of Greater New Haven* (New Haven, 1951); Idem., *Our Yankee Heritage: The Making of Bristol* (Bristol, 1954); and Idem., *Our Yankee Heritage: New England's Contribution to American Civilization* (New York, 1954).

17. Anonymous to Hoover, Dec. 11, 1952, FBI.

18. Special-Agent-in-Charge (hereafter SAC) to Director, Jan. 13, 1953, FBI.

19. Beals to Barnes, Jan. 17, 1953, CBC. Beals wrote a similar but shorter letter. See Beals to Celia T. Critchley of the Bristol Public Library, Jan. 19, 1953, CBC. (Apparently, she had an interest in the case.)

20. New Haven office to Director, June 18, 1953, FBI.

21. Report from Washington office, Sept. 1, 1953; Report from SAC, Los Angeles office, July 9, 1953; and Report from agent in St. Louis, Feb. 18, 1954, all in FBI.

22. Report from New York office, Aug. 4, 1953, and Report from U.S. legation in Mexico City, Sept. 28, 1953, both in FBI.

23. SAC, to Director, Washington office, April 16, 1953, FBI.

24. Director to SAC, New Haven office, Aug. 19, 1954, FBI.

25. Nixon apparently read a reprint in the *St. Louis Post Dispatch* of Beals's article "Tragic Guatemala," published in *The Progressive* (May, 1955): 14–16.

26. Memorandum by anonymous FBI agent, July 12, 1955, FBI.

27. Memorandum by anonymous FBI agent, July 14, 1955, FBI.

28. Carleton Beals to Ralph Beals, June 20, 1958. See also Carleton Beals to Alberto (Rembao), July 28, 1957, and Carleton Beals to Bertha Klausner, Aug. 8, 1957 and Idem., Sept. 9, 1957, all in CBC.

29. *New York Times*, Feb. 24, 1957, 1, and Matthews, *The Cuban Story* (New York, 1961), 15–44.

30. Beals, "Rifle Rule," *Christian Century* 73: 1355–1356.

31. Beals to McWilliams, Jan. 6, 1957, CBC. Beals used the term "Novembrista" probably because Castro made a dramatic, inflamatory speech to Cuban émigrés in New York City on November 1, 1955. The term "Novembrista" was quickly supplanted by "26 of July Movement." Rolando E. Bonachea and Nelson P. Valdes eds., *Revolutionary Struggle, 1947–1958, The Selected Works of Fidel Castro* (Cambridge, Mass., 1972), 70–71.

32. McWilliams to whom it may concern, May 31, 1957, and McWilliams to Fernando Ortiz, May 31, 1957, both in CBC.

33. Beals, "Rebels Without a Cause," *The Nation* 139 (June 29, 1957): 565–568. For a hostile account of Castro's early life, see Luis Conte Aguero, *Los dos rostros de Fidel Castro* (Mexico, 1960). For another view, see G. Rodríguez Morejón, *Fidel Castro: biografía* (Havana, 1959).

34. Mario Llerena, *The Unsuspected Revolution* (Ithaca, 1978), 101–102, 124–125.

35. Beals to the editor, *The Nation* 140 (Sept. 21, 1957): 140.

36. Llerena, *Revolution*, 124–125.

37. Ibid., 202–203.

38. Beals to McWilliams, Dec. 12, 1958, CBC.

39. Smith ed., *Background to Revolution* (Quote from the "Introduction," 13.) For a comprehensive history of Cuba—U.S. relations, see Herminio Portell Vilá, *Historia de Cuba en sus relaciones con los Estados Unidos y España*, 4 vols. (Havana, 1938). For a Cuban leftist's point of view, see Emilio Roig de Leuchsenring, *Los Estados Unidos contra Cuba republicana* (Havana, 1964).

40. Beals, "Revolutions Without Generals," *The Nation*, 188 (Jan. 17, 1959): 43–46.

41. McWilliams to Beals, Jan. 9, 1959, CBC.

42. Beals to McWilliams, n.d. and Beals to Jim ?, Jan. 21, 1959, both in CBC.

43. *Diario Nacional*, Jan. 13, 1959, 1, Printed Matter, CBC.

44. *El Avance*, Feb. 6, 1959, Printed Matter, CBC.

45. Paul J. McNicol to J. Edgar Hoover, Translation of Portel Vilá's article in the Feb. 5, 1961 issue of *Libre*. Report on Carleton Beals; June 19, 1961, USIA Records, Washington, D.C.

46. Beals, "As Cuba Sees It," *The Nation* 188 (Jan. 31, 1959): 83–85. Quote from Beals, "Cuba in Revolution," *Christian Century* 76: 131.

47. "Cuba in Revolution," *Christian Century* 76: 131–132.

48. Thomas, *Cuba*, 1173–1175.

49. Beals, "The Squeeze on Castro," *The Nation* 189 (June 24, 1959): 64–65. In a much more extensive survey, Robert Scheer and Maurice Zeitlin reached similar conclusions about the coverage of Cuba in high circulation magazines such as *Time, Life, US News and World Report* and *Reader's Digest*. See their *Cuba, An American Tragedy* (Harmondsworth, England, 1964), 316–336.

50. Beals, "The Squeeze on Castro," *The Nation* 188: 402–404.

51. Thomas, *Cuba*, 1241–1261, 1458–1460.

52. Ortiz to Beals, Feb. 16, 1959, CBC.

53. O'Connor to Beals, May 29, 1959, CBC.

54. Dawson to Beals, Feb. 18, 1959 and Idem., March 18, 1959; Beals to Dawson, March 10, 1959, all in CBC.

55. McWilliams to Beals, June 23, 1959; Idem., Oct. 29, 1959; and Idem., Dec. 17, 1959; and Beals to McWilliams, Oct. 31, 1959, all in CBC.

56. Beals to Bertha Klausner, Sept. 28, 1959 and Robert T. Wolfe (Executive Director of the Housing Authority of the City of New Haven) to Beals, Nov. 27, 1959, both in CBC.

57. *Brass Knuckle Crusade* (Hastings House, 1960) and *Cyclone Carry* (Chilton, 1962).

58. *The New York Times*, Nov. 20, 1960, 30; *Saturday Evening Post* 34 (June 19, 1961): 10; and *Newsweek* 58 (Oct. 23, 1961); 22–23.

59. *Middletown Press*, April 12, 1960 and Idem., April 21, 1960, both in Printed Matter, CBC.

60. "Beals's Self-Defense," *New Haven Register*, June 26, 1960, Printed Matter, CBC.

61. Hollander, *Political Pilgrims* (New York, 1981), 223–277, 347–399.

62. Thomas, *Cuba*, 1272–1288.

63. *El Mundo*, May 26, 1960, Printed Matter, CBC.

64. *Hoy*, May 17, 1960; *Revolución*, May 18, 1960; and *Verde Olivo*, May 29, 1960, all in Printed Matter, CBC. Beals also appeared on a television interview program *Telemundo Pregunta*, where three Cuban journalists questioned him.

65. *El Mundo*, May 15, 1960, Printed Matter, CBC. On the meeting with Guevara, see Beals, *Great Guerrilla Warriors* (New York, 1971), 9.

66. Beals, "Report from Havana," *The Nation* 191 (July 23, 1960): 45–49.

67. Beals, "Cuba's Invasion Jitters," *The Nation* 191 (Nov. 12, 1960): 360–362.

68. *The Nation* 191 (Nov. 19, 1960): 378–379 and McWilliams, "Second Thoughts," *The Nation* 229 (July 14, 1979): 38.

69. Gay Talese, *The Kingdom and the Power* (New York, 1966), 4–5.

70. Report on Carleton Beals, June 19, 1961, USIA, Washington, D.C.

71. Carleton to Carolyn, March 22, 1961, CBC.

72. Secretary of State, circular, March 24, 1961, (D.S. classification illegible).

73. Carleton to Carolyn, May 3, 1961, CBC.

74. Edward P. Kardas to U.S. State Department, May 8, 1961, DS 920.6211/S-861 XR737.00.

75. Carleton to Carolyn, April 19, 1961 and Beals, Text for radio talk, Montevideo, Uruguay, n.d., both in CBC. New Haven office to Director, Report on Beals's trip, May 26, 1961, and U.S. legation to Director, Memorandum, Rio de Janeiro, June 29, 1961, both in FBI.

76. CB Interview, August 1977; Beals's article in *Independent*, July 1961, 1, 3; New York Office, Report on Beals, August 31, 1961, FBI; and Maurice Halperin, *The Rise and Fall of Fidel Castro* (Berkeley, 1972), 327–335.

77. Beals to Revueltas, n.d. (probably June 1961), CBC.

78. Beals to Schapiro, June 29, 1961, CBC. In his account of Prensa Latina in the *Independent* (July 1961, 1, 3) Beals claimed that while Revueltas was not a Communist, he was a "pliant, false-front man," who would not defend the independence of the news agency against the aggressive rise of Communist influence in Cuba.

79. *Independent*, July 1961, 1, 3. For similar views of Third World attitudes toward U.S. dominated news media, see Jeremy Tunstall, *The Media Are American* (New York, 1977) and Anthony Smith, *The Geopolitics of Information* (New York, 1980).

80. Gibson to Beals, July 10, 1961, CBC.

81. Summary report on Carleton Beals, Feb. 2, 1961, FBI.

82. CB, Interview, August 1977.

83. Summary report, Feb. 2, 1961, FBI.

84. Hoover to SAC, New Haven, March 2, 1961; New York office, Memorandum, Oct. 13, 1961; and New Haven office, Memorandum, Oct. 25, 1965, all in FBI.

85. Paul J. McNicol to J. Edgar Hoover, June 19, 1961 enclosed with "Carleton Beals," Report, June 5, 1961. Copy, USIA.

86. SAC to director, New Haven, Jan. 26, 1962, FBI.

87. New Haven Office, Untitled report, Sept. 10, 1963, FBI. (Deletion by FBI.)

88. SAC, to director, SAC, Dec. 30, 1964, FBI.

## Chapter 13

1. *New York Times*, July 28, 1979, B15.

2. For example, see Beals, *Brass-Knuckle Crusade; Cyclone Carry;*

*Eagle of the Andes* (Philadelphia, 1963); *Land of the Maya* (New York, 1967); *Nomads and Empire Builders* (New York, 1965); *War Within a War; the Confederacy Against Itself* (Philadelphia, 1965); and *The Great Revolt and Its Leaders* (New York, 1968).

3. This lengthy manuscript is in the CBC.

4. Much of the personal information in this chapter is based upon the author's six visits with Beals from 1973 to 1978.

5. Beals, *Latin America: World in Revolution* (New York, 1963) especially 220–226, 280–331.

6. McWilliams to author, April 28, 1978, Author's Papers and *The Nation* 229 (July 14–21, 1979): 38.

7. Lawrence Goodwyn, *Democratic Promise* (New York, 1976), 552–614 and Smith, *Geopolitics of Information*.

8. Diggins, *The American Left* and Salvatore, *Debs: Citizen*.

9. On Cuba, see Hollander, *Political Pilgrims*, 223–277. (Hollander did not include the Mexican revolution.)

10. There is an immense literature on these conceptual frameworks for the study of political, social and economic change. Some outstanding studies among many are Kalmon Silvert, *Man's Power* (New York, 1970); Eisenstadt, *Modernization:* and Idem., "Studies of Modernization" *History and Theory* 13; 225–252; Guillermo O'Donnell, *Modernization and Bureaucratic-Authoritarianism* (Berkeley, 1973); Alex Inkeles and David H. Smith, *Becoming Modern* (Cambridge, Mass., 1974); and Marshall Berman, *All That Is Solid Melts into Air* (New York, 1982).

11. Among many recent publications on imperialism are Benjamin Cohen, *The Question of Imperialism* (New York., 1973); Bath and James, "Dependency Analysis of Latin America," *Latin American Research Review* 11: 3–54; M. Platt, "Dependency in Nineteenth Century Latin America" Stanley J. and Barbara H. Stein, "D.C.M. Platt "The Anatomy of 'Autonomy,'" both in *Latin American Research Review* 15: 113–149; and Smith, *The Pattern of Imperialism*. Two important discussions of Third World intellectuals' theories on economic development as a way to reduce subservience to the U.S. and western Europe are Ignacy Sachs, *The Discovery of the Third World* (Cambridge, Mass. 1976), 125–156 and Gunnar Myrdal, *Economic Theory and Underdevelopment* (Reprint 1971, New York, 1957), especially 100–106.

A journal that has contributed much to the discussion on imperialism from a leftist point of view is *Latin American Perspectives*, which publishes Latin American and U.S. scholarship. For example, see *Latin American Perspectives* 8 (Summer and Fall, 1981), subtitled "Dependency and Marxism."

12. Spanish translations include *El Oro de las bananas* (Santiago de Chile, 1940); *América ante América* (Santiago de Chile, 1940); *Con Sandino en Nicaragua* (San José de Costa Rica, 1928); *Fuego sobre los Andes* (Santiago de Chile, 1942); *Panorama Mexicano* (Santiago de Chile, 1942); *La proxima lucha por Latinoamérica* (Santiago de Chile, 1942); *América Latina: mundo en revolución* (Buenos Aires, 1963) and *Porfirio Díaz* (México, 1982). A French translation, *L'Amerique latine, monde en revolución* appeared in Paris in 1966.

# Bibliography

The main purposes of this relatively short bibliography are to provide the reader with a convenient listing of the primary sources that figured prominently in this study and to present, in the last section, a brief historigraphical essay on some of the main issues in Beals's writing. One of the most difficult problems in biography is the author's tendency to understate, or perhaps to ignore, what "the other side" had to say in relation to controversial points surrounding the central character. It is hoped that this last section will provide the interested reader with some stimulating choices for further reading by writers who, in many cases, took exception to the views that Beals espoused

## Manuscript Collections

Carleton Beals Collection, Mugar Memorial Library, Boston University.
Ralph Beals Papers, Ralph Beals family, Los Angeles, California.
Victor Calverton Papers, New York Public Library, New York.
Carrie Chapman Catt Papers, Library of Congress, Washington, D.C.
Lewis Gannett Papers, Houghton Library, Harvard University, Cambridge, Mass.
Ernest Gruening Papers, Elmer E. Rasmuson Library, University of Alaska, Fairbanks, Alaska.
Samuel Guy Inman Papers, Library of Congress, Washington, D.C.

Dwight Morrow Papers, Amherst College, Amherst, Mass.
James Sheffield Papers, Sterling Memorial Library, Yale University,
New Haven, Conn.
Frank Tannenbaum Papers, Columbia University, New York.
Bertram Wolfe Collection, Hoover Institution, Stanford University,
Stanford, California.


**Government and University Archives**

Archivo General de la Nación, Mexico City, Mexico.
Archivo General de la Secretaría de Relaciones Exteriores, Mexico
City, Mexico
National Archives, Records of the United States Department of
State, Washington, D.C.
National Archives, Records of the United States War Department,
Washington, D.C.
United States Central Intelligence Agency Records, Washington,
D.C.
United States Information Agency Records, Washington, D.C.
United States Department of Justice, Records of the Federal Bureau
of Investigation, Washington, D.C.
Office of Admissions and Records, University of California,
Berkeley, California.
University Archives, Bancroft Library, University of California,
Berkeley, California.


**Personal Interviews and Correspondence**

Carleton Beals, Interviews with author, January 7, 8, 1973, June 4,
5, 6, 7, 8, 11, 12, 13, 14, 15 and July 1, 2, 1973, Killingworth,
Conn.
Carleton Beals to author, November 3, 1972; November 25, 1972;
December 1, 1972; September 9, 1973; January 12, 1974; April
17, 1974; August 23, 1974; October ?, 1974; December 26, 1974;
Author's collection.
Carolyn Beals, Interviews with author, June 14, 15, 1981, Killing-
worth, Conn.
Ralph Beals, Interview with author, July 6, 1975, Los Angeles,
Calif.
Ernest Gruening, Interview with author, March 20, 1974, Wash-
ington D.C.

Ernest Gruening to author, September 20, 1973 and October 11, 1973, Author's collection.

Carey McWilliams to author, June 20, 1974; June 21, 1974 and April 28, 1978, Author's collection.

Katherine Anne Porter to author, January 28, 1976, Author's collection.

Felipe Texidor, Interview with author, June 24, 1975, Mexico City.

Ella Wolfe, Interview with author, July 24, 1984, Palo Alto, Calif.

Ella Wolfe to author, July 30, 1984, Author's collection.


### Articles by Carleton Beals

Carleton Beals wrote over two hundred articles during his career. The most convenient listing of his articles can be found in the *Reader's Guide to Periodical Literature* from 1919 to 1965.


### Books by Carleton Beals

The following list includes information on publishers, translations, illustrations and reprints.

*Mexico: An Interpretation.* New York: Huebsch, 1923. *Mexiiko: Och Mexikanska Problem.* Stockholm: Hugo Gebers Vorlag, 1924.

*Rome or Death: The Story of Fascism.* New York: Century, 1923.

*Brimstone and Chili.* New York: Knopf, 1927.

*Con Sandino en Nicaragua.* San José, Costa Rica: Comité Pro-Sandino, 1929.

*Destroying Victor.* New York: Macaulay, 1929.

*Mexican Maze.* Illustrated by Diego Rivera. Philadelphia and New York, Lippincott, 1931. Fifth edition, *Enredo Mexicano.* Mexico: El Universal, 1933. *Panorama Mexicano:* Santiago, Chile: Zig Zag, 1941. Westport, Greenwood, 1971. (Book club ed. also 1931.)

*Banana Gold.* Illustrated by Carlos Mérida. Philadelphia and New York: Lippincott, 1932. Reprint: New York: Arno Press, New York Times, Hoover Institution, 1970. *El Oro de las bananas.* Santiago, Chile: Zig Zag, 1940.

*Porfirio Díaz: Dictator of Mexico.* Philadelphia and New York: Lippincott, 1932. Reprint: Westport, Greenwood, 1971.

*The Crime of Cuba.* Photographs by Walker Evans. Philadelphia and New York: Lippincott, 1933. Reprint: New York: Arno Press, New York Times, Hoover Institution, 1970.

*Fire on the Andes.* Illustrated by José Sabogal. Philadelphia and New York: Lippincott, 1934. *Fuego sobre los Andes.* Santiago, Chile: Zig Zag, 1942.

*Black River.* Philadelphia and New York: Lippincott, 1934.

*The Story of Huey P. Long.* Philadelphia and New York: Lippincott, 1935. Westport: Greenwood, 1971.

*The Stones Awake.* Philadelphia and New York: Lippincott, 1936.

*America South.* Philadelphia and New York: Lippincott, 1936. *America ante America.* Santiago, Chile: Zig Zag, 1940.

*The Coming Struggle for Latin America.* Philadelphia and New York: Lippincott, 1937. Halcyon House Blue Ribbon Reprint: New York, 1940. *La Próxima lucha por Latino America.* Santiago, Chile: Zig Zag, 1942.

*Glass Houses.* Philadelphia and New York: Lippincott, 1938.

*American Earth.* Philadelphia and New York: Lippincott, 1940.

*Panamerica: A Program for the Western Hemisphere.* Boston: Houghton Mifflin, 1940.

*Rio Grande to Cape Horn.* Boston, Houghton Mifflin, 1943.

*Dawn Over the Amazon.* New York: Duell, Sloan and Pearce, 1943. Literary Guild Edition, New York, 1943. New Zealand reprint, 1945 (?)

*Lands of the Dawning Morrow.* Indianapolis, New York: Bobbs Merrill, 1948.

*The Long Land: Chile.* New York: Coward McCann, 1949.

*Our Yankee Heritage: The Making of Greater New Haven.* New Haven, Conn.: Bradley and Scoville, 1951; 2nd ed. 1957.

*Stephen F. Austin: The Father of Texas.* New York: McGraw Hill, 1953.

*Our Yankee Heritage: The Making of Bristol.* Bristol: Bristol Public Library, 1954.

*Adventure of the Western Sea: The Story of Robert Gray.* Illustrated by Jacob Landau. New York: Henry Holt, 1956.

*Taste of Glory.* New York: Crown, 1956.

*John Eliot: The Man Who Loved the Indians.* New York: Julian Messner, 1957. Junior Literary Guild, 1957.

*House in Mexico.* Illustrated by Tom O'Sullivan. New York: Hastings House, 1958.

*Brass Knuckle Crusade: The Great Know-Nothing Conspiracy.* New York: Hastings House, 1960.

*Nomads and Empire Builders.* Philadelphia and New York: Chilton, 1961. Reprint: New York: Citadel Press, 1965.

*Eagles of the Andes.* Philadelphia and New York: Chilton, 1962.

*Cyclone Carry: The Story of Carry Nation.* Philadelphia and New York: Chilton, 1962.

*Latin America: World in Revolution.* New York: Abelard Schuman, 1963. *L'Amerique Latine, Monde en Revolution.* Paris: Payot, 1966. *America Latino, mundo en revolución.* Buenos Aires: Palestra, 1967.

*The War Within a War.* Philadelphia and New York; Chilton, 1965.

*Land of the Mayas, Past and Present.* Illustrated by Marianne Greenwood. New York: Abelard-Schuman, 1966.

*The Great Crusade and Its Leaders.* New York: Abelard-Schuman, 1968.

*Stories Told by the Aztecs Before the Spaniards Came.* Illustrated by Charles Pickard. New York: Abelard-Schuman, 1970.

*Colonial Rhode Island.* New York: Thomas Nelson, 1970.

*Great Guerrilla Warriors.* New York: Prentice-Hall, 1970. Reprint: New York: Tower, 1970.

*The Nature of Revolution.* New York: Thomas Y. Crowell, 1970.


## Dissertations and Theses

Beelen, George D. "Harding and Mexico: Diplomacy by Economic Persuasion," Ph.D. diss., Kent State University, 1971.

Beals, Carl B. "The Self-Sufficient City-State," Master's thesis, Columbia University, 1917.

Christopulous, Diane. "American Radicals and the Mexican Revolution, 1900–1925," Ph.D. diss., State University of New York at Binghamton, 1980.

Horn, James J. "Diplomacy by Ultimatum: Ambassador Sheffield and Mexican-American Relations, 1924–1927," Ph.D. diss., State University of New York at Buffalo, 1969.

Ignasias, C. Dennis. "Reluctant Recognition: The United States and the Recognition of Alvaro Obregon of Mexico, 1920–1924," Ph.D. diss., Michigan State University, 1967.

Jackman, Frances J. "America's Cuba Policy During the Period of the Machado Regime," Ph.D. dissertation, Catholic University, 1964.

McMullen, Christopher Jay. "Calles and the Diplomacy of Revolution: Mexican-American Diplomatic Relations, 1924–1928," Ph.D. dissertation, Georgetown University, 1980.

Zelman, Donald L. "American Intellectual Attitudes Toward Mexico, 1908–1940," Ph.D. dissertation, Ohio State University, 1970.

## Essay on selected secondary works

Beals's leftist approach to the general subject of U.S.-Latin American relations can be contrasted to the conservative positions taken in Samuel Flagg Bemis, *The Latin American Policy of the United States* (New York, 1943), Dexter Perkins, *A History of the Monroe Doctrine* (Boston, 1955), and Graham Stuart and James L. Tigner, *Latin America and the United States* (Englewood Cliffs, New Jersey, 1975). Lester Langley takes a moderate, even-handed perspective in *The United States and the Caribbean in the Twentieth Century* (Athens, 1985) as does Cole Blasier in *The Hovering Giant* (Pittsburg, 1976). Studies that share much in common with Beals's view of U.S.-Latin American relations are Gordon Connell-Smith, *The United States and Latin America* (New York, 1974), Alonso Aguilar, *Pan-Americanism from Monroe to the Present* (New York, 1968), Vicente Sáenz, *Hispanoamerica contra el coloniaje* (México, 1956) and Juan José Arévalo, *Anti-Kommunism in Latin America* (New York, 1963, translated by Carleton Beals). Bryce Wood's *The Making of the Good Neighbor Policy* (New York, 1961) is especially valuable because of the attention given to the influence of press opinion on the work of diplomats. Richard Immerman's *The CIA in Guatemala* (Austin, 1982) represents an important breakthrough in research in government sources and confirms some of Beals's accusations in the early 1950s.

The subject of U.S.-Mexican relations was of particular importance to Beals. Robert Freeman Smith's *The United States and Revolutionary Nationalism in Mexico, 1916–1932* (Chicago, 1972) remains one of the best studies on this subject in spite of its overestimation of the influence of business on Woodrow Wilson's policies. Lorenzo Meyer has contributed several valuable works in this area including *Los grupos de presión extranjeros en el México Revolucionario, 1910–1940* (Mexico, 1973) and *Mexico and the United States in the Oil Controversy, 1917–1942* (Austin, 1973). Some useful surveys of U.S.-Mexican relations are Karl Schmidt, *Mexico and the United States, 1821–1973: Conflict and Coexistence* (New York, 1974), Robert J. Schafer and Donald J. Mabry, *Neighbors - Mexico and the United States* (Chicago, 1981), and Josefina Vázquez and Lorenzo Meyer, *The United States and Mexico* (Chicago, 1985).

From 1918 through the 1930s Beals gave much of his attention to Mexico and its revolution. In recent years this period in Mexican history has become the subject of an important historical debate in which one school, often called revisionist, holds that while Mexico underwent political and military upheaval, there was no significant redistribution of power or wealth. The traditional school accepts the notion that the revolutionary governments were often flawed by corruption and inefficiency but, by contrast with the revisionists, asserts that fundamental social and economic change did occur. Examples of the traditional view are William Sherman and Michael Meyer, *The Course of Mexican History* (New York, 1983) and James Wilkie, *The Mexican Revolution: Federal Expenditure and Social Changes* (Berkeley, 1970). Donald Hodges and Ross Gandy in *Mexico, 1910–1976: Reform or Revolution* (London, 1979) and Arnaldo Córdova in *La ideología de la Revolución Mexicana* (México, 1973) and *La política de masas del cardenismo* (México, 1974) use somewhat different approaches to conclude that the revolution was a state-directed populist movement that reached its climax under Cárdenas and faltered seriously after 1940. Two of the leading revisionist works are Ramón Eduardo Ruiz, *The Great Rebellion, Mexico 1905–1924* (New York, 1980) and Nora Hamilton, *The Limits of State Autonomy: Post-Revolutionary Mexico* (Princeton, 1982). Many of the twenty-three volumes in the series *Historia de la Revolución Mexicana* published by El Colegio de México contain revisionist interpretations of the revolution. For example, see Jean Meyer, Enrique Krauze and Cayetano Reyes, *Estado y sociedad con Calles* (México, 1977) and Lorenzo Meyer, *El conflicto social y los gobiernos del maximato* (México, 1977) and Lorenzo Meyer, *El conflicto social y los gobiernos del maximato* (México, 1978). Luis González's penetrating account of the Cárdenas years in *Los días del presidente Cárdenas* (México, 1981) contains both traditional and revisionist elements.

The problems surrounding social and economic change in Latin America created important issues for Beals and his contemporaries and continue to generate debate among students in this field. Thomas Skidmore and Peter Smith have written an innovative textbook, *Modern Latin America* (New York, 1984), that combines some insightful observations on these issues with a thorough exposition of dependency analysis. Three studies that consider socio-economic change in a world-wide context are Samuel P. Huntington, *Political Order in Changing Societies* (New Haven, 1968); Theda Skocpol, *States and Social Revolutions* (Cambridge, 1979) and Jack Goldstone (ed.), *Revolutions: Theoretical, Comparative and Historical Studies* (New York, 1986). Frederick Pike's provocative ideas on the corporate state and its capacity to resist and to assimilate change are summarized in his *Spanish America, 1900–1970* (New York, 1970). The important topic of mass participation in politics is explored in Michael Conniff (ed.) *Latin American Populism in Comparative Perspective* (Albuquerque, 1982). On the question of social and economic change in Central America, the best starting points are R. Lee Woodward, *Central America: A Nation Divided* (New York, 1985) and the same author's "The Rise and Decline of Liberalism in Central America: Historical Perspectives on the Contemporary Crisis," *Journal of Interamerican Studies and World Affairs*, 26 (August, 1984), pp. 291–312. On the failure of a promising reform movement in Cuba in the post-Machado period see Luis Aguilar's *Cuba 1933: Prologue to Revolution* (Ithaca, New York, 1972). A comprehensive survey of twentieth century Cuba is in Hugh Thomas's *Cuba: The Pursuit of Freedom* (New York, 1971). Ramón Eduardo Ruiz wrote a brief but highly readable study, *Cuba: The Making of a Revolution* (New York, 1968). An informative introduction to Peru and its Andean neighbors is Frederick Pike's *The United States and the Andean Republics* (Cambridge, Mass., 1977) and a valuable analysis of the social roots of political change in modern Peru is Steve Stein's *Populism in Peru* (Madison, 1980). A pioneering study on the influence of Marxist ideas in the region is Sheldon Liss's *Marxist Thought in Latin America* (Berkeley, 1984).

Beals's views of revolution and reform do not fit conveniently into the ideological categories along the liberal-leftist spectrum in the United States, but some of the works that help to approximate the location of his thoughts in this context are: Daniel Aaron, *Writers on the Left* (New York, 1961); John P. Diggins, *The American Left in the Twentieth Century* (New York, 1973); Richard Pells, *Radical Visions and American Dreams* (New York, 1973); and Harvey Khler, *The Heyday of American Communism* (New York, 1984). Paul Hollander's *Political Pilgrims* (New York, 1981) provides a major critique of the writings of liberal and leftist observers from the United States who witnessed and wrote about the revolutions in Russia of the 1930s and Cuba and Vietnam in the 1960s. Although Hollander does not include the Mexican revolution, his observations have implications for any evaluation of the work of Beals and his contemporaries in Mexico from 1918 to 1940. Robert Packenham's *Liberal*

*America and the Third World* (Princeton, 1973) examines the attitudes and policies of U.S. liberals on revolution and social change in the Third World since 1947. Beals often disagreed with these liberal views as a result of his left-wing populist position.

For suggested reading in journalism and communications history see footnote 3 in Chapter I.

# Index